NEW DAY, NEW LIFE

LIVE, LAUGH, LOVE, WORK, PRAY
HOME OR AWAY

Mark C. Overton

Five Inspirational Books in One Volume!

Copyright © 2020 by Mark C. Overton

ISBN   Softcover   978-1-951469-61-0

This Book is licensed for your personal enjoyment only. It may not be re-sold or given away to other people. If you would like to share this book with another person, please purchase an additional copy for each recipient. If you're reading this book and did not purchase it, or it was not bought for your use only, please go to Publisher and purchase a copy. Thank you for respecting the hard work of this author.

Unless otherwise noted, all Scripture quotations are taken from the Holy Bible, New International Version®, NIV®. Copyright © 1973, 1978, 1984, 2011 by Biblica, Inc.® Used by permission of Zondervan. All rights reserved worldwide. The "NIV" and "New International Version" are trademarks registered in the United States Patent and Trademark Office by Biblica, Inc.® Scripture quotations marked NIrV are taken from the Holy Bible, New International Reader's Version®, NIrV® Copyright © 1995, 1996, 1998, 2014 by Biblica, Inc.® Used by permission of Zondervan. All rights reserved worldwide. The "NIrV" and "New International Reader's Version" are trademarks registered in the United States Patent and Trademark Office by Biblica, Inc.® Scripture quotations marked TLB are taken from The Living Bible copyright © 1971. Used by permission of Tyndale House Publishers, Inc., Carol Stream, Illinois 60188. All rights reserved. Scripture quotations marked KJV are taken from The King James Version of the Bible. Scripture quotations marked ESV are from the ESV® Bible (The Holy Bible, English Standard Version®), copyright © 2001 by Crossway, a publishing ministry of Good News Publishers. Used by permission. All rights reserved. Scripture quotations marked NKJV are taken from the New King James Version®. Copyright © 1982 by Thomas Nelson. Used by permission. All rights reserved. Scripture quotations marked NLT are taken from the Holy Bible, New Living Translation, copyright 1996, 2004, 2007 by Tyndale House Foundation. Used by permission of Tyndale House Publishers, Inc., Carol Stream, Illinois 60188. All rights reserved. Scripture quotations marked NASB are taken from the NEW AMERICAN STANDARD BIBLE(R), Copyright (C)1960,1962,1963,1968,1971,1972,1973,1975,1977,1995 by The LockmanFoundation. Used by permission.

Printed in the United States of America.

To order additional copies of this book, contact:
Bookwhip
1-855-339-3589
https://www.bookwhip.com

NEW DAY, NEW LIFE

LIVE, LAUGH, LOVE, WORK, PRAY
HOME OR AWAY

Mark C. Overton

Five Inspirational Books in One Volume!

You Only Live Once
I Like to Start with Something Funny
What Love Really Means
Work Excellence Chapter & Verse
LORD Teach Me How to Pray

INTRODUCTION

Live, Laugh, Love, Work, Pray
Home or Away

Though there is no place like home, one in seven kids between the ages of 10 and 18 will run away at some point according to runaway statistics. Similarly Scripture gives us a depiction of people who are away from God; they may run because of their love for sin or bitterness due to a tragic life event. Regardless of reason, they're encouraged to *Live, Laugh, Love, Work, Pray h*ome or away. And to come home and find their way back to him and a *New Day, New Life.*

The Urban Dictionary tells us home: "means something different to each person who uses it. A person's home can be the place where they live, the place they grew up, or the place where the people they care about live."

To some folk, home is where you can rest your head and your heart now and everything feels safe; the place where you are not alone. Home is a place you instantly feel comfortable in. Usually a home has family, friends, school, job, and whatever makes that person happy.

For Dorothy and her dog, Toto, Kansas was home. You may have watched *The Wizard of Oz,* a 1939 American musical fantasy movie considered one of the greatest films in cinema history. When a tornado rips through Kansas, they are suddenly whisked away in their house to the magical Land of Oz They follow the Yellow Brick Road toward the Emerald City to meet the Wizard to help her get back home now. One of its most famous lines is "Click your heels together three times and say 'There's no place like home' and you'll be there."

To "E.T," home also represented a place of residence, origin, or base of operations. *E.T. the Extra-Terrestrial*, a 1982 American science fiction film, tells the story of Elliott, a lonely boy who befriends an extraterrestrial stranded on Earth. One of "E.T's" beloved quotes is "E.T. phone home." Elliott and his siblings help E.T. return to his home planet, while attempting to keep him hidden from their mother and the government.

On the other hand, National Runaway Safeline statistics tell us between 1.6 and 2.8 million youth run away in a year. Folk may decide to leave home for many different reasons – from a desire to live independently, to forming a relationship and living with that person, getting bullied or threatened, experiencing domestic violence, lacking acceptance, moving into a shared accommodation, or choosing to leave home because of conflict, arguments or restrictions, etc. People run away for their own reasons; they feel anywhere is better than where they are. Isaiah 53:6 tells us, "We all, like sheep, have gone astray." Much as sheep tend to wander off physically from the flock, so human beings tend to waywardly wander off spiritually from God.

Scripture also tells us a famous parable about "The Prodigal Son," who made the decision to run away from his spiritual home – from God, his faith and everything familiar (Luke, Chapter 15). I heard this story from my pastor and he somewhat told it this way. In this story, the Father represents God, our heavenly Father. The sons represent us. It is a depiction of what happens when someone runs from him.

When dad died, he would divide his money between his two sons. But, the younger son was impatient. He didn't want to wait until his dad died. He wanted his share of the money now. This was more than just going to see the world. The junior was cutting loose from the way of living, thinking and acting handed down to him – everything his father believed and stood for. The fledgling left home and all it represented for life on his own. He ran.

When leading a chapel men's group, I've also seen some people make this same decision and "run away" from God [and their spiritual home]. Real talk, I'm not a pastor, counselor or psychologist; yet, people run for various reasons. However, as a seminary student, I strive to rightly handle the word of truth. Being trained under qualified teachers and learning from godly scholars, my own experiences and beliefs are given shape and expression for your knowledge and truth.

Some people run because God's boundaries feel like restrictions or punishment. They're a grown-ass woman or man and don't want limits or rules. They want to do their thing, their way and don't want to feel others' judgment or disapproval. I'm glad they hold on to what Proverbs 22:6 tells us: "Train up a child in the way he should go; even when he is old he will not depart from it" -- Live, *Laugh, Love, Work, Pray* home or away.

Others run because they imagine a life filled with fun and freedom. Fantasy trumps reality. What they don't have seems better than what they do. Like Frank Sinatra, who first sang "I Did It My Way," they want to do it their way. They run because they want to prove they don't need anyone or anything. Do you think the runner has thought through what happens after the fun or possible consequences of their decision?

People also run because disappointment with people leads to anger towards God. They respond to a deep or profound hurt by leaving him and everyone connected to him. It's misplaced anger.

Folk run because of poor relationship choices. Their foolish friends convince them life on the run will be better. They run because it's easier to run than to face the results of failure. They mess up and don't feel like there is a place for them anymore. They fear rejection, so they flee rejection.

Sometimes, they run because of an addiction. Something else takes control of their life. They are no longer in control. They've given control away. Some people run out of habit. It's what they've done their whole life. They were raised to run by parents who ran. It's inter-generational and an unfortunate learned behavior.

A few people run because they are lonely. It's not so much they are running from something as they think they are running too something. They imagine their new life will be filled with fun and friends. Regardless of the reason, there is nothing sadder than to watch someone run. You know where it's headed. You know the end result. So many people run from him, from church, from what was right.

Looking at the prodigal son, we learn what happens when you run. It is a decision that leads to consequences: The first consequence of running is you leave home. How obvious is that? That's the point of running. And, when you leave home, you run away from the safety of home and leave the protection of your heavenly Father behind.

When you leave home, you run away from the security of home. Security is the feeling of knowing you belong and you have a place to call home. Anyone who travels a lot knows what I am talking about. When I served in the military and went out of country, I initially felt a little out of place – like I didn't quite fit.

In fact, because travelling overseas increases the risk of foreign intelligence targeting, agents provided foreign travel briefings when travelling abroad. Although taking every precaution, you don't feel completely secure. When the plane lands back in the United States and you step off the plane, you may breathe a sigh of relief.

And for children to know "home" will still be there after school or when they come home from college for a weekend spells security. Mom, dad and family will be there. No one is going to abuse you. They are proud of you and will be excited to see you. It feels good to be home; there's nothing like the security and privacy of home.

When you leave home, you're running away from dwelling in the shelter of the Most High. You're not only running away from the safety and security of home, you run away from the blessings of home (provision --food, clothing, shelter, protection, belonging, etc.). When you leave home, you also run from the love of home. Oh – don't get me wrong. He still loves you. You're just not there to experience it. Really, that's enough consequence. That should be enough to make you come home – life without the safety, the security, the blessings and the love of home. Who would want to live that way – away from his blessing, protection and love?

And if that's not enough, when you continue running the consequences continue like the younger son who squandered his share of money on wild living. He ran away to party and wasted everything he had. When you run from God, you make bad decisions. You do things you never thought you'd do. It's not your plan. You don't plan to make stupid decisions. But, you make bad decisions. You do dumb things. That's just what happens when you run.

Like the young son losing all the money, when running from God, you lose (e.g., money, families, marriages, businesses, job, careers, innocence, reputation, families, friends, life, etc.). It's painful to watch -- seeing the cost of a runner's decision. It hurts so badly. When you run from him, your plans (relationships, financial, etc.) fail. You left home. You ran from him. You never planned it this way! It's not as good as it looked and it's not what you expected. When you are in the situation, you say, "How did this happen? How could this happen to me? How did I ever become this? This was never my plan!"

The youngest son was going to be rich and free – having fun with dad's money. Far from the comfort, security and blessings of home, he found himself working in a pigpen. He was supposed to be special, instead, he was with the pigs. When you run, you end up embarrassed and ashamed. You knew better. At least you should have. Most of the time, this is the biggest hurdle for a runaway. "I'd love to come home, but what will people think? What will they say?" You can't let guilt and shame keep you away from home. You can't run forever.

In peeling back this fantastic devotional's content, you'll find five newly revised, inspirational books in one volume – Live, Laugh, Love, Work, Pray. *New Day, New Life* guides you through stages of your journey in life—from adolescence to later adulthood for starters! Discover God's promises that never fail. Experience over 100 short clean jokes that will have you rolling on the floor laughing and happier than at the end of a workday on Friday! Learn what love really means. Kiss the "Monday Blues" goodbye forever and feel truly inspired and motivated to transform every workday into Friday! Eliminate disruptions and attention deficit disorder when you pray using the same method as Jesus' teaching on prayer! Whether you're home or away, it's my prayer these encouraging messages for daily living hit home with you. Regardless of your location, I hope they hit the mark as your daily bread and inspire you to stay or come home.

Well, enough of waiting to guess what will people think? It's not a shot in the dark people who are genuine followers of Jesus Christ will celebrate with, love, and accept you. And the critics and cynics who question your commitment? Don't listen to them. Overcome the embarrassment and shame and come on home. And like all the people who helped spend his money and partied with him, what happened to this runner may happen to you. When you run from God, one day you'll discover you are alone. The people who got drunk and partied with you are nowhere to be found --you are alone.

Maybe this story has described you. You left relationship with God – you left home. When you did it, you didn't realize the consequences, but now you do. Maybe you are all the way there -- experiencing all of the consequences. Or maybe you are just seeing some of the consequences and recognize – "Uh-oh, that pattern is happening to me. I can see – it's where I'm headed." So, what do you do? Look what the youngest son did.

What brought him to his senses? The consequences. The reality of his situation. The good news is his dad brought him up to *Live, Laugh, Love, Work, Pray* at home. And he may have while away. He looked around at his situation, with the pigs, hungry and alone. He'd be foolish not to come to his senses! And, isn't it time for you to come to your senses? What will it take for you? Are you finding meaning in this lifestyle? How many broken relationships is it going to take? How much do you have to lose? How many bad decisions do you have to make? How many plans have to fail? Isn't it the right moment to come home? Isn't it time to come home? Why not come home before it gets that bad? Isn't it time?

The youngest made the decision – "Even if all I can do is get a job with my dad, it's better than this. I'm going home. I'm going back to the safety, security, blessings and the love of home." He was going back to *Live, Laugh, Love, Work, Pray* at home. No matter how far you've gone, no matter how long it's been, you can always come home.

Alright, you're ready and all set – take off because it's never too late to come home to a *New Day, New Life*. No matter how many bad decisions you have made and consequences you have suffered, you can get a head start on where you're at in your journey in life. Plunge into the book reflecting your current situation: *Live, Laugh, Love, Work, or Pray*. Even if you are embarrassed and ashamed. Tomorrow is another day. You can always come home to a *New Day, New Life*.

PART I
LIVE

YOU ONLY LIVE ONCE

31 Days to Make Your Life Count

DEDICATION

"Go into all the world. Preach the good news to everyone. Anyone who believes and is baptized will be saved. But anyone who does not believe will be punished."

-- Mark 16:15-16 NIRV

I dedicate *The Good News Book Series* to my mother, Gloria McGriff; she trained us siblings up in the church and encouraged our education. The joy of avidly reading books by my wife, Margarita Overton, also encourages me to write.

CONTENTS

Foreword 13
Introduction - Following God's Promises and
    Receiving His Blessings 16

One – Burdens 22
Two – Children 25
Three – Comfort 28
Four – Compassion 31
Five – Faith 34
Six – Fear 37
Seven – Finances 40
Eight – Forgiveness 43
Nine – Godly Living 46
Ten – Healing 49
Eleven – Holy Spirit 52
Twelve – Hope 55
Thirteen – Humility 58
Fourteen – Judgment 61
Fifteen – Love for Enemies 64
Sixteen – Marriage 67
Seventeen – Nearness 70
Eighteen – New Life 73
Nineteen – Obedience 76
Twenty – Patience 79
Twenty One – Peace 82
Twenty Two – Prayer 85
Twenty Three – Protection 88
Twenty Four – Provision 91
Twenty Five – Repentance 94
Twenty Six – Rest 97
Twenty Seven – Resurrection 100

Twenty Eight – Salvation. 103
Twenty Nine – Success 106
Thirty – Temptation 109
Thirty One – Wisdom 112

Conclusion - Living Up To Expectations. 115

FOREWORD

I love singing the Russell Kelso Carter's hymn, *Standing on the Promises*: "Standing on the promises of Christ my King, Through eternal ages let his praises ring; Glory in the highest, I will shout and sing, Standing on the promises of God." Great song, but what does it mean – this standing on the promises? How do you stand on God's promises? What does the word promise mean to you? A promise is a vow, a commitment, a guarantee. Or so the book definition is, but when I say promise, what do you think of? Do you think of the crooked car salesman who told you there was nothing wrong with the car, and it's the cheapest one they had? Or maybe the politician who promises he won't raise taxes and he's on your side. Or perhaps it hits even closer to home. She promised to take you for better or worse, or for richer or poorer. And when poorer and worse came, her promise left with her. Stand on a promise – I don't think so; the last promise I stood on was broken.

A couple of years ago, we had a pretty bad ice storm on a Friday night. One of our pastors arrived at the church Saturday morning to get ready for our Saturday night service for young adults. The parking lot was covered with ice. A couple of other people were already there busting up the ice so folk could get to church. The volunteers went in and got coffee to warm up, and he stayed outside and started working. He was glad they went inside because it wasn't long before he lost his balance. Both feet and the shovel went in the air, and the pastor landed on the hard ice. He saw nothing but sky overhead. Thankfully, no one was around. But now he had to get up – without falling again. The pastor had no such luck. He fell one more time and saw nothing but sky. Thankfully, no one was around. He slowly got up this time using the shovel. Now my colleague had another problem, the pain was unbearable. Lots of pain, and he was cold. And to go inside was defeat. After all, the helpers had worked for a long time without stopping. The Young Adults Pastor had been out there 15 minutes, and now he was going in. However, it hurt so badly. He was so cold and carefully made his way inside. My coworker found the guys, but for ego's sake, he couldn't tell them why he had come inside. He could barely sip his coffee and his rear end was hurting so bad. My associate wasn't about to tell them why he was inside. All pain and embarrassment because he couldn't trust what he was standing on. The ice was hard to walk on and painful when he fell. In life, broken promises are hard to stand on too; they're even more painful when what you were standing on-- a rock-solid foundation gives way.

Something to stand on won't give way in tough times and for followers of Jesus Christ; we stand on the promises of God. The promises of God are found in his Word – the Bible. It's our rock-solid foundation. The Bible is more than a book of stories about what happened 2,000 years ago. From its promises, we draw strength, find hope, and most of all, we learn about the God who loves us. His word is powerful. His promises are real. It's the rock-solid foundation our faith is built upon. It's his promises found in his Word we stand on.

In the end, 'promise' means different things to different people. Mark, who joined FirstNLR in 2015, has structured this book's 31-day roadmap of God's conditional promises around three guideposts: the promise's meaning, an engaging story of fulfillment, and fruitful application. The stories are inspiring. But more than the information, motivation and practical guidance, what stands out is the appeal and journey to trust in and live out God's promises. You can receive 31 days of Almighty God's blessings and favor every day and every month of the year. Similar to the story of Ezekiel in the Old Testament (Ezekiel 2:9 – 3:9), Mark had an encounter with the Promises of God. No, Mark didn't eat a scroll with God's words. However, they are a part of his life like the food he eats becomes part of him. He's an active member of our greeting and homeless ministries and supports outreach and Mission initiatives.

The Bible is also God's story of bringing salvation to us. God loved you and I so much, he gave us life and created us for relationship with him. When we sinned and broke relationship, he gave us Jesus his son to restore the relationship with him. Afterwards, he gave us the Holy Spirit so we would not be alone. He gave us the

Bible. The Bible explains all of this and tells us this story. The Bible is our guidebook for living and can transform your life. His Word is to be the light guiding you in a dark world. His Word is to be your comfort in a storm. It's what you stand on. When you need a promise to stand on and won't fade away, you go to the Bible. It's filled with encouragement, blessing, guidance, and direction. It's our guidebook for living. Like Ezekiel eating the Word, you and I have to do the same thing. Take his Word, break it down, and absorb it. Eat his words and grow. Fill your life with the Bible. God gave us his Word. Respond to his gift and realize you need more of the Bible in your life.

Let me give you a couple of ways you can fill your life with Scripture:

1. Create and follow a plan to read the Bible. Spend time reading a portion of the Bible until you think you understand it and can apply it to your life. Move on.
2. Memorize Bible verses. Memorizing the Bible gives you a foundation to stand on when you're overwhelmed by life. So I've got a question for you – what promise are you standing on? Your own best guesses? Somebody else's promises? Maybe the reason you keep falling and the reason you have so much pain is because you're standing on the wrong thing. Stand on his promises. Read God's promises, memorize them and here's one more way to get more of the Bible in your life.
3. Join a Sunday school class. In addition to meeting great people, Sunday school is one of the best places to learn more about God and faith. God's promises don't fail. But sometimes you need all the help you can get standing. Sunday school is the place and reason why you and I need more of the Bible in our life. When life's hard, I can stand on the rock-solid promises of God. What you stand on determines if you'll make it when life becomes difficult. These are God's promises from his Word. And as you hear or read God's gift to you, eat his words – *You Only Live Once*.

Rod Loy
Senior Pastor, First Assembly North Little Rock

INTRODUCTION

Following God's Promises and Receiving His Blessings

We make many types of promises -- from marriage vows to military oaths, specific actions or completion of tasks. Happy couples recite blissful wedding vows and pledge commitment and loyalty to their new spouse till "death us do part." We will love our partner for life. We all crave for such unwavering devotion to tie the knot. In my marriage, we're faithful to, covenant, and honor "*MO2-4L+*"—*Mark and Margarita Overton for Life* joyfully – the promise of "forever" and a fairy-tale ending. What God has joined together, let no man put asunder. Most of us have a similar vision with at least one person in our lives.

Often before marriage, head over heels in love and love is blind, couples wear beautiful promise rings and take the next big step in their commitment to one another in the life ahead of them – from "I Promise" to "I Do." Lifelong friends, college graduates, and their "alma mater," veterans and the armed services, and citizens and their countries also reflect commitment and loyalty through their faithful allegiances.

When I served active duty in the United States Air Force, the oath of enlistment signified a public statement of commitment: "… I will support and defend the Constitution of the United States against all enemies, foreign and domestic; I will bear true faith and allegiance to the same; and I will obey the orders of the President of the United States and the orders of the officers appointed over me according to regulations and the Uniform Code of Military Justice."

In mentioning the President of the United States, you may remember some of the countless Presidential promises. In 1986,

President Ronald Reagan proclaimed, "We did not –repeat, did not -- trade weapons or anything else for hostages, nor will we." In 2003, President George W. Bush announced aboard the USS Abraham Lincoln, "Mission Accomplished," declaring an end to major combat operations in Iraq. Earlier in 1988, his father, President H.W. Bush promised during the Republication nomination, "Read my lips; no new taxes." In 2008, "President Barack Obama claimed, "If you choose change, you will have a nominee who doesn't take a dime from Washington lobbyists and PACs [Political Action Committees]."

You also may be familiar with Martin Luther King Jr.'s "I Have a Dream" speech, which encouraged America there is room for everyone to 'cash in' on the rights they have been promised.

In a sense, we have come to our nation's capital to cash a check. When the architects of our republic wrote the magnificent words of the Constitution and the Declaration of Independence, they were signing a promissory note to which every American was to fall heir. This note was a promise all men, yes, black men as well as white men, would be guaranteed the unalienable rights of life, liberty, and the pursuit of happiness.

In addition, we sometimes make promises in dire situations: "If you get me out of this situation, I promise to serve you." "If you get me through this, I will make a difference." If he would do something, you would do something, or stop doing something in fact. To help you through the situation, you feel you owe mighty God something and make a confession of faith. Scripture tells us when making a vow to God, keep your promise and don't delay in fulfilling it. He has no pleasure in fools or a fool's errand; fulfill your vow. The bottom line: it's better not to make a vow than to make one and not fulfill it.

It's also awesome when you avoid making a promise in haste; you create rash or quick decisions. In the book of Judges, Jephthah made a vow to the LORD while fighting the Ammonites. If triumphant over the Ammonites, he would present as a burnt offering the first person at his house greeting him when he returned. The LORD answered him and gave him victory. What Jephthah didn't expect was his one and only child to come running out of the door to greet him upon his return home. Two months later, he offered her as a burnt offering to uphold his vow.

Our words have the power of life and death; people expect you to honor your promise, a personal commitment. We prize keeping a promise being "as good as our word." As Mahatma Gandhi encouraged, "A promise made is a promise kept." When you make a promise, you will honor your promise. You sealed the deal, and you meant what you said. You're sincere about it. You signed the pledge and knowingly believe what you promised.

You want to do what you said you'd do. You want to. Yet, like sensing a gut check of unsureness, thoughts, and feelings may be unsettled in your mind. Your feelings, capacity, willingness, circumstances, or benefit can change over time. You don't want to face the agonizing reality, and you feel bad. Like a New Year's resolution or info commercial guarantee falling short, you sort of always knew -- you wouldn't be able to fulfill the promise.

Not to steal the thunder, God honors his promises. Like opening an e-mail from a trusted source, you can trust the sender. This banging message is from mighty God. The promises of God are also rock-solid and indisputable. God makes these assurances himself instead of offhand, off-the-cuff, empty promises. He doesn't under-promise or make broken, pie in the sky promises. You shouldn't expect a breach of promise; a promise is a promise.

Truly I tell you, God's promises are 'Yes' and 'Amen;' his 'yea' is his 'yea,' and you can take that to the bank! The Scripture says, God fulfills his promises. He will not break his covenant, and he will not go back on his word – not even one word of what he said. Beyond the shadow of a doubt, God's promises never fail! You can always count on God. You can always believe God's Word. And you can always trust in God's promises; they are guaranteed to satisfy.

God's Word contains thousands of Bible promises, and you can claim them in faith. Researchers have said the Bible includes over 7,000 promises, and around 1,500 Bible verses contain the word "if." In each promise, God pledges something will (or will not) be done or given or come to pass.

You may recognize two kinds of promises in the text from the LORD—unconditional and conditional. You may remember his covenant never to send another flood to destroy the entire earth. This unconditional pledge is one whose fulfillment rests solely with God; it's made without attaching any conditions whatsoever.

Like an "if-then" statement, a conditional promise declares the LORD is willing to act under certain circumstances; it appeals to you to cooperate. What do I mean? Romans 10:9 tells us: "If you declare with your mouth, "Jesus is LORD," and believe in your heart God raised him from the dead, you will be saved." Let's be clear: this type of promise is subject to certain qualifications or requirements. When you act, you must react. It's not all up to our awesome God; we also have skin in the game and a part to play in the relationship! Right? Isaiah 1:19 reassures us: "If ye be willing and obedient, ye shall eat the good of the land."

A computer programming language performs different computations or actions based on whether a condition evaluates to true or false. Like its conditional statement (i.e., if-then-else), God decrees a profound, conditional promise. The people must meet both requirements to eat the good of the land. If they do one and not the other, they do not eat of the good land. In this statement, blessings follow obedience to God. To receive these flow of blessings into your life, you must cooperate and follow the conditions he has given; it's a two-way street. God expects something from you in return.

To satisfy these Scripture's guarantees, you must come to faith in Christ; you submit to his will and trust him. You must meet his conditions first. Your responses to his promises result in blessings or curses. I've identified the promises in God's Word for daily Christian living and explained what they mean. The catch is to know your responsibilities and how to fulfill them. You can elevate your faith and further become immersed in his Word to truly put your devotion in motion. The LORD declares and expects you to fulfill your words.

As you read these conditional promises, look for the word "if" or the promise may also imply the related condition. You can hang your hat these promises are for you in this day and age; they are for daily Christian living. They show a lot of promise. Though of times past, these guarantees still affect you today – every believer in every age. The certainty of God's promise still stands as when God made his promise to Abraham (Genesis 12). God doesn't change, and he sets no limits on time period or recipient. You can't presume to know exactly when, where, or how God will fulfill his promises in your life. Because these promises are backed up with Scripture, you can claim these conditional promises as your own. Honest as the day is long, my word is my bond; he promises you a 'rose garden.'

Tailored for success, this inspiring devotional provides 31 days of targeted, conditional promises of God. In unpacking its content, you'll find each day is structured into a promise, story of fulfillment, and fruitful application – your daily bread. Like Baskin-Robbins' original '31 flavors,' you can receive 31 days of almighty God's favor every day and every month of the year. Each month, you can start anew and absorb yourself more in the teachings. They're alphabetically listed in areas from burdens to wisdom to make it easy for you to navigate through the table of contents; choose and dwell in your best-fit promise taking you to your goal. This book is easy to go back to again and again; it inspires and enables you to be doers of the word. Fortify your faith by releasing God's promises into your life.

By opening this book, you've shown interest in where you are and desire to be. Review God's many promises with a heart of trust and gratitude. My hope is, you'll be encouraged each day to receive and act on these relevant promises. You'll dislike getting to the end of the devotional. Read for the second round if you like. I have a deal for you — a deal I do not believe you can refuse. If you satisfy the condition he has set, I believe you'll position yourself to receive his blessings. And the icing on the cake is none of God's promises ever fail.

Well, enough of waiting for the LORD to fulfill his promises. Take the leap [of faith] and avoid wasting a lot of time hemming and hawing. Go for the "A" and use this book as your guide to help live out your part of these conditional promises. MLK Jr. affirmed, "If we wait to we're ready, we'll be waiting for the rest of our lives." Do it now; you don't have to start tomorrow. Don't focus on the problems; focus on the promises.

You desire to receive and live out God's promises; you want to excel and grow. You want change in your life. You are a person of vision and dreams. You want something special and great from your life. Most of all, you'll gain the advantage of God's blessing in your life. "*You Only Live Once,* but if you do it right, once is enough," stated an American actress. Make your life count and live up to expectations in applying these 31 rock-solid promises. They're a perfect for an amazing day! Imagine a new story for your life and live it.

Alright, you're all set and ready to jump into this book. Jump for overflowing blessings and dive in anywhere you like – the book was penned to allow you to do dive right in. And if you want to get a head start on Salvation and the most powerful blessings in Scripture, leap now to Day 1 –– where all the living up to expectations starts! Friends, I urge you, declare this day the LORD is your God and you will walk in obedience to him. Keep his decrees, commands, and laws. Hang on every word; obedience brings blessings. Yes, LORD – the promise of a new day. All the people shall say, "Amen!"

DAY 1

Burdens

*Cast your cares on the LORD
and he will sustain you;
he will never let
the righteous be shaken.*

Psalm 55:22

Express Promise

Scripture tells us of this promise's meaning. Whatever your burdens, trials, troubles, crosses, distresses, cares or fears, you can lay them on his shoulders. Whereas anxiety reacts with fear and worry, the LORD shows concern and acts with reason and empathy in taking care of your concerns. By faith and prayer, you can commit to him and confidently expect a good outcome.

Carry Out

We all may have experienced the loss of a loved one. Last year in September, The LORD called a beautiful person home to rest. I experienced the unimaginable, devastating, heartbreaking, grief-stricken loss of a first cousin; she was like a sister, and I was at a loss for words. Growing up with my cousin was always a blast; we rode around in her Gremlin, listened to her girls' [Whitney Houston and Janet Jackson] music, and hung out after Friday night football games. She was so real, caring, warm, and down-to-earth; she had a great sense of humor and the best laugh.

Before going into surgery, she gifted us with her signature laugh and soft smile; she lit up the room. From the love expressed, so many others also saw my sweet cousin as a hard worker and faithful friend with a heart of gold. My cousin was a lovely person inside and out; she brought out the best in us. She made us better. I'm sure you have a loved one like this in your life. Though my heart hurt and her loss felt so unreal, I held up and held on to God's promise of strength and sustenance; I pushed forward and praised through pain. My cousin will always be in my heart.

Like Ruth and Job, you may have lived through difficult times too. During the story of Ruth, we meet her mother-in-law Naomi. After the death of her husband and sons, Naomi returned to Israel and Ruth traveled with her (Ruth 1:1-22). Though discouraged and bitter, Naomi and Ruth had an amazing bond because of God's goodness. Naomi faced trials and emerged victorious in God's hand.

Similarly, even though Job lost his houses, riches, cattle, and children, he still chose to praise God for his goodness (Job 1: 1-21).

Job recognized everything he had in life came from the hand of the LORD. He continued to maintain his trust in the faithfulness of God. In the same way, you may have experienced personal heartbreaks like the loss of a family member or close friend or loss of a job or income; you can sympathize with an overwhelming or shattering feeling of losing a child.

Go and Do Likewise

Is conflict in a relationship or anxiety with your children, job, college or health your current situation? In each, by faith and prayer, cast your burdens upon the LORD. Remain in his assurance and all will work for your good. You'll feel strengthened by his Spirit; it'll sustain you during your life struggle. Don't worry about anything; pray about everything. God wants to walk beside you through difficult times. He'll sustain, bear up, and supply your wants, and satisfy you. When you face trials or tragedies, turn to God.

DAY 2

Children

Children, obey your parents in the LORD, for this is right. "Honor your father and mother"—which is the first commandment with a promise—"so it may go well with you and you may enjoy long life on the earth."

Ephesians 6: 1-3

Express Promise

When you cast your burdens upon the LORD, he will carry you in the arms of his power like a nurse cradles a child. By the same token, Scripture tells us of the meaning of this promise: children obey your parents and honor the duty of parents. Children, obey your parents in everything consistent with your duty to the LORD. In all things lawful, the will of the parent is a law to the child. This is right and reasonable. Children should honor (i.e., love, reverence, obey, assist) their father and mother.

Carry Out

I grew up in a Central Texas city providing a strong quality of life without the typical problems associated with urban growth and development. We got solid values to last a lifetime. Everyone treated each other like family and neighbors were 'extended' parents. Our hood was the 26th Street or 'Purple Jacket' gang. We wore the school colors of a former all-black high school.

My siblings and I grew up with strong work, faith, and education ethics. For extra money, we mowed lawns, picked pecans, recycled soda bottles, and caught and sold crawfish for fishing bright and early. Give a man a fish and you will feed him for a day. I also worked on a small farm where the owner had cows, pigs, etc. We also went to the store for neighbors; they gave us enough money to buy the item with spare change for a treat. These jobs taught us many valuable lessons about work: integrity, excellence, teamwork, and followership, to name a few. We were encouraged and expected to achieve.

Football is king in Texas; some say football is a religion or Texas is about "God and guns!" We not only looked forward to Friday night football, but we also had a church-going childhood and school was mandatory – our weekly model. And if we misbehaved, acted up, or popped off in school, the principal spanked us with a wood paddle–ouch! Afterwards, momma whooped us with a switch too. I was whipped into compliance! Needless to say, we understood well the duty of children is to obey their parents.

The story of Shadrach, Meshach, and Abednego exemplifies an example of obedience and faithfulness. They refused to worship the golden statue of Nebuchadnezzar, king of Babylon. God rewarded their obedience by protecting them when they were thrown into a blazing inferno heated seven times hotter than usual (Daniel 3:1-30).

Go and Do Likewise

We're children of God through faith; children of God do what is right and are heirs of God and co-heirs with Christ (Romans 8:17). So, raising and training your child begins with the Bible (2 Timothy 3:16). Prayerfully meditate for your children's obedience. Train up your children by first directing them to the Savior and obeying all God's regulations. The LORD will make you the head, not the tail; you will always be at the top, never at the bottom (Deuteronomy 12:28). As a parent, if you maintain obedience to God's laws, your children and successive generation most likely will too. (Leviticus 25:18).

DAY 3

Comfort

Praise be to the God and Father of our LORD Jesus Christ, the Father of compassion and the God of all comfort, who comforts us in all our troubles, so we can comfort those in any trouble with the comfort we ourselves receive from God.

2 Corinthians 1:3-4

Express Promise

The Bible tells us children are a reward from God (Psalm 127:3) -- how comforting! It is my hope you are also encouraged by the meaning of God's promise of comfort. He says to not let your heart be troubled. All comforts come from God. Scripture tells us he is as tender as a mother; he comforts us as a mother comforts a little one. Jesus came to this earth to give us hope and comfort. He promised the Holy Spirit would be sent to be our Comforter. In facing loss, we can find comfort; we can see our loved ones again at Christ's coming. God sends people to comfort you, and he wants you to be a comfort to others.

Carry Out

Comforted by faith God is in control, one of my high school classmates shared praise through problems. She initially went to the emergency room because of a gallbladder condition; however, after a chest X-ray, doctors discovered a spot on her lung. When she followed up with her primary care physician, she was referred to a lung specialist. These pulmonary appointments are usually several weeks out. And it so happened, the clinic had an opening. She scheduled a lung biopsy, which an available appointment is normally 2-3 weeks out. Six days later she had the biopsy and after 13 days received her results -- a malignant tumor. After an imaging test, technicians found no other "spots." And she had surgery to remove part of her cancerous lung. Though my classmate was the one with bad news, she comforted us by sharing how thankful she is for all God has given her. Doctors did not leave any stone unturned, and it so happened, she is now cancer free.

The Book of Psalm put it this way, how God comforted David. He had escaped for his life from a jealous King Saul and wrote a powerful testimony: "Even though I walk through the darkest valley, I will fear no evil, for you are with me; your rod and your staff, they comfort me" (Psalm 23:4).

Like with David, God is our comforter in times of trial, anxiety, and hopelessness. Open your heart to also comfort the sick, dying, lonely, disheartened, shut-in, defeated, and those who need Christ's love. The God of all comfort comes to you as you pray; seek him with all of your heart. He is there when no one else seems to care.

Go and Do Likewise

Trust God and allow him to provide you comfort. You sleep when you're comfortable and rested. However, when you face tough times, you may not sleep well because of discomfort in your Spirit. In spite of the situation, believe God will comfort you each day. You can also be comfortable in the uncomfortable when you're in the will of God. Like Jesus being comfortable sleeping in the boat when the storm was all around him (Matthew 8:23-27), you can trust in the LORD if you have an uncomfortable condition at work, school, etc.

DAY 4

Compassion

Whoever is kind to the poor lends to the LORD,
and he will reward them for what they have done.

Proverbs 19:17

Express Promise

While comfort or mercy may refer to God's outward doing in response to conditions of sorrow or suffering, compassion denotes inward affection for others deriving from one's heart. God's promise of compassion tells us to show concern for the poor, the homeless, the orphans, and the widows.

When having compassion and giving to the less fortunate, you alleviate and lessen their necessities and glorify God. When you enrich the poor, you can enrich yourself. The LORD takes what is done to them as done to himself. God has blessed the poor of this world to be rich in faith and heirs of his kingdom (Luke 6: 20-21).

Carry Out

During my childhood, I watched my mother cook and take Sunday dinners to friends shut-in and anonymously give money to church families in need. While I served in the active duty United States Air Force, I continued to show these deep feelings of compassion; I was actively involved in base and community activities.

After transitioning from the Air Force and accompanying my active duty spouse, I sustained making service my heartbeat of compassion and served in the church. At First Assembly of God of North Little Rock (First NLR), where 'Every Soul Matters to God,' I show care and invest in others by participating with the homeless and greeting ministries and other outreach initiatives.

In 2015, as one of fifteen teams, my spouse and I served on the Hospitality and Greeters Team. After the meal, I made a blooper when talking with a guest. He had a medical condition and asked for assistance from potential resources nearby. I was amiss in asking a homeless person, "Where do you live?" He said, "I live under a bridge." My wife wouldn't let me live down my embarrassing slip-up. We led the guest to our prayer team. In short, we helped out with the clothing team the next year.

Like the parable of the Good Samaritan (Luke 10:25-37), you can also show mercy and compassion to your neighbors. Scripture also prompts us, "If anyone has material possessions and sees a brother or sister in need but has no pity on them, how can the love of God be in that person? Dear children, let us not love with words or speech but with actions and in truth" (1 John 4:17-18).

Go and Do Likewise

Most of us don't find giving to the poor or caring for the ill difficult. God commands us to give generously to the poor (Deuteronomy 15:10). Jesus was also moved by passion to help a person, even if it was inconvenient (John 11:33). Most folk will feed or pray for the homeless; you can show passion and take the next step and establish a friendship and aid a life change (Luke 14:13). It's my hope and prayer you continue to connect with God's heart for the poor. Many more areas of society can also benefit from fostering a compassionate view: civil rights, treatment of animals, or the environment, to name a few.

DAY 5

Faith

Have faith in God," Jesus answered. "Truly I tell you, if anyone says to this mountain, 'Go, throw yourself into the sea,' and does not doubt in their heart but believes what they say will happen, it will be done for them. Therefore I tell you, whatever you ask for in prayer, believe you have received it, and it will be yours.

Mark 11: 22-24

Express Promise

A heart of compassion contributes to a heart of faith (Mark 6:34). Like the inward affection of compassion, faith denotes a direct connection with God. The meaning of this promise speaks of having a strong, firm faith or confidence in the power and faithfulness of God. We are to be fully confident he will make good his declarations and fulfill his promises in due season. "Now faith is confidence in what we hope for and assurance about what we do not see" (Hebrew 11:1). On this foundation, approach God in prayer. When you fully expect and are sincere, persistent, and determined in asking, you'll receive what you ask, as our LORD declares.

Carry Out

We can all get antsy about a job raise or promotion. You've been faithful over small things, and you want to expand your territory and be faithful over larger things. Faith requires you "give up something," or you're willing to abandon everything; the higher the risk, the higher the reward.

By faith, my best friend and his spouse put up their house for sale to relocate from Ohio to Alabama, their home state. It took 18 months to sell their house. In leaving his civilian government job, he was possibly giving up a top-level supervisory position. His spouse moved to Alabama in advance after their home sold and he commuted every 2 weeks. When his partner's medical condition worsened, he asked his boss to telework every 2 weeks. After his supervisor said, "No," my friend made a dramatic new move to resign from his job.

He continued to apply for jobs in Alabama. Once accepting a job, the Washington DC contractor was unaware my friend had resigned his government job. My colleague received a telework job he could work from home, earned the same pay, and resided nearby for family – Hallelujah!

If you have faith like a mustard seed, Scripture tells us you can say to this mountain, "Move from here to there," and it will move. Nothing will be impossible for you (Matthew 17:20). In the book of

Daniel, he influenced King Darius, his employer, to believe in the only true God. (Daniel 6:26). By doing a job well in your sphere of work, you can also practically 'show and tell' others with whom you work about Christ. In addition, the story of Hannah's plea for a son inspires us to pray and believe (1 Samuel 1: 10-11, 19-20).

Go and Do Likewise

Regardless of your current situation and even when you have to 'give up something,' love God with all your heart and mind (Deuteronomy 6:5). The more you think about God, the more connected you are. He is in your mind, and you can have more self-control over your thoughts. Also, ask him for help to spiritually guide you. He is faithful to answer. You don't have to have mountain-moving faith; your faith needs to be present. God will meet you at your level of expectation or faith. Nothing is too hard for him, and with him, all things are possible.

DAY 6

Fear

*I sought the LORD, and he answered me;
he delivered me from all my fears.*

Psalm 34:4

Express Promise

Fear is the opposite of faith. From time to time, we refuse to operate in faith because of fear. God's promise of delivering us from all fears tells us how David's prayers helped to silence his fears. He sought the LORD and the LORD delivered him from all his fears. He provided for David not only from the death he feared, but also from the worry David was put into by the dread of it. Look unto God with an eye of faith and prayer, and be lifted up in comfort and joy. Be secure in the hope of his compassion.

Carry Out

Everybody has a dog story. Who doesn't love a dog story? I have plenty of stories about man's best friend: Sadie, our pet beagle, as well as former family dogs like Champ, Wolfkin, and Buttons. We've always had canines in our family: Lacy, Cocoa, Kojac, Nikita, Baker, Jack, Crumpet, Prince, Winston, Bella, and Cojo. Well, I also have a dog story about my past neighbor's full grown, jet-black Doberman pinscher.

Late one evening after returning home from a friend's house, I parked my car on the street and walked toward my parent's house. They may have turned in early, and the garage doors were down. So, I proceeded toward the front door. Suddenly, I caught a flash of white in my peripheral vision galloping from my right out of total darkness… my neighbor's Doberman. Armed to the teeth, they gleamed pearly white. His approach was "Feed me!" I couldn't beat a hasty retreat to my car, so my M.O. was to get into the house. With leaps and bounds, I pounded the door and hoped it would be unlocked. I felt like Casper, the friendly ghost. I was so fearful I wanted to permeate through the door. The LORD –through my momma – delivered me from my fear and opened the door. Thank God, I didn't go to the dog! My unspoken prayer was heard, and answered on time!

I experienced the type of fear of being afraid of something – 90 pounds of a meat-eating canine. However, I overcame my timidity and had enough self-discipline to make it to the front door (1

Timothy 1:7). I was brave as a lion. Like the meaning of the promise, Isaiah 41:10 encourages us, "So do not fear, for I am with you; do not be dismayed, for I am your God. I will strengthen you and help you; I will uphold you with my righteous right hand."

Go and Do Likewise

Like these stories, you can also take practical steps to stand on this promise actively; believe God for whatever needs you have. Instability, conflict, lack of peace, and uncertainty can create fear. Fear can paralyze you and cause you to get off the mark; fear can result in the fight-or-flight response. In addition, fear can separate us from God as sin separates us from God.

When you trust God, you refuse to give in to anxiety. Being disconnected from God contributes to tension. You leave your comfort zone and believe in faith versus fear. You turn to God even in your darkest times and trust him to make things right. The key to overcoming fear is total and complete trust in God! If you trust God, you can't have fear. Keep faith instead.

DAY 7

Finances

Bring the whole tithe into the storehouse, there may be food in my house. Test me in this," says the LORD Almighty, "and see if I will not throw open the floodgates of heaven and pour out so much blessing there will not be room enough to store it.

Malachi 3:10

Express Promise

Trust in God lessens the fear of having a poverty spirit or a scarcity mindset. This promise denotes bringing the tithe 'into the storehouse,' which were large rooms built for this purpose (e.g., meat, sacrifices, etc.) If lacking, the LORD will supply not only plenty, but also in proportion to the tithes and offerings you give.

Bringing all your tithes denotes paying tithes in full and on time. Strive not to hold back the tithe. In the Old Testament, the law required Israelites to set aside a tenth of all their fields produced each year. The law also obliged additional tithes: for the Levites, festivals, and orphans and widows, doubling the taxation to about 23 percent (Deuteronomy 14:28-29). The only place a percentage is required is the old covenant. In the New Testament, honor God by gladly returning some of the blessings he gives. We have the sacrifice of Jesus Christ.

Carry Out

It's offering time! Some of you may be wondering why people at church are so excited about the opportunity for giving. Feast or famine, my spouse and I faithfully give out of honor for God. When she first became a new believer, she developed a close relationship with a family strong in their Christian faith. One of their encouragements was the concept of tithing. She was a single parent struggling with an Airman's [or first grade] pay. She felt she couldn't afford to tithe. Her friend lovingly said, "You can't afford NOT to tithe."

Her ah-ha moment sealing the deal was after she had tithed and paid bills and had $70 left over for groceries. She clipped at least $20 in coupons and was still $30 short. She carefully selected groceries based on one coupon for each item in the cart. Unexpectedly, the store manager walked up and said, "Here, it looks like you can use this." He handed her a $35 voucher! God knew her needs, and he provided the way! That's good!

Consider too the parable of the talents (Matthew 25:14-30) and shrewd manager (Luke 16:1-14). One master entrusted his wealth to servants when he went on a journey and returned; the other master accused his manager of wasting his possessions respectively. We're also encouraged to use our God-given gifts in his service (1 Peter 4:10).

Go and Do Likewise

Like these servants and manager, Scripture advises you to have wisdom when managing money. Know what your expenses are and what income figures you're dealing with. Wise people save or invest for the future (Proverbs 21:20). When spending money, employ good decision making and control. Give back to the LORD joyfully, and he will richly bless you; you're a good steward over God's possessions. Use your money to help others, but with good judgment and God's direction. Be wise and a good steward of money. If careful to follow all these instructions, you will be blessed as he promised.

DAY 8

Forgiveness

If we confess our sins, he is faithful and just and will forgive us our sins and purify us from all unrighteousness.

1 John 1:9

Express Promise

You cannot serve both God and money. The condition of this promise is, if we fully acknowledge and confess our sins, he is faithful to his promise to forgive us. He will do what he has assured us he will do in absolving our flaws, faults, weaknesses or shortcomings. The LORD is upright, denoting he is equitable, and his disposition is proper. He is just, which means he will be true to his promises, pardoning those who believe in him. The forgiveness of sins is an act of mercy as opposed to an act of justice. You have his word he is ready to let you off if you bring to bear true atonement and faith. You can't receive forgiveness if you don't repent, believe, and confess. He will cleanse you from all unrighteousness by forgiving all past, known, and unknown. He ultimately removes all the blemishes of guilt from your soul.

Carry Out

As I watched true crime shows on television, I was not only astounded by the evil of some people, but also the families and victims' forgiveness of murderers. If you spend any amount of time watching true crime TV, you will quickly notice the shows almost always involve one particular type of crime: murder. Often, too, the focus is on exotic, bizarre and especially grisly or gory details of murder. The killers are glutton for punishment. Like me, you may be one of the millions of people wound up and fascinated by these true crime shows.

God is just, and his love is so amazing! Families feel love and compassion and find it in their heart to forgive; people petition the kangaroo courts to set the offenders free or help them start a new life. They chose not to hang on to anger and revenge. They let go and forgave to help bring healing. Jesus did something special for all of us when he died on the cross. He canceled a real debt and paid for our sin. Christ took punishment for us. We no longer have debt. He paid it in full (Matthew 27: 32-65).

We all mess up. The LORD has forgiven you, so you also must forgive (Colossians 3:13). Jesus forgives us for our thoughts, deeds, actions, motives, or heart's intent not lined up with his word. He is the reason we can forgive others. We love and forgive because he first loved and forgave us (Luke 23: 33-34).

Go and Do Likewise

Like Jesus' petition on the cross, we should forgive one another as God has forgiven us. In humility, die to self. Jesus also said we are to forgive others "seventy times seven" in response to Peter's question, "LORD, how many times shall I forgive my brother when he sins against me? Up to seven times?" (Matthew 18:21-22). Have empathy for others. Folk can have bitterness or ill will toward you or offend, hurt, lie to, or reject you. We also offend God every time we sin. So, it's a lot easier to forgive when you remember you need forgiveness too (2 Corinthians 2:5). I'm so glad his grace covers us!

DAY 9

Godly Living

Worship the LORD your God, and his blessing will be on your food and water. I will take away sickness from among you,

Exodus 23:25

Express Promise

Forgiving someone who hurt you is never easy. But with God, it is possible. When you worship and enjoy the LORD, the precept with this promise is his blessing will make your bread and water more refreshing and nourishing than a feast of other things without blessing. He will take away your sickness; he will prevent or remove it. He promises where you live will not be visited by widespread, dreadful diseases. He will fulfill the number of your days. Thus, through godliness, you have the promise of the life now.

Carry Out

We're all told exercise is good. It is part of being healthy and the struggle to exercise is real. My spouse and I also toil to get enough exercise, like lots of people. I can't count the number of exercise equipment and programs we've invested in; we even converted a bedroom into our 'fitness room.' We recently got another fitness device to impel us to get up and get moving more. This wearable product changes the way we move; it prompts us with hourly messages like "Feed me 250 steps" or "It's step o'clock." My spouse jests "we're managed" like robots. And it's amazing how much this gadget motivates us. We're not addicted to or compulsive about exercise. However, instead of moaning when I have to mow the yard, I excitedly see it as an opportunity to get in lots of steps. And to top off reaching our daily activity goal, my spouse and I frequently burn off steam jogging or walking in place, doing jumping jacks, or walking throughout the house as though we have an inside track or path. We look to get extra steps in whenever possible, being a slave to the activity tracker. In a sense, the activity tracker "manages" our perspective and motivation.

Is our Christian life a bit similar? Paul encourages, "Train yourself to be godly" (1 Timothy 4:7). Physical training may have some value, but spiritual training -- training in godliness -- is of value both in this life and the next. "Godliness" should be seen as good, clean-living enjoyment of life and of God—God-oriented living. Consider the duties to qualify as an overseer or deacon, denoting godliness in action (1 Timothy 3:2-3, 8). Regarding Christians in the church at Ephesus, Paul was steadfast healthy doctrine produces healthy deeds (1 Timothy 1:3).

Go and Do Likewise

Godly people live in such a way as to please God. Godliness is an attitude of seeking to please the LORD. Scripture tells us to live as children of light and find out what pleases the LORD (Ephesians 4:17). Godliness is not avoiding sin in order to escape punishment. It is avoiding things which we know don't please God because we love him more than we love sin or our own way. Godliness fulfills the first great commandment: "Love the LORD your God with all your heart and with all your soul and with all your mind and with all your strength" (Mark 12:29-30). Trust in Jesus and his promises and grow in godliness.

DAY 10

Healing

He said, "If you listen carefully to the LORD your God and do what is right in his eyes, if you pay attention to his commands and keep all his decrees, I will not bring on you any of the diseases I brought on the Egyptians, for I am the LORD, who heals you."

Exodus 15:26

Express Promise

Have faith in God. Know you're healed. It is here promised if you will attentively listen to the voice of the LORD your God, he will put none of these diseases (plagues, leprosy, skin, etc.,) on you. If disobedient, the hardships inflicted on your adversaries should be brought to bear on you. Though the danger is implied, the promise is conveyed. God is the great Physician --Jehovah Rapha, The LORD Who Heals; the LORD Who makes bitter things sweet. He is your sustainer, provider, comforter; he is your guide, your strength, and friend. The LORD is our life and the number of our days. He will heal you, sustaining you in health and healing your ailments.

Carry Out

It goes without saying, I planned on being home for my brother's surgery. Doctors had discovered a polyp after an exam. Along with family residing in town, I wanted to be there for my brother and available to help. We talked about how he would medicate, and any help needed, especially since he would be recovering at home.

I stayed at the hospital with family during the pre-op visit and surgery, which started behind schedule. It was welcomed to receive a pastoral prayer for healing before surgery, uplifting my brother's spirit and care. And the good news is, my brother made it through surgery after 5 hours and to his recovery room almost 3 hours later. After an overnight stay, we were back home by noon after he was discharged. My brother's speedy recovery reminded me of a story I heard through the grapevine about this 92-year old man. He wasn't feeling well one day, and so he decided to go to the doctor and have a check-up. A few days later, the doctor saw him out walking down the street with a beautiful young lady by his side. And he seemed to be as happy as could be. The Doctor was kind of surprised. He said, "Wow, you sure are doing a lot better." The man said, "Yes Doctor, I took your orders. You said get a hot momma and stay cheerful." The doctor said, "I didn't say that! I said you got a heart murmur. Be careful!"

Like the story of healing the royal official's son, you can be confident Jesus has the power to heal. Jesus healed this man's son even without being in the boy's presence. The man believed Jesus would heal his son at his word (John 4:47-53).

Go and Do Likewise

You too can believe, without a doubt, he will heal when you ask him. Sometimes healing may come here on earth or in heaven. Regardless, trust God for healing and have faith in his supreme will. In due course, our full bodily healing waits for us in heaven. In heaven, there will be no more pain, sickness, disease, suffering, or death. Strive to be less anxious with your physical state now and a lot more alarmed with our spiritual condition. You can center your heart on heaven where you don't have to cope with physical struggles anymore.

DAY 11

Holy Spirit

If you, though you are evil, know how to give good gifts to your children, how much more will your Father in heaven give the Holy Spirit to those who ask him!"

Luke 11:13

Express Promise

Thankfully, God wants to help us and heal us — spirit, soul, and body. The precept joined with this promise says if you, who are, at any rate, evil, and inclined to a needy and pessimistic temper; yet, you know how to give good gifts to your children, your heavenly Father will give much more. You should give what is best and provide in the best manner and time; present every necessary good. God will give you the best and most excellent gift of all, his Holy Spirit; you must sincerely and earnestly ask.

Christ encourages fervency and constancy in prayer. It's an essential duty to ask for this gift. Be encouraged and believe, if you ask right, what you ask will not be in vain. Our heavenly Father is more than ready to bestow on you all these blessings when you ask for them. For as surely as God's power enables him, his goodness inclines him, and his promise binds him, to give the Holy Spirit to you when you ask in the manner; the meaning of this promise points you in the right direction.

Carry Out

Many poets used symbolism to deepen the meaning of their poems. In the 7th grade, I wrote my first poem entitled, "*An Endless Bondage*," which also exhibited symbolism in the following excerpt:

> I feel as a lost person in a world struggling for peace.
> I feel like a civil rights activist caged from justice.
> Yet, I know freedom will result from this bondage one day because
> this bondage is within myself.

Allegory is often used by writers to enrich their writing. We also use symbols to represent everyday life: white stands for life and purity. Additionally, we can use objects to imply something else: an olive branch is considered a symbol of peace. Any time there is something standing for more than its literal meaning, this can be an example of symbolism.

Another example of symbolism is the Holy Spirit, which refers to the third Person of the Trinity (the Father, the Son, and the Holy Spirit); the Holy Spirit is God himself living inside of us. Scripture describes it as, "Christ in you, the hope of glory" (Colossians 1:27). So, we receive the Holy Spirit by receiving the LORD Jesus Christ as our Savior. In addition to names and titles, other symbols which refer to the Holy Spirit are: fire, rest, sacrifice, oil, wine, water, dove, and wind; it's a sign of new life.

Go and Do Likewise

As you encounter a bewildering variety of symbols each day, let's remember the Spirit's presence as the dove at Jesus' baptism symbolized the gentle Savior bringing about peace to mankind through his sacrifice (Matthew 3:16). As a believer, the Holy Spirit already dwells within you and is not a million miles away. You can be continually filled (Ephesians 5:18) with the Holy Spirit by: daily spending time in prayer and Bible study (Acts 4:31) and obeying his commandments (John 14:15).

DAY 12

Hope

*Be of good courage, and he shall strengthen your heart,
all ye hope in the LORD.*

Psalm 31: 24 (KJV)

Express Promise

God, the source of hope, will fill you with joy and peace because you trust in him. You will overflow with confident hope through the power of the Holy Spirit (Romans 15:13). When you're of good courage, you're encouraged to be strong, namely, in the LORD, and through confidence in his promises; they will not fail you. The LORD will strengthen your heart. Trust God, and he will pass on resilience and endurance to you.

LORD, pardon our complaints and fears; increase our faith, patience, love, and gratitude. Teach us to delight in difficulty and in hope. Put your hope in the LORD; rely on him for grace and glory and to supply of all your wants. When you hope in the LORD, you have reason to be of good courage and to be strengthened. For as nothing truly evil can come about you, so nothing truly good for you will be withheld from you.

Carry Out

We all like to celebrate starting anew. "Even with holiday festivities, 'Jesus is the reason for the season' and look forward to next year and his and our story getting even better!" That's normally our signature closing for our *MO2-4L Praise Newsletter,* celebrating our year in review. When spending time with family in Texas during the holidays, another part of our M.O. is watching college bowl games.

One of the most memorable national championship college games I ever watched was the 2006 Rose Bowl Game. It featured the only two unbeaten teams: the defending Rose Bowl champion, Texas Longhorns, against the two-time defending national champions, the University of Southern California Trojans. The highly anticipated matchup was a back-and-forth contest; Texas secured the victory (41-38) in the game's final 19 seconds on a fourth down and five yards to go for a first-down.

Gideon is also a textbook example of an underdog. Scripture tells us the LORD gave the Israelites into the hands of the Midianites for 7 years because of their evil ways. When the Israelites cried out to the LORD because of Midian, he turned to Gideon to go and save Israel out of Midian's hand. This story is so hopeful because with God all things are possible. He thinned down a force from 22,000 to 300 men, and Gideon defeated an army of 135,000 Midianites. The victory was the LORD's; God received the glory. (Judges 6-7).

Go and Do Likewise

Like Gideon, don't ever lose hope, even if the possibilities appear hopeless. You can have the victory as long as God is on your side. You can anchor your hope in his word and promises. Numbers do not matter with God. When we have him, we are the majority. Similarly, you can also have hope like Nehemiah. Though the task may be great, the workers few, and the haters many, what's done in God's name and for God will succeed and prosper, bringing him glory (Nehemiah 1-6).

DAY 13

Humility

For those who exalt themselves will be humbled, and those who humble themselves will be exalted.

Matthew 23:12

Express Promise

Believers can show the world the hope they have inside by way of joyful, humble readiness to endure offenses and serve. How reasonable are the conditions of this promise when you humble yourself and lift up others, God will reward your humility? The Pharisees prescribed conformity to the Law of Moses. Pride was their ruling sin; it plagued them to appear as fanatical hypocrites and more religious than others. They demanded respect and were puffed up about their titles. We may judge according to external appearance, but God searches the [inward] heart.

Carry Out

When I had my chief master sergeant pin-on ceremony, I felt so humbled by the occasion not only as a measure of success, but also as an opportunity to help others more. The moment of being selected for promotion to chief master sergeant, the highest enlisted rank in the US Air Force, is a dream come true and a blessing; it was one of the happiest days of my life. Besides passing on 'words of wisdom,' the recognition is primarily an opportunity to share your gratitude.

Like others, during the occasion of promotion and retirement, I had a host of people to thank who lent a helping hand: God Almighty versus Lady Luck, the chaplain, senior leaders and supervisors, my commander, chiefs, mentors, friends, my Airmen, family, facility location, co-workers and peers, and attending audience. My eyes were wide open to the blessings given me, and it was so natural to express my gratefulness with a humble heart. The privilege of leading others gives you the kind of humility to use the words *we, team,* and *us!* The honor of leadership allows you to put other people first.

Scripture describes the Pharisees' behavior as arrogance instead of humbleness. Everything they did was done for people to see; they did everything for show (Matthew 23). Contrast the Pharisees' brazen conduct with Jesus' humility. He was born in a lowly barn, he put others before himself, and he never bragged. His servant leadership guides his followers. John the Baptist also encourages us to be humble, testifying about Jesus, "He must become greater;

I must become less." (John 3:30). Along with Jesus and John the Baptist, Paul is an awesome example of humility. He saw himself as the "least of the apostles" and the "chief of sinners" (1 Corinthians 15:9).

Go and Do Likewise

Everybody wants to be humble; nobody wants to be humbled. God has promised to show favor to the humble, while opposing the proud (Proverbs 3:34). Accordingly, come clean and put away pride. Avoid taking credit, admit your mistakes, learn from and praise others, go last, help others succeed or serve someone. If you put yourself on a pedestal, you place yourself in conflict with God who will, in his grace and for your own good, humble you. But when you humble yourself, God imparts you with more favor and elevates you.

DAY 14

Judgment

"Do not judge, or you too will be judged. For in the same way you judge others, you will be judged, and with the measure you use, it will be measured to you.

Matthew 7:1-2

Express Promise

Nothing may change you as much as the humility in striving to understand instead of judging others. The principle with this promise is we must not self-judge and shun making our word the law to one and all. We must not judge hastily or pass judgment upon each other without merit or foundation. We should see the best in folk. Judging can hold you back from godliness. Our LORD's words imply to evade passing judgment harshly and critically. Sidestep judging people without full, clear, and certain know-how of their fault or behavior and with an attitude of love.

With the aim of being not judged with harshness, don't judge others. If you judge considerately, making proper allowances for folks' weaknesses, showing concern and letting go of their faults, God and man will take care of you likewise. And with what measure you allot, he will apportion to you. So, it's up to us, whether or not we're dealt with hard-heartedly or graciously.

Carry Out

As a retired chief master sergeant myself, being a military spouse in Guam was a new role for me. My role as a key spouse accompanied my spouses' duty position as a command chief. As a key spouse, I supported the base commander's spouse expectations; she advocated the leadership team extends chiefs' spouses as part of the wing leadership team. I was blessed to be a part of the leadership team, and I'm grateful to our chiefs' spouses' team again for their volunteerism and service!

The chiefs' group and their spouses had welcomed my spouse and me at our home when we arrived to the base in November. We hit the ground running, initially meeting with spouses at base events. To help form the team and build rapport, I suggested a first spouses' potluck social at our on-base home in early December. Well, needless to say, several of the male chiefs were vocal about their spouses attending the get-together. We make judgments every day. In this case, the emphasis may have been on getting together with spouses too soon instead of with chiefs and their spouses, which happened months later. As a last-ditch stand, I worked together with another chief's female spouse to help bring the event together. This opening helped fortify the chiefs' spouses to support Airmen and their families at Team Andersen.

The Bible declares two-faced ways of thinking is wrong (Matthew 23). Isaiah also prophesied about hypocrites: "These people honor me with their lips, but their hearts are far from me." (Mark 7.6).

Go and Do Likewise

Believers are advised against judging others dishonestly or wickedly; Jesus commends "right judgment" (John 7:24). You are to be discerning and talk the whole purpose and will of God. You are to gently deal with fellow believers who slip-up and care enough to speak the gospel into the lives of those around us. Judgment belongs to God.

DAY 15

Love Your Enemies

But love your enemies, do good to them, and lend to them without expecting to get anything back. Your reward will be great, and you will be children of the Most High, because he is kind to the ungrateful and wicked.

Luke 6:35

Express Promise

Mercy triumphs over judgment (James 2:13). How rich are the particulars of this promise to show compassion and generosity? If you lend, you do not have to be afraid or awed; you will lose what you give. Give with a resolve to lose it; however, overcharging is forbidden and stealing is prohibited, especially without cause. When you clearly see folk reduced to lack and cannot pay interest, you should show love and mercy like the example of our heavenly Father.

Carry Out

As a part of our polarized culture, two core American values — freedom of religion and freedom from discrimination — continue to clash. Pitted against each other are religious freedom believers opposing same-sex marriage and LGBT [lesbian, gay, bisexual, and transgender] supporters; they discriminate because of their sexual orientation is prohibited. When listening, viewing, or reading what's happening in the news or blogs, you may have also heard these back-and-forth stories: from Chick-fil-A's anti-LGBT activism; right for same-sex couples to marry; announcement transgender people will not be allowed in the military; or a baker who refused to sell wedding cake to a gay couple.

In the military services, it's also emphasized all will be treated with dignity and respect, while all remain focused on accomplishing assigned missions. Similarly, when Jesus said we are to love our enemies, he upped the standard for relationships -- the law of love. The second commandment tells us to love our neighbor as ourselves; yet, it didn't imply you should hate your enemy. Jesus declared we should love our enemies as well as our neighbors (John 13:34-35).

Let's go ahead and admit it's a moot point: living up to this expectation seems impossible! For better or worse, a few folk may feel you're "enemies." They seem to hate on you. If you've offended them, they reject your expression of regret regardless of your actions. You may have upset coworkers or they may be haters; they've set themselves against you. Family members may hold a chip on their shoulder against you for whatever reason. Some people may simply dislike you; you can't change them and letting go is utmost. Even though your nemesis acts like a jerk to you, you don't have to conduct yourself like a jerk toward your foe.

Go and Do Likewise

No matter your opponent's actions, open your hearts to them and act toward them with kindness; choose to love them (Matthew 5:44). Jesus realized every sincere example of love grows out of a constant and total surrender to God. Love grows into an action rather than a feeling. And pray for them too. Pray for God to transform their hearts by the Holy Spirit. Walk out love for enemies by living out Day 8 (forgiveness), seeing the goodness in your adversary, and searching for their understanding. So, what's pronounced is hard, but it's not impossible. With God, all things are possible.

DAY 16

Marriage

Wives, submit yourselves to your own husbands as you do to the LORD. For the husband is the head of the wife as Christ is the head of the church, his body, of which he is the Savior. Now as the church submits to Christ, so also wives should submit to their husbands in everything. Husbands, love your wives, as Christ loved the church and gave himself up for her to make her holy, cleansing her by the washing with water through the word, and to present her to himself as a radiant church, without stain or wrinkle or any other blemish, but holy and blameless.

In this same way, husbands ought to love their wives as their own bodies. He who loves his wife loves himself. After all, no one ever hated their own body, but they feed and care for their body, as Christ does the church—for we are members of his body. "For this reason a man will leave his father and mother and be united to his wife, and the two will become one flesh." This is a profound mystery—but I am talking about Christ and the church. However, each one of you also must love his wife as he loves himself, and the wife must respect her husband.

Ephesians 5:22-23

Express Promise

Marriage is for people who will love their enemy. Throughout your lifetime, your spouse will be both your best friend and at times, your enemy. However, if you love your spouse during times of calm and uproar, you will have victory in your marriage. The cherished belief linked with this promise proposes wives yield to husbands except where God prohibits. The duty of husbands is to love their wives. There will be letdowns and shortcomings on both sides; yet, the association isn't altered. All the duties of marriage are included in unity and love. As possessing Christ's authority in your husband, whose image they bear, a wife's fulfilment to her husband is of paying to Christ himself. For the husband is the guardian of the wife as Christ is the head of the church. In such a way, the husband should apply his influence over his wife.

Carry Out

Our culture perceives marriage as a relationship can drain the life out of you or make you feel miserable. You may have heard of this view reflected in TV shows like "Married with Children;" "the old ball and chain" or "kitchen pass" labels; or bachelor and bachelorette parties as the "last chance" to have fun before you give up your freedom. God's intent is for marriage is to be fulfilling. He designed and created marriage as a good thing -- a beautiful, priceless gift. You may have had a childhood vision of what marriage should look like. Some married couples have unrealistic expectations of their bridal and each other.

Like this husband I heard about in this situation, you may undergo trials and challenges in marriage. He was quietly reading his newspaper when his wife snuck up behind him and hit him in the head with a frying pan. He said, "What was that for?" She said, "That was for the piece of paper I found in your pocket with the name Mary Lou on it." He said, "Aw honey, that's one of the horses that I bet on at the race track last week." She apologized and went about her business. Two days later, she hit him on the head with a bigger frying pan. When he came to, he said, "What in the world was that for? She said, "Your horse called."

With God as your source and first strand in your marriage, you can make it through. A cord of three strands [God, husband, and wife] is not quickly broken (Ecclesiastes 4:12). Gain great comfort from his word and design of a husband and wife unit (Genesis 2: 18, 22-24). Scripture tells us of great, true love marriage relationships: Adam and Eve, Mary and Joseph, Abraham and Sarah, and Jacob and Rachel, to Ruth and Boaz.

Go and Do Likewise

You want to also enjoy life and enjoy your marriage. Learn to trust and lean on God and his word. It's my hope your spouse and you continue to grow in understanding of each other in a spirit of oneness and unity. As you walk in the fruits of the spirit of love, joy, peace, patience, kindness, gentleness, goodness, faithfulness, and self-control, you will receive deep revelation and knowledge to apply to your marriage day-by-day.

DAY 17

Nearness

*What other nation is so great as to have their gods near them the way the LORD our God is near us whenever we pray to him?
But if from there you seek the LORD your God, you will find him if you seek him with all your heart and with all your soul.*

Deuteronomy 4:7, 29

Express Promise

You can realize the beauty in marriage which God intended for you when drawing nearer to him. God exemplifies his nearness by his wonders, grace, promises of his presence, and principally by his readiness to hear our prayers. Considering our many appetites and our heart's unethical desires, carefully guard your heart. Let us clasp to our faithfulness by love, and cleave to him. Your prayer success depends upon your faithfulness. Scripture tells us: "Come near to God and he will come near to you." (James 4:8) and "Return to me and I will return to you" (Zechariah 1:3) (Malachi 3:7).

Carry Out

It's a family thing! Though I was excited to be out of country for the first time in 1985 during my initial, 12-month overseas assignment in the Republic of Korea, I still felt a little lonely. There is no time like a joyful season spent with family and friends. Initially, I resolved not to embrace the Korean culture. My base sponsor appealed to me for the first 3 months to 'get off the yard' and visit the local villages and nearby cities.

This Christmas found me on duty in a locale many of my friends couldn't pinpoint on a map. Operating as a detachment during an isolated remote duty at Pilsung Range, also known as Korean Tactical Range, may have added to the loneliness. Also contributing to the isolation was most members lived and worked in the same building. Topping off the seclusion, winters were bone-cold and there were about 45 Airmen and 250 Korean Airmen -- all men! When I finally "got off the yard" and explored the new culture and colorful scene, I overcame being homesick by drawing near to Korean traditions; yet, there is no place like home.

When Adam and Eve chose to disobey the command of God, their sin also caused them to withdraw from the nearness of God; sin separates us from God. (Genesis 3: 6-10). The Exodus was also a time when God set himself apart from all other "gods." He distinguished Israel by his presence. In addition, Jesus was the One who left his home to draw us to himself. The people of God looked forward to a future day when they would enter into an intimate communion with God – omnipresence and nearness of God!

Go and Do Likewise

The rest of the Bible is about the plan and purpose of God to deal with man's sin so we can once again enjoy fellowship with God in his presence. While I finally "got off the yard," home is always near because it's where I'm from and who I am – an ambassador for Christ. And with Jesus, I'm never alone. Likewise, God is ever near in the sense he sees and hears what men are doing -- "The Nearness of God." Talk with him, live by his decrees, repent, and allow his Spirit to dwell in your heart and mind. Draw near to God, and he will draw near to you (James 4:8).

DAY 18

New Life

*Therefore, if anyone is in Christ, the new creation has come:
The old has gone, the new is here!*

2 Corinthians 5:17

Express Promise

But as for you, the nearness of God can be your good; you can make the new life in Christ your refuge (Psalm 73:28). The direction connected with this promise says Christ's real followers exist in him in place of themselves; they divinely know him and become a servant of God by being alive in devotion and residing in his Spirit. As a new believer, his sense of right and wrong is progressive, stimulated, and stands apart from wrongdoing by Jesus' blood. His will is exposed to the will of God. All old man views and habits pass away. The new man acts upon fresh values with new ends. Though the same man, he is transformed in character and conduct. He has new, godly life.

Carry Out

Deciding to join the military was an initial career decision. The next twenty-six years, I lived 'a great way of life,' as the Air Force recruiting slogan promoted. After basic military training in San Antonio and technical training school in Wichita Falls, Texas, I was assigned to 11 permanent duty locations. They included three places in Texas, two sites in the Republic of Korea, two locales in Washington, DC, and Japan, Germany, Turkey, and Florida.

I was also temporarily assigned to the following spots: Panama, Italy, England, Belgium, Macedonia, and throughout Germany, including the former East Germany. Additionally, I've traveled as a tourist throughout the Pacific and European theaters in countries such as the Philippines, France, and Bulgaria.

Also, as a spouse supporting my wife when she was in active duty, permanent duty locations included assignments in Georgia, Guam, and Arkansas. Having served over half of my life in the military, this 'great way of life' was also a 'new way of life,' which began in Air Force Basic Training in San Antonio, Texas.

Many Bible characters also have had to start over: meek Moses from prince to fugitive to shepherd to leader (Exodus 2-6); Gideon from hiding to hero (Judges 6-7); Esther from orphan to Queen (Esther 1-2); David from teen shepherd to King of Israel (1 Samuel

16); and the heroes and heroines in the Hall of Faith (Hebrews 11:32-39).

Go and Do Likewise

Like the champions of faith, you too can receive your reward now because of your faithfulness. You understand God cannot lie and he will deliver the promise in the right and proper time. You can also be the next story of a new beginning. In addition, he is the God of second chances and third chances and beyond. You can make a new beginning and if you have not asked forgiveness and believed in Christ, begin there. Like beauty and the beast, you can still make a new life in Christ. Come to know Christ personally, put away the old self, be renewed in the spirit of your mind, and put on the new man.

DAY 19

Obedience

Whoever has my commands and keeps them is the one who loves me. The one who loves me will be loved by my Father, and I too will love them and show myself to them."
John 14:21

Express Promise

Come near to God and he will come near to you. Wash your hands, you sinners, and purify your hearts, you double-minded (James 4:8). The first verse of this promise points out the continual steps leading up to Christ's full appearance. The first step is the moral concern and everyday adherence of our LORD's decrees. The unquestionable proof of our love to Christ is to obey his laws. Regarding one's love for Christ, the next step reveals the Father loves the believer in an exclusive way. When a follower's heart shows genuine love to Christ, obedience will trail. In the third step, the special love of the Son shadows the special love of the Father, and goes along with the Son's full appearance.

Carry Out

It's important to obey traffic laws when driving. At a time, I used to be pretty lead-footed. During my active duty Air Force days, I remember two occasions when traveling to different cities where I got pulled over and ticketed, not once, but twice. Aargh! Like most motorists stopped for speeding, though warranted, I'd rather a club-wielding police not issue a ticket. In an attempt to get out of the ticket, I wish I had the wit of this senior citizen I heard about. He was cool as a cucumber. He was driving down the freeway in his brand new Corvette with the top down going 80 miles hour when he saw flashing red lights from a state trooper in his rear view mirror. Without thinking about it, he floored it… took off to 100 miles an hour. He heard the sirens behind him. He finally pulled over and said, "Officer I'm so sorry, I don't know what I was thinking." The state trooper said, "Listen, it's Friday, 4 o'clock and my shift is over in 30 minutes. If you tell me a reason why you're speeding I've never heard before, I'll let you go." The man thought about it and said, "Officer, years ago my wife ran off with a state trooper and I thought you were bringing her back." The officer said, "Have a great weekend!"

Though obedience is easier said than done, you can find encouragement from others who have been there too. In Jesus Christ we find the perfect model of obedience. He lived a sinless life. As his 'disciple,' we follow Christ's example as well as his commands; our motivation for obedience is love (John 14:15). King Saul also turned away from following the LORD's commands (1 Samuel 15:22). In addition, the story of Noah shows he firmly obeyed God (Hebrews 11:7)!

Go and Do Likewise

Obedience is tough. It becomes a contest when we feel lured to believe we stand to lose more through our obedience than we might gain. You may have to be dutiful to a boss, parent, crack troop, or traffic law. Obedience is a part of our faith coming from our submission, surrender, and compliance to God's will; we continually apply our faith. Living out faith, in Day 5, required "giving up something." In obedience, you give up your will, control, and trust; your life becomes Christ-centered versus self-centered.

DAY 20

Patience

Let us not become weary in doing good, for at the proper time we will reap a harvest if we do not give up.

Galatians 6:9

Express Promise

Remain on the course Christ has set through your obedience; wait on the LORD despite all obstacles and trials. The facts of this promise are splendid. With an outlook of joy, let us not be weary or discouraged in well-doing. No matter what work and exhaustion, whatever expense and difficulty, cope with it. For in due season, when the crop comes or when it's right with God, you shall reap. Expect an abundant harvest if you stay strong. Give your best according to your ability, at whatever time or place, and in whatever way you can. Do well in every possible way and to all men, especially believers.

Carry Out

How many of your like to fish? It's not a baited question. Sure, there are ladies who like to fish, but by a show of hands of your husbands or guy friends, "How many know they're a good fisherman? Hit me up on Facebook; I would like to talk with you after reading this. I love fishing; I love to eat fish. I don't claim to be a good fisherman, but every now and when you throw your line out and reel in a big fish, you want to say, "Thank you Jesus. Hallelujah. Thank you LORD," "Yeah," or whatever expression suits you. There was a joke about fishing I was going to tell you. Oh no, I forgot the line! The gentle hint I'm about to tell you will shock you – fishing requires patience.

While in Japan, our men's fellowship group went fishing at a fish pond. One young boy saw a big red fish swimming near the bank of the pond. He quickly baited his line and put the bait out there in front of the fish. So fisherman, "What do you think happened next?" As a matter of fact, the fish swam away. Like fast food, fast service, and fast solutions, we want things now. The young boy re-tried this bait-and-hook technique for 10 minutes and finally gave up -- hook, line, and sinker. It's my hope you'll also be encouraged by the faithfulness of Abraham and Sarah and patience of Job.

Abraham and Sarah's impatience evoked them to take matters into their own hands to produce a child, Ishmael. Yet, God fulfilled his original promise by the birth of Isaac through Sarah when Abraham was 100 and Sarah was 99 years old (Genesis 17: 1-15). While impatience like Abraham and Sarah's can at times have long-term effects, Job was perhaps best known as a person of patience. Thus, the common saying, "The patience of Job." Job showed patience to continue to trust him. Job waited for his answer to Job's trials (Job 1:8-22).

Go and Do Likewise

Patience is a virtue. Like fishing and Abraham and Sarah or Job, patience brings about suffering on some level – whether boredom, being childless, or facing trials. Even as we wait, he reveals his will to us and works all things together for our good and his glory. When you go tough times of testing, you often do not see why God allowed it to happen until at a later time. Patience isn't a weakness. It shows great strength, especially when exercised on behalf of others.

DAY 21

Peace

Do not be anxious about anything, but in every situation, by prayer and petition, with thanksgiving, present your requests to God. And the peace of God, which transcends all understanding, will guard your hearts and your minds in Christ Jesus.

Philippians 4:6-7

Express Promise

If you desire peace, an inner feeling of calmness, you must also desire patience. Patience and peace go hand in hand. The lead up to this promise inspires you to be careful for nothing. Those who agonizingly worry may expect to feel alone and self-reliant among life's problems and risks. Let believers be of one mind and ready to help each other. Pray on all occasions with all kinds of prayers and requests. Prayer and supplication with thanksgiving generally denote worship. Though different, they are attached. The peace of God, the calm feeling of being reconciled to him and having his favor and blessings, sustains you from weariness. This calm before the storm will cling your heart and mind to Jesus Christ, the Prince of Peace. This type of harmony comforts you in your times of trial.

Carry Out

After a return trip from Texas to Arkansas, I was approaching the outskirts of Little Rock when I encountered a motorist on Interstate Highway 30 on her cell phone. Without an opportunity to pass, I continued to follow the vehicle. It's not clear what made the driver slam on her brakes, but she may have perceived I interrupted her morning talk or texting. As for me, I may have had the "Drive friendly, the Texas Way" attitude. I interpret this saying as moving out of the left lane when sitting at the speed limit, which blocks others from passing. Immediately when the opportunity became available, I passed the vehicle to get ahead of the driver.

Looking back in my mirror, she appeared to display non-verbal motions, weaved in and out of traffic, and exited the highway. I'm glad we were able to keep half of our peace and not throw arrows. We didn't lash out, lose our peace or reach for crabs at the bottom of the barrel. Folk can hold their peace and bury the hatchet by: talking versus arguing, being the bigger person as a giant instead of midget or hero versus zero, or rising above as an eagle as opposed to a crow. I strived to give peace in place of power and be a champ for God rather than a chomp for men.

In the book of Acts, James, was a role model for keeping the peace when the apostles and elders met to consider if the Gentiles must be circumcised and required to keep the Law of Moses (Acts 15: 5, 6, 13, 19). His compromise of non-circumcision and abstinence offered a peaceful solution and gained the apostles' consensus.

Go and Do Likewise

Clearly, the point of this scripture is we can achieve peace thru understanding. Like a roadmap to peace instead of road rage, James dealt with a possibly contentious issue bringing peace and honoring God. In this instance, let's encourage others to embrace the peace and harmony they too can feel with him. Can you change the things you don't like about the world and still be enclosed in calmness? Can you accept the world as it is while still trying to change it? Rest in Jesus' presence and receive peace. Let the peace of Christ rule in your hearts (Colossians 3:15).

DAY 22

Prayer

"Ask and it will be given to you; seek and you will find; knock and the door will be opened to you. For everyone who asks receives; the one who seeks finds; and to the one who knocks, the door will be opened.
"Not everyone who says to me, 'LORD, LORD,' will enter the kingdom of heaven, but only the one who does the will of my Father who is in heaven. Many will say to me on that day, 'LORD, LORD, did we not prophesy in your name and in your name drive out demons and in your name perform many miracles?'

Matthew 7:7-8, 21-22

Express Promise

Prayer: LORD, make me an instrument of your peace. The encouragement covered by this promise guides you to ask God for supernatural aid. Ask, as a beggar asks you to donate. Ask, as a traveler asks directions. All are welcome to the throne of grace when you come in faith. Believers are urged to seek help from him in all problems of any kind -- a key path and reassuring appeal covered by this promise. Search, as for a thing of value you have lost or as the businessperson pursues goodly treasures. Seek, and you will find. When you knock, persistently endure in your work and your efforts will not be in vain. Knock, as one desires to enter into a house knocks at the door– like I knocked at the door on Day 6. Provided you ask what is acceptable to his will and in harmony with his laws, he will give to you. For every one asks, receives his goodness and faithfulness, especially believers. Whatever you pray for, according to the promise, he gives to you if he sees it fit for you.

Carry Out

Often I see a post on social media with someone asking "Please pray for so-and-so" for an individual facing an ailment or some sort of hardship. Many people comment on the post such as "Prayers being sent your way" or "Praying." When sending a prayer, do folk pray, especially if the recipient is a stranger? Do they truly intend to pray or mask feeling good about themselves? Do they believe random, heartless prayers will fulfill their request? Is "keeping the person in your thoughts" a more sensible response? Others make a note of the request and pray on the spot or during their time they daily devote. Giving the benefit of the doubt, I'm encouraged by the member soliciting for prayer on someone's behalf. They may believe in and relate with God; they may feel he hears and responds to prayers.

Establishing the right relationship with the everlasting Father helps to realize the privilege of answered prayers. Consider, for instance, the answered prayer of Elijah and Jesus. Elijah first blessed a widow and her son by amazingly causing her food not to run out

(1 Kings 17:7-15). Later, he prayed for the child's life to return to him and God answered right away. (1 Kings 17:21-22)

In the night, Jesus was betrayed and arrested; he pleaded with his Father to avoid the torture and death he knew awaited him. He ended his prayer with a statement of complete obedience to God: "…not as I will, but as you will." His ultimate desire was to do what God wanted him to do, and this is the part of the prayer God answered. (Matthew 26:39). Calvary covered it all; that's so good!

Go and Do Likewise

So, when others ask for prayer, they believe he is going to answer prayer, even if the answer is "no" or "not yet." Regardless of the answer or timing of the answer, mighty God always listens. You can also embed prayer in your life by establishing a time, place, and method for prayer.

DAY 23

Protection

*Whoever rests in the shadow of the Most High God
will be kept safe by the Mighty One.
He will cover you with his wings.
Under the feathers of his wings you will find safety.
He is faithful. He will keep you safe like a shield or a tower.*

Psalm 91:1, 4 (NIRV)

Express Promise

A prayer for God's hedge of protection: "I run to you, LORD, for protection. Don't disappoint me" (Psalm 71:1). The principles of this promise are when you make him your dwelling and sanctuary, you'll abide by the Almighty's shadow, which signifies he protects. You rely on him in your dangers and difficulties and live a life of continual relationship with him. Choose him as your protector by faith and find all in him you need or can desire. You'll find a quiet and safe relaxing place under his divine care. Believers may consider with comfort they're under the same almighty Protector. He will protect you with the greatest love and warmth. And under his wings of overwhelming power and wisdom, he will be your shield. His shield is most high. His defense is strong and certain; he promises great security to believers in danger.

Carry Out

It was an early Saturday morning returning from holiday leave in my hometown in Central Texas to my first duty station in San Antonio. I was eager to get back to Kelly Air Force Base because the weather and roads were worsening. The roads were slick, and it was forecasted to snow hard. Like many of my fellow safe drivers, the thought of driving in winter can cause crushing, knee-knocking, unbearable fear – at least in the back of your mind. Everything stops because a great deal of the population has no experience in driving in snow and ice conditions. So, the driver's fear is even though you know how to drive in those extreme conditions doesn't mean you're safe.

My driving appeared to get better after entering onto the interstate highway. After initially skidding, my driving on ice slowed down to a crawl, and the snow continued to fall as I headed south. In Round Rock, a driver swerved from another lane and caused me to brake hard. To add insult to injury, my 1981 Monte Carlo and I went sliding off the road and down into an entrenched ditch. The state expressway wasn't previously separated by modular concrete barriers. I walked to a nearby grocery store and called home. My momma and dad, an Army veteran more skillful in driving in icy conditions, drove from home, picked me up, and safely transported me to Kelly Air Force Base. I'm so grateful for my parent's undying love and protection!

I also love the comfort and Bible stories like baby Moses (Exodus 2: 1-10), Esther (Esther 4-8), David and Goliath (1 Samuel 17), and Daniel (Daniel 6), which speaks of God's protection.

Go and Do Likewise

I hope these stories of fulfillment encourages you in your "safe place." Wherever you seek safety, God's presence is with you and provides the strength and protection you need. Honor him and do what is right and you can trust the LORD for protection. The LORD is your Shepherd; he will take care of you, and you will not want (Psalm 23). Stay in the herd -- a part of his family, and receive his protection. His angels will encamp around you.

DAY 24

Provision

So don't worry. Don't say, 'What will we eat?' Or, 'What will we drink?' Or, 'What will we wear?' People who are ungodly run after all those things. Your Father who is in heaven knows you need them. But put God's kingdom first. Do what he wants you to do. All those things will also be given to you.

Matthew 6:31-33 (NIRV)

Express Promise

By spending time in God's presence, we are inviting him to pour out his blessings to protect and provide in our lives. In this promise, you're fortified not to worry regarding how he will provide for you during your lifetime. Prune ungodly distraction, separation, anxiety, or unbelief. For your heavenly Father knows you have needs. He has promised food and clothing, and you may expect them. Do not worry about tomorrow. Do not worry about the things of this life and become preoccupied with them. Seek first his kingdom. When you're in short supply, the whole matter is to trust him for your daily needs. Once you understand how much he loves you, your worries will fade. Learn to turn your worries or cast all your anxiety over to Christ.

Carry Out

It was an uncomfortable situation. I've been in "transitional seasons" multiple times where the resources I used to see come in to help provide abruptly died out (e.g., retirement, relocation, etc.). Now, I was in between banker's hours jobs again. I looked forward to converse with my wife; it was a talk we had to iron out and better late than never. Familiar with songs like Gwen Guthrie's "Ain't Nothin' Goin' on but the Rent" and Destiny's Child's "Bills, Bills, Bills" didn't ease the approach.

For better or for worse, life always seems to present you with opportunities. My spouse and I hammered out a promise to get through this together as a part of the process of moving forward. Job loss made money tighter, and we trusted God to provide. Like when I initially transited from the military and relocated to a new city, I'm so grateful for my service to country and my retirement pay helped fill the gap. It's not a fickle fortune and I thank him for his blessings! In 5 months, I burned the midnight oil and applied for 64 cutting edge, information technology jobs, interviewing for 10 jobs before landing my current position. Thank him for daily providing!

Learning to trust God for daily providing reminded me of the Prophet Elijah's experience. Soon after Elijah voiced his decree of a dry spell in Israel, God sent him to a desolate place where he used the Ravens to daily supply Elijah bread and meat, and he drank for Elijah and for the woman and her family (1 Kings 17:1-15). Food for thought, they were likely hungry as wolves.

Go and Do Likewise

Jehovah-Jireh, "The LORD Will Provide," will generously provide all you need. You will always have everything you need and plenty left over to share with others. As believers, even in the "dark times," our dependence and hope come from the LORD. As he used ravens and a widow to provide for Elijah, God can bless you abundantly. Whether a check in the mail or a financial gift received at the right moment, you can depend on him. Everything is under his command, and he provides exactly what's needed and when needed. He is your source.

DAY 25

Repentance

"But if a wicked person turns away from all the sins they have committed and keeps all my decrees and does what is just and right, that person will surely live; they will not die. None of the offenses they have committed will be remembered against them. Because of the righteous things they have done, they will live.

Ezekiel 18:21-22

Express Promise

Repentance influences the way we behave; it motivates us to obey God's commandments and accept his provisions for salvation. Claim this promise over your life; if the evil person will turn from wickedness by repenting, he will surely live. The wicked man would be saved if he turned from his evil ways. The word repent means to feel regret, turn from your sin, and turn to Jesus Christ for forgiveness. He will not assign to wicked men the way they transgressed in the past. In the righteousness which the wicked has done, he shall surely live. He will divert penalty and forgive. He will not reveal or credit the evil person's wrongdoings on him; they shall be as if they were gone. He desires all men to be saved and to come to the understanding of the truth, and is not willing any should perish. True believers watch and pray, and continue to the end, and they are saved.

Carry Out

Many couples commonly throw mud at constant matters like money, sex, work, parenting, and housework. Rather than become a grace giver versus rock thrower, most argue about these five burning issues over and over again; these irritants speak to our sense of love and regard. In the end, an offense leads to one of us apologizing to the other for an action. My desire is to back up the "I'm sorry" with a sincere desire to change as opposed to smoothing over things, whitewashing, avoiding the real issue, getting out of jail free, manipulating or getting off the hook.

Like when Jesus forgave the woman caught in the act of adultery (John 8:1-11), a change or repentance is required so as to deserve forgiveness. Similar to a child breaking house rules or a criminal being arrested, he said, "Go now and leave your life of sin." In addition to admitting you erred, change in heart is also needed (2Corinthians 7: 9-11). Otherwise, the offender may violate again. Like John the Baptist (Matthew 3: 1-6), Jesus preached repentance rather than speaking of an apology (Matthew 4:17). He talked about a true change of heart. Unlike the apologies of athletes and politicians or Bible characters like Pharaoh (Exodus 9, 10), Balaam (Numbers 22:34), or Judas (Matthew 27:4), David turned to God and genuinely repented. It is to him we must turn for help, and it is against him we have sinned (2 Samuel 12: 13).

Go and Do Likewise

What David told God applies to us too. By repentance, you can obtain forgiveness of sins and enjoy fellowship with him. He uses his people, like Nathan, to confront people with their sin (2 Samuel 12:1). Like Zacchaeus (Luke 19:1-9), repent and grow. Pray the Father makes you aware of your own heart's content and open your eyes to being repentant. True apologies can happen only when you take responsibility for your own behavior, acknowledge the other's point of view, and make changes. If applicable, change your lifestyle and behavior. Only he can change hearts. In this regard, repentance is the work of God. By repenting, you can confess your flaws and your dependence upon Jesus Christ himself. You change your mind, and the mind change leads to a change in your life.

DAY 26

Rest

"Come to me, all you who are tired and are carrying heavy loads. I will give you rest. Become my servants and learn from me. I am gentle and free of pride. You will find rest for your souls. Serving me is easy, and my load is light."

Matthew 11:28-30 (NIRV)

Express Promise

"In repentance and rest is your salvation," says the sovereign LORD (Isaiah 30:15). Review God's promise of rest with a heart of trust and gratitude. Come to the Father those working hard and are weary and burdened. Specifically, this promise refers to those who are tired from Satan's bondage, the world's love and search of its prides, life's distresses and various trials, and desire for his resolution, peace, and rest. While waiting to enjoy these blessings, people may become heavy laden with blame, iniquities, and his discontent. When you come to him as a Father, you must recall he is LORD of heaven and earth; come to him with reverence as to the sovereign LORD of all. Draw near to him with confidence, as one able to defend you from evil and to supply you with all good. In coming to Christ, you petition him in faith and prayer for such blessings as you want. And he alone will freely give you rest as a gift: from anger and the useless guilt and power of sin; worldly likings, cares, anxiety, and sorrows; trials, and troubles of life. You have his word all things will work for your good, and you will have peace and comfort in your heart and find rest for your soul.

Carry Out

You may spend 100,000 hours working in your job over a lifetime. The words "work" and "toil" are mentioned over 480 times in The Bible, supporting the importance of work to God. Work is so important in Exodus 34:21, he gives this command: "Six days you shall labor, but on the seventh day you shall rest." Similarly, the Merriam-Webster Dictionary defines retirement as "withdrawal from one's position or occupation or from active working life." Your culture may promote the goal of retirement as ceasing all labor to live a life filled with leisure. You may have 'retired,' but you want folk to think you are in no way tired. I heard about this 85-year old woman. She went on a blind date with a 92-year old man. She came home frustrated, and her daughter said, "Mom, what's wrong?" She said, "I had to slap him three times." The daughter said, "You mean he tried to get fresh?" She said, "No, I thought he was dead." Though you grow older, you still use your talents and skills to help others.

Like the words "work and toil," "rest and relax" is a repeated theme thru Scripture, beginning with creation week in the Book of Genesis. God created for six days; then he rested; he set the standard for mankind to follow (Genesis 2:2-3). The Ten Commandments made resting on the Sabbath a requirement of the Law (Exodus 20:8-11). And now Jesus is our Sabbath rest. We can rest in him always instead of 1 day per week.

Go and Do Likewise

Most of us don't think of taking on anything huge when we reach a certain age. But you can still do great things for God, no matter how old you are. He desires rest for us because it does not come naturally to us. Get your rest, and trust mighty God will take care of things for you. When you're refreshed, and you're capable, you can finish the work he has called you to do. He will provide you with the needed strength. Instead of being put 'out to pasture' or feeling "weary and burdened," draw near to him, and he will give you rest (Matthew 11:28).

DAY 27

Resurrection

"Do not be amazed at this. A time is coming when all who are in their graves will hear his voice. They will all come out of their graves. People who have done what is good will rise and live again. People who have done what is evil will rise and be found guilty.

John 5:28-29 (NIRV)

Express Promise

"The rest of the dead did not come to life until the thousand years were ended. This is the first resurrection" (Revelation 20:5). In this promise, you'll also discover God will do exactly what he's promised. Whoever hears his word and believes him has everlasting life; he will not judge you. The hour is coming and has now come when all are in the graves will hear the Son of God's voice and live. He will raise those who were dead in sin to newness of life. He will raise the dead in their graves. Our LORD declared his authority and character, as the Messiah. He has all knowledge, almighty power, and 'last word' to judge. By faith and hope, believe his testimony so you repent and do not come into blame on grave day.

Carry Out

It's not every day you get the chance to start something over again. When you burn your bridges, there are no do-overs. The good news is, there are second chances, new starts or resets. Everyday can be a new start to a brighter day. Like many veterans transitioning into or from the military services, one of my resets was shifting to civilian life again. Some people may have been a high school dropout or drank too much and got popped. Other individuals may have had the wrong major in college or hurt or screwed over a friend. What we've learned in hindsight, all were platforms for learning and growing from our mistakes. You can't turn back the hands of time.

One of my wife's and I favorite TV shows is *"Dancing with the Stars."* In the finals, a couple will choose a dance style for their redemption dance; the last time performed, they likely received their lowest score. In an irony of fate, the judges normally reward the couple a higher score for their redemption dance. Consider for instance the second chances of Bible characters raised from the dead like the blessed event of Jesus' Resurrection:

- Elijah raised the widow's son (1 Kings 17:17-24)
- Elisha raised the Shunammite's son (2 Kings 4: 20-37)

- Jesus raised a widow of Nain's son (Luke 7:11-16), a synagogue ruler's daughter (Mark 5:35-53), and Lazarus (John 11:1-44)
- Peter raised Tabitha (Acts 9:36-41)
- Paul raised Eutychus (Acts 20:7-12)
- God raised many holy people upon Jesus' death (Matthew 27:51-53)

Similarly, Jesus died and rose again. Death was powerless to hold him in the grave. The second coming of Jesus Christ is soon (John 14:1-3). Stay woke! He will raise to life the righteous dead and along with the righteous who are still alive on the earth (1 Thessalonians 4:16-17).

Go and Do Likewise

When you trust Christ's blood, you can be sure you'll have eternal life with him (2 Corinthians 4:14). You have the assurance of Salvation, a blessed event. Because he died, you are given the gift of "second chances" and can resist wrongdoing, grow in obedience, and love others as you have been loved (Romans 6:11-12). Glory to God for the power of Christ's death!

DAY 28

Salvation

If you declare with your mouth, "Jesus is LORD," and believe in your heart God raised him from the dead, you will be saved.

Romans 10:9

Express Promise

Jesus' death and Resurrection is central to believers and their Salvation. In Genesis 3:15, the first promise of salvation is recorded in the Bible. The rest of the Bible is the story of how God fulfills this promise of salvation so sinful men can once again draw near to a holy God. In this promise, you'll explore in its meaning believers don't oppose confessing with your mouth and believing with your heart. One is viewed as the essential result and expression of the other; they're regarded as equal to each other in acknowledging Jesus as LORD. We must devote and give up to him our souls and our bodies: our souls in believing with the heart and our bodies in confessing with the mouth. In being raised from the dead, Jesus was delivered over to the grim reaper for our sins and raised to life to justify our flaws. Like spelled out in Day 27, the proof of the promise and expectation of Jesus would have been incomplete without the Resurrection. His death would not have had its saving worth and value.

Carry Out

While visiting family in Texas for the Thanksgiving holiday weekend, I was touched to read about a church teaming up with local businesses to feed travelers. The annual meal was served at rest stop areas on both sides of the interstate highway. Similar to the story of where Jesus fed 5,000 people with a loaf of bread and two fish (Matthew 14: 19-21), the team was able to feed over 600 families and members free. They weren't persuaded to drop money in the bucket; it was all a gift.

Salvation is also a free gift. God has given us eternal life and this life is in his Son, Jesus Christ. In other words, the way to possess eternal life is to possess God's Son. There are no works for you to do; it's done. A guy asked Rick Warren, an American evangelical Christian pastor and author, "What can I do to be saved?" Pastor Warren said,

"You're too late! You're about 2,000 years too late! What needed to be done for your salvation has already been done, and you can't do anything about it. Jesus Christ already did it. He paid for your salvation on the cross, and it's now a free gift to you. That's why when he was hanging on the cross, he said, "It is finished." He didn't say, "I am finished," because he wasn't. He's still alive today. The "it" is your salvation. The plan to provide grace for every person is finished." (Romans 3:24)

Go and Do Likewise

It's my hope you value the price he paid at the cross. Salvation is a gift of God; it's the greatest gift you're ever going to be offered (John 3:17). Comparable to saving for your favorite vacation spot or bucket list adventure, Jesus is worth it! This is the good news of the Bible: His own Son who became a man, lived a sinless life, died on the cross for our sin, and was raised from the grave. He promised salvation to all who believe in his Son (Romans 1:16–17); He promises eternal life (1 John 2:25). There is no greater blessing than the free gift of his salvation; it's all a gift!

DAY 29

Success

Never stop reading this Book of the Law. Day and night you must think about what it says. Make sure you do everything written in it. Then things will go well with you. And you will have great success.

Joshua 1:8 (NIRV)

New Day, New Life

Express Promise

Once you have accepted Christ as your savior, engage in regular prayer, read the Bible, and get plugged into a local church. Success is developing a deeper, personal relationship with Christ. Proclaim this promise over your life encouraging you with the promise and presence of God. Constantly meditate on his Word by reading the Bible. Diligently study it day and night keeping with his will and your duty. Observe to do according to what is written and understand it. By obedience and faithfulness, when you speak the Word, all will go well. You will make your way prosperous and have good success.

Carry Out

As a retired Chief Master Sergeant, I every so often share words of wisdom with Airmen about career success. Airmen seek guidance from a guy who started at the bottom and rose to the top. In my 26-plus years in the air force, I've run across a lot of people with their own secrets, pillars, or keys to success; you need more than a "magic formula" to achieve a successful career in today's air force. Your career is what you make it. The great thing about the military is everything you need to be successful is right there in front of you. If you want to go to school, take advantage of tuition assistance and programs available to you. If you want to be promoted, study for promotion and do what it takes regardless if you're a 'dark horse' eligible for the first time.

Similar to this promise of reading the Book of Law, I burned the midnight oil and buried my head in the sand to prepare for my promotion test. I was busy as a bee and planned, read, highlighted, dissected, memorized, reflected, studied, and critically studied our professional development guide. I was selected for promotion to the coveted award of chief master sergeant. I charted a course to career success and helped others to grow and prosper.

Comparable to reading the promotion guide, ponder for instance these other verses about reading the Bible. Ezra, the priest, read from the break of day till noon (Nehemiah 8.3). Scripture also tells us faith comes from hearing the message of Christ (Romans 10:17). Since Jesus is the Word, folk must hear the Word by speaking it in order for people to hear about faith in Christ. God himself inspires scripture (2 Timothy 3:16-17) and his Word will achieve what he sent it out for (Isaiah 55:11).

Go and Do Likewise

We could easily devote more energy to self-improvement methods. It's better for new and growing believers to learn sooner than later. When you're off path at the start, you can be off by miles later. Read through this promise verse by verse; reading it out loud brings the Word of God to life. His words are alive, active, powerful, and inspiring. When you memorize his words, you can draw on them like Jesus when tempted in the wilderness by Satan (Psalm 119:11). His Word will help defend you when you're tempted or tested; he will carry you through severe trials. Read it, use it, and you'll love it. Success is being faithful, one moment at a time by honoring him with a pleasing attitude. Like Joseph (Genesis 39:2), stay faithful in every moment. Success always leaves footprints.

DAY 30

Temptation

You are tempted in the same way all other human beings are. God is faithful. He will not let you be tempted any more than you can take. But when you are tempted, God will give you a way out. You will be able to deal with it.

1 Corinthians 10:13 (NIRV)

Express Promise

Consider when you're tempted by success. Decide to trust God, and you can resist temptation. However, this promise encourages you you're able to bear temptations common or suited to man. He permits the temptation by allowing the conditions which enable the enticement to arise. With each temptation, he makes a way to escape from it. He will make your burdens according to your strength. He knows what you can bear. God is faithful. Be fully encouraged to flee from sin and to be faithful to him. You cannot fall by temptation if you cleave fast to him.

Carry Out

I heard about this lady who was shopping with her husband. He asked her not to buy any new clothes. Well, she saw this dress in the window and decided to try it on; she liked it so much, she bought it in secret. A couple of days the later, the husband discovered it. He was so upset. She explained to him when she tried it on, it looked so good, Satan tempted her to buy it, and she couldn't resist it. He said, "Why didn't you do what the Scriptures said and say, 'Get behind me Satan?'" She said, "I did, and he told me it looked even better from a distance."

Though you may know about the enticement of Jesus (Matthew 4:1-11), Sampson and Delilah (Judges 16), and David and Bathsheba (2 Samuel 11:1-4) among other Bible characters, this incident makes me reflect on Adam and Eve yielding to Satan's original temptation (Genesis 3:1-7). Satan is crafty and deceptive, not straightforward. Like with Eve, his pattern for tempting us typically allows our own inner yearnings which relate to the lures of the world. He recognizes temptation is most powerful when you're all alone and tests you on the authority of God's Word, character, and judgment. In addition, Satan intrigues you with the possibility of gratification but doesn't allude to the glaring omission.

Like Eve saw the fruit, the lady shopping saw the dress as a delight to the eyes. It looked as if it would meet a real need, either sex or comfort. And the results seemed initially beneficial. Hopefully, her purchase didn't alienate her from her husband like Adam and Eve's sin led to them to separate from one another and from God. If temptation and sin defeat you, he provides the way of deliverance: "you are healed by his wounds." (1 Peter 2:24).

Go and Do Likewise

God doesn't leave you alone. Like the story of Joseph and Potiphar's wife, you can resist and flee your temptation by keeping your focus on him (Genesis 39:9). He gives you a way out. Stay steadfast in living with a mind to please him even when you're alone; you can resist Satan's devious charms. Satan is a personal adversary; pray, rebuke, and cast down, Jesus will deliver you from evil spirits and his forces of darkness. Pray, and He will answer your prayers and grant you strength to persevere in faith and resist every type of temptation. Do not be deceived what you see, hear, or feel. Stand on the truth (John 8:32). Be on alert, remain on guard, and stay firm in your faith when you're undergoing a temptation or sorrow.

DAY 31

Wisdom

Trust in the LORD with all your heart.
Do not depend on your own understanding.
In all your ways obey him.
He will make your paths smooth and straight.

Proverbs 3:5-6 (NIRV)

Express Promise

God is faithful; he will not let others tempt you beyond what you can bear. But when you are tempted, he will also provide a way out so you can endure it (1 Corinthians 10:13). Last but not least, the conditions of this promise are, if you trust in the LORD with all thy heart, lean not on your own understanding, and in all ways acknowledge him, he will make your ways safe and good. Rely on his wisdom, power, and goodness, and promises for direction and help in all your affairs and dangers. Trust in the LORD with all your heart. Believe he is able and wise to do what is best. You acknowledge him by knowing him; you follow his directions, expect success from him, and manage your activities. You please and glorify him. It is promised, he will direct your paths.

Carry Out

A question many students ask is, "What will I do when I finish high school?" For some, the answer is "get a job." For others, the answer is "to travel and see the world or to continue education." I decided to 'continue my education' at a local college before enlisting in the United States Air Force to 'see the world.' The immediate result of my decision was gratefully serving my country; my service continues to be a blessing in disguise!

However, I obligingly experienced many second and third order consequences, which were different yet directly linked to my initial decision: permanent change of station or assignment, unaccompanied tours, temporary duty including short or no-notice deployments, alerts, recalls, extended hours or shift work and the real possibility the government would call me to make the ultimate sacrifice in the line of duty.

The people of Judah also stood at a crossroad and on the cusp of a major decision when their nation had been inflicted with disaster. God promised them two things: he'd restore their land if they stayed in Judah or death or they'd depart this life if they went to Egypt. They decided to 'pitch their tent' in Egypt; they made a choice based on their own wisdom and direction versus his, and they eventually passed away (Jeremiah 42: 8-22).

At Gibeon, Solomon also made a wise decision when he asked God for wisdom (1 Kings 3:5-12). Wisdom and understanding are important gifts he gives us. When you decide to have faith in your life, and you do it in obedience to him, he will always lead you down the right path. He is with you.

Go and Do Likewise

As you face your own tough, important decisions, let's remember to look to God's Word to find what wisdom situationally looks like (James 3:17). Wisdom isn't gained by disobeying him, but by fearing and obeying him. When you walk in relationship with Jesus, he will guide you in knowledge and understanding to build your life on the strong foundation of his wisdom (Matthew 7:24). Praise him for ordering your steps and instructing you in the way which you should go. As you follow him, I believe your path will become clearer each day.

CONCLUSION

Living Up To Expectations

Some last words I'd like for you to take to heart is: now he has given us his great and precious promises, let's live up to expectations of his plan and purposes in our lives. With this devotional, you can commit, immerse, and realize these 31 days of God's conditional promises. Your dedication to living up to expectations is a result of your actions. To rise to expectations of living victoriously now, you must fully devote and thus act to suddenly achieve results. You can instantly show you consider this task of successfully living up to expectations a priority by walking in faith and carrying through your part – obedience and cooperation -- of his conditional promises.

God is faithful, and expectations is confidence. It is difficult for a child to please his father unless he has confidence in him. It is impossible for a wife to please her husband, or a husband a wife, unless they have confidence in each other. Likewise, you cannot please him when you have no confidence in him or doubt the truth of his promises. He has confidence in you to achieve what he destined you to achieve.

Scripture says in reward of your obedience [of walking in his statutes], you will have fruitful seasons. I receive that! God seeks your obedience because he wants you to show your love for him. As you picked up about conditional promises, you cannot sow disobedience to him and expect to reap his blessing. This is what the LORD says: the wicked should not expect to retain their dishonest or unlawful gains (e.g., crime doesn't pay) (Ezekiel 33: 31) and the doubtful man should not expect answers to prayer. In contrast, the Bible encourages those who trust in the LORD to expect good things from him; he will not disappoint the believer's expectation.

What we sow, we reap (Galatians 6:7). Let us not deceive ourselves: We will reap the harvest of our lives. Slap somebody [with a high five]! He will meet you at your level of expectation.

You may have heard about the story of Israel's wilderness detour (Exodus 12). Because of little faith – grumbling unbelief and disobedience, God led them in an indirect way through the wilderness. This route was toward the Red Sea instead of through Philistine territory, which was the shortest route to the Promised Land – an 11-day journey. Instead, the Israelites explored the land for 40 years; they never stepped a foot into the land 'flowing with milk and honey.' Like the "Hall of Fame" of Old Testament characters of faith (Hebrews 11), we too should be able, by faith, to act on things not seen. Scripture says without faith it is impossible to please him. If we have faith, we can see results. Yet, the condition is faith. A real believer will go before she sees any results; the results come *after* we obey – by faith.

As we live up to expectations, let's look unto Jesus, the author and finisher of our faith. By faith, a woman who had been subject to bleeding for 12 years, came up behind Jesus in a crowd and touched his clothes to be healed. Her faith made her well; her condition was healed. We can also measure up and meet God's expectations. Like the courage of Joshua and Caleb, two of the twelve spies who scouted out the Land of Canaan as a future home for the Israelites, keep faith in him and don't be afraid (Numbers 13:27-28). It's my hope and encouragement you speak faith first, go do it; don't settle or give up in living up to expectations.

In living faith, does life feel like it's mediocre or do you believe you're not good enough? Sometimes, we "get our hopes up" based on what we assume or what others rebrand as fake news, deflections, denials, or lies. The moment you're born, you're projected to grow, learn, mature, develop, succeed, and share your success. Regardless of your stage in life, others place expectations on you – or you place expectations on yourself. You're expected to work or study hard and make the most money or get the best grades. All is well with your children, image, career, health, relationships, church, and community, but you can do better. Yet, like eating foods unfulfilling or satisfying and, worse, have no nutritional value, life may feel like "empty calories." A lot of things are similar — we participate in activities hoping to be successful in life, but in the end, wonder how we can possibly live up to all of the heavy weight of expectations felt in life.

A lot of time we feel like everything is a burden. Too many people drag through the day with feelings of inadequacy, despair or undue stress. They seek approval from everyone, feel they're not good enough, or don't fit in with, satisfy, or suit expectations. People want to avoid making someone disappointed by letting down or not doing something they're expected to do. They don't want to be perceived as substandard, lackluster or an underachiever missing the mark.

People spend a lot of time trying to be all each person wants them to be; they dress themselves in masks based on the expected role play. Folk lose themselves. They become fixated on the notion of everybody loving and approving them. They get lost in the crowd, fall short of their potential, and give in to being their best in life. Believe me, pride, selfishness, and distractions may also prevent you from meeting expectations. When people do not meet expectations, hurt follows; we often place blame on something or someone who did not live up to our expectations.

Rise up for battle! If you'll spend less time trying to live up to people's expectations and more time living up to God's, you have the free will to live up to expectations you may feel in life. You can rise to expectations because you're uniquely gifted. According to 1 Corinthians 12:12, "As a body, though one, has many parts, but all its many parts form one body, so it is with Christ." There is unity and diversity in the body. Our gifts, talents, and abilities work in unison and together for his Kingdom.

As we previously grasped, the preamble to the Constitution says, "That all men are created equal, that they are endowed by their Creator with certain unalienable Rights." And though God created mankind in his own image, he did not create us equally. Look around; all people are different. He designed men and women to be different in many ways. We think differently, process emotions in a different way, make decisions in our own way, and learn another way. He created you to be none other than you. We're blessed by him; every skill we have is from the LORD.

Like the sports underdog stories of the 1980 men's USA Olympic hockey team and "Buster" Douglas' knockout of heavyweight champion Mike Tyson in 1990, David and Goliath also exemplified a story of an underdog who beat the odds. God had planted expectations on David's heart (e.g., the lion and bear) to kill Goliath long before Goliath was ever a problem.

You may have heard of the story where the armies of the Philistines and the Israelites prepared for more battle (1 Samuel 17). According to the story, the 9-feet 6-inch giant Goliath proposes a battle of champions—one will represent the Philistines and one the Israelites. The loser's side will become servants to the winner's side – winner takes all. Goliath repeated this challenge for 40 days; everyone was too afraid to accept his challenge. David came to the camp and undertook the challenge to fight Goliath; he let King Saul know he had killed a lion and a bear while shepherding. Saul straps David in Saul's armor; he expected David to go out and fight like him [Saul]. David couldn't fight like Saul; he had to fight like David. David rose to expectations and showed how to face a giant; he killed Goliath.

Like with David, God supplies all of your needs, and you shouldn't be concerned about whether you are good enough to live up to something others want from you. You can be as good as what is expected or promised. You can be good enough, fit in with, satisfy, and suit expectations. You can live up to your reputation. While acknowledging the truth of facing the giant, David's perspective of him determined his view of the circumstance. He recognized the spiritual aspect of the battle and faced the giant with faith; he expected victory and glorified him.

Rise up for battle! Like these underdogs, you're not created to be a copycat of the person putting expectations on you. God has expectations for you. Keep striving. Keep going and rise again (Proverbs 24:16). You can live up to expectations and fulfil his words by obeying him. In these promises and his word, he has given you everything to be successful. As uncovered about conditional promises, he has expectations of you. You can rise up and meet his expectations placed on you.

Similarly, people in Jesus' day were expecting the Messiah, but, when he came, they had some unlikely expectations of what he'd do. They wanted the Savior to free them from Rome. They incorrectly expected Jesus to establish his kingdom. When he did not fulfill their expectations, they were unsatisfied and mad enough to kill. They called out "Crucify him!" As throughout his life on earth, Jesus rose to God's expectations.

At the Garden of Gethsemane, Judas betrayed Jesus on the night before Jesus' crucifixion (Matthew 26:47-56). Leaving to pray alone, he twice asked his Father to remove the cup – God's judgment -- he was about to drink. Each time he yielded to the Father's will, an angel from heaven built him up. Unquestionably, our Savior's readiness to die on the cross was the night's central impact; he paid the penalty for our sins. Thank him for his unspeakable gift; he gave us the victory through his son, our LORD Jesus Christ. Finally, Jesus met his expectations; he rose from the grave to make us right with him. Thank you God; we praise your glorious name!

Rise up for battle! Like Jesus, you should also look to God and trust him. He fills the earth with the knowledge of his glory as the waters cover the sea. His promises are undeniably ironclad. The LORD is not slow in keeping his promises. Your expectations he will fulfill his word is called faith. You can expect him to do exactly what he says he will do. When based on his Word, he will never fail to meet your expectations. Scripture tells us the law of the LORD is perfect and the statutes of the LORD are trustworthy (Psalm 19:7). It would be great if we were all perfect; however, we can start anew. Let your light shine, even if your light is a candlelight.

Hear the word of the LORD: "If God is for us, who can be against us?" (Romans 8:31) So, dear friends, take the pledge and soar like an eagle [fly with other eagles high above the clouds] or scratch like a chicken [walk around with other chickens not doing much of anything]. You have the choice. My hopes and prayers are you choose to be in covenant with the LORD. We're blessed in not only hearing the word, we're blessed in our doing!

It's a new year; make it a new you (Isaiah 43:18). Growth requires change, and it's your choice to accept or refuse what God promises you. The promise is in you (Jeremiah 20:7-11); you can still make it to the Promised Land. Scripture also tells us, "If you wait for perfect conditions, you will never get anything done" (Ecclesiastes 11:4 TLB). You can't have faith without first having hope.

Real time, let's cross the line of no return and go forward—hear, trust, and obey the Word, get baptized in the name of the LORD Jesus Christ for the remission of sins; let's live holy (1 John 1:5) and not look back – *You Only Live Once*!

PART II
LAUGH

I LIKE TO START WITH SOMETHING FUNNY

Over 100 Tested, Short, Clean Jokes

CONTENTS

Introduction – A Smile Doesn't Cost a Cent,
    but it Gains a Lot of Interest 125

Part I – Spiritual Joy **133**
One – Male Wisecracks 134
Two – Female Quips 152
Three – Marital Jests 161
Four – Family Witticisms 167
Five – Children Rib-Ticklers 169

Part II – Non-Spiritual Humor **172**
Six – Animal Bits 173
Seven – Sports Antics 176
Eight – Occupational Laughs 177

Conclusion – Take Charge of Your Own Joy 182

INTRODUCTION

A Smile Doesn't Cost a Cent, but It Gains a Lot of Interest

Have you heard the one … about the Closing Hymn? If you're wondering whether or not the "closing hymn" reminds you of one of Joel Osteen's favorite jokes, you've heard well -- I feel your eagerness. But before I share this with you or tell you this favorite …

Every day is a gift from God and if you're not excited about today being a day to celebrate, what truly brings you joy?

So, a preacher was winding up his temperance sermon with great fervor: "If I had all the beer in the world, I'd take it and throw it into the river." And the congregation cried, "Amen!"

"If I had all the wine in the world, I'd take it and throw it into the river." And the congregation cried "Amen!"

"If I had all the whiskey and demon rum in the world, I'd take it all and throw it into the river." And the congregation cried "Hallelujah!" The preacher sat down. The song leader stood tentatively and announced: "For our closing song, let us sing Hymn # 365: Shall We Gather at the River."

The preacher may have suddenly sat down; however, we're led to believe it's no joking matter the assembly will be as happy as a clam and instantly jumping for joy when they gather at the river.

The Problem for Which This Book Provides an Answer

Does life suddenly feel like it's mediocre? You're working hard, making good money, and your health is well too. Yet, like eating unfulfilling or satisfying foods, and worse, foods having no nutritional value at all, life may now feel like "empty calories." A lot of things are alike —activities in which we participate in and hopes of having a good time. And in the end, they can leave you feeling miserable about yourself. Happiness is temporary and based on circumstances; joy is everlasting, regardless of the circumstances.

Is your joy full today? When something is full, there isn't room for any more. It's a feeling of complete fulfillment. What's your pleasure -- wine, women [men] and song? What takes you to your happy place -- happy songs, happy days, happy anniversaries, happy holidays, happy dances, happy meals, happy birthdays, happy endings and happy New Years?

Bro, too many people drag through the day with a sour attitude, no enthusiasm. Accordingly, they hardly ever smile. They never laugh anymore --the average child laughs 200 times per day and the average adult laughs 14 times a day. Thus, everything is a burden. As a result, they have a sad disposition, seem less than giddy, or wake up grouchy. They feel frustrated, on edge, aggravated, uptight, stressed, or feel people push their buttons.

God never created us to endure life. Be the first to hear about it -- he created us to enjoy life and have unbridled joy! Sis, for this reason, we're not supposed to go around with a long face, negative, discouraged, and grumpy.

Whether you receive these rib-tickling Christian jokes as a believer or a speaker retelling them to your targeted audience, these short, clean jokes are a must to make you laugh quick and easy. Double the pleasure, double the fun! They will help you radiate joy now instead of faked happiness.

Why This Book Is Important to Read

As believers, you and I are expected to be the most joyful people on earth. Right? People may ask, "Why are they so joyful? They must be high [as a kite]!" Yes LORD -- hardcore Christian living! But I want to take it a step further. Everywhere we go, we should be so full of joy – as happy as a dog with two tails -- we instantly brighten other people's days. A smile doesn't cost a cent, but it gains a lot of interest.

> This *is* the day the LORD has made; we will rejoice and be glad in it (Psalm 118:24 NKJV)

You have the joy of the LORD! Avoid wasting a lot time hemming and hawing; good luck with getting your joy back!

Before you learn how you can take charge of your own happiness, let's first understand *I Like to Start with Something Funny* is all about: over 100 reliable clean, short jokes lock, stock and barrel. They're remarkably hilarious! Regardless if you're receiving (e.g., listening, reading, etc.) or sending (e.g., joke telling, presenting, etc.), they are proven ice breakers! You'll suddenly get a big delight in every comical joke read or told. They are to make you laugh and they also help to ensure your joy is full and complete, and glorify God. He who laughs last, laughs longer.

Framing – Unhappiness Occurring Every Day You Wake Up

In unpacking this book's importance, you'll discover the sequential organization in telling a funny joke – framing, telling and responding. They parallel the main parts to a speech and attendance at a church – "opening" (invitation to church), "body" (friend attends church), and "conclusion" (pastor clinches the deal). As we dig into this arrangement, the humorous joke can be a powerful weapon in your armory, especially when:

- The speaker is naturally funny.
- The enriching joke adds significance to the message, event, people, and the speaker
- The elevating joke doesn't detract from what you are trying to accomplish; people are able to focus on the message

Telling: Short, Clean Jokes Breaking the Ice and Grabbing the Audience's Attention

Following the framing, the whimsical joke can be told straight from the "horses" mouth. A large number of preachers question whether they should tell a joke when they get up to give a sermon. One pastor who started banging his sermons with good-natured jokes is Joel Osteen, Senior Pastor at Lakewood Church, the largest Protestant church in the United States, in Houston, Texas. He is also widely known as "The Smiling Preacher" and a man who maintains a constant positive outlook in spite of circumstances. He's encouraging, uplifting and down to earth. And he always touches viewers with a lighthearted joke and warm smile.

If you've heard an inspirational pastor providing hope and speaking in a conversational tone on the television, Sirius XM radio or on-line podcast at least once, there's a good chance you've been listening to or watching Joel Osteen. He likes to "start his sermons with something funny" and he has a collection of humorous jokes in his wheelhouse. Of course, these little clever jokes are neither doctrinal nor theological -- they are to make you laugh.

He'll crack you up-- say funny things and doesn't mangle the punchline. It doesn't matter what medium you use to watch or listen to Joel; he's a figure of fun every time. And I'm not pulling your chain. He is positive, he's good -- and you can be "funny" too (i.e. when retelling the best fit joke to your glee club, etc.).

How about you? Maybe you're trying to be a comedian or want to break the ice for presentations at work or school. OK, no problem. You won't suck severely or get heckled, booed or jeered. Telling these good-hearted jokes won't be trash, lame, or get you cancelled – WHOMP WHOMP. These warmhearted jokes will result in joy-filled chuckles instead of a Debbie Downer or Negative Nancy outlook. Are you getting this? I promise when trying to tell these good-humored jokes to your family, friends and co-workers, you won't screw up, get stuck, have an "Oh, crap" moment or say, "Oh, this is messed up. HELP anyone." Your crowd will be as happy as a lark and satisfaction is guaranteed!

Keep believing and you'll experience big things -- for real. You can be the big cheese and strike while the iron is hot! Yo, you got this. Start as an underdog and end as a champion; these cheery jokes will resonate and get a great response from family and friends! Like the 5 "Bs" of a presentation, Be Brief Brother (Baby), Be Brief, you get an advantage of these short, clean jokes. Sweet -- they help to keep your laugh shack set concise and effective!

What do I mean? As an icebreaker, they give you a leg up and support King Henry VIII's statement to each of his seven wives, "I won't keep you long." Using your gift of the gab, you'll be seriously laughing and having a happy day; you'll have a field day and be a happy camper. Your squad will also roll with the punches and get a kick out of it; they will "get it" and "die" laughing!

Hardy har -- imagine yourself telling these little, knee-slapping jokes. They're analogous to having a good speech "opening" (invitation to church), "body" (friend attends church), and an inspirational "conclusion" (preacher as the finisher of a powerful message).

As the "opening" of the message, the upbeat joke takes on the concept of primacy, instantly pushing the envelope so people remember most vividly what they hear at the beginning of a speech. Are you with me? The first minute is the key to grabbing the attention of your audience. It is when you introduce your communication, favorably engaging and drawing them to you and your point now. Studies show the average attention span is 8 seconds. With these short, clean jokes, your high-key audience will suddenly be tuned in and ready, willing and able to listen -- they won't bail.

For real! As an icebreaker, the funny joke instantly grabs the interest of the witnesses with a limited time span for the upcoming sermon. As the punchline "closer," the entertaining joke helps contribute to the concept of recency, extending to folks who will strongly recall what you say at the end. Are you following me?

Let's picture the comical joke's role as one of a smiling church greeter, exhibiting a friendly welcome at the door, enabling the visitor or attendee to feel (at least the slightest bit) welcomed, and "preaching the sermon." Like the greeter -- the personification and the representative of the church, the lighthearted joke helps to set the entire tone of the presentation.

Similarly, when it comes to persuading, inspiring, or influencing your fans (e.g., "stans" – stalker fans), a priceless joke as your opening (i.e., punchline closer) is by far the most important moment of your delivery. It will help to lighten up, create an immediate bond and get viewers hyped and on your side; they'll increase viewers tuning in and promote being more receptive to your topic. Accordingly, these tested jokes reduce tension and provide showbiz value to your talk. Thus, the jolly joke allows spectators to see you're human and identify with you and it lets everybody in the room yuck it up and have some fun too.

As a follower [of Christ], the good-spirited joke can also break the ice for your hungry parishioners to hear the Good News. From the start, you enlighten your listeners with a touch of gentle humor. In putting icing on the cake, these good-hearted jokes add to an opportunity to express God's love through Christ and help set the tone of the upcoming worship service.

Responding: To Short, Clean Jokes to Encourage Laughter and Bring Joy

After telling the humdinger joke, the expected response is laughter now for your funny bones. The joke teller hopes the onlookers "get it" and are laughing their behind off. He who laughs last, didn't get it. Conceptually, with the slapstick joke as the "punchline closer," an "invitation" to accept Christ or what you're presenting becomes the deciding moment. Thus, the impact of a playful joke (i.e. the punchline closer by the minister or you) and why *I Like to Start with Something Funny* is important; the jokes are all they're cracked up to be.

In your capacity as a beneficiary of these good-hearted jokes, this book will be a guiding light to God's goodness and further take his vision of joy to the world! No matter what your circumstance, you'll crack up reading through these sidesplitting jokes; they'll instantly send you joy and always keep a smile on your face – "Of all the Things You Wear, Your Expression is the Most Important" (Janet Lane-Claypon).

How This Book Is Organized

You can park your car on this medium, increasing your capacity to read *I Like to Start with Something Funny* for pleasure, knowledge and information longer; reading doesn't offer as many distractions as other mediums. Though reading this book is worth the wait, reading or telling these tested, short clean jokes delivers instant gratification. To get the most out of reading this book, the book's structure – "spiritual joy" and "nonspiritual humor" -- helps you to more easily return to certain parts and remember the content better.

Believe me, these good, clean jokes will have your full thoughtfulness and keep you fully engrossed. They're also further categorized to easily identify the protagonist who becomes the "butt," mark or target of the zinger and who is being poked fun at, knocked or egged on. However, don't expect to cringe by seeing bottom of the barrel food, diet, or ethnic joke groups being rubbed in. Your get-together will be infectiously laughing so hard their cheeks will hurt or feel tickled pink and may say, "You're so crazy (or cray-cray –slang for "crazy" … in a nice way)!"

When deciding to retell these laughable jokes, you can also navigate through the table of contents to choose your best-fit, short, clean joke to retell to your targeted crowd. You get me? They're a quick read. While the effect may be different when listening to them from Joel himself, like reading a book about Mount Everest, the outcome will be quite the cliffhanger. They will break the routine of a dry, monotonous, mundane day and amuse you and your gathering.

I have a deal for you --- a deal I do not believe you can refuse. When reading for personal edification and entertainment, you'll instantly love all of these hilarious jokes and suddenly want more of them. You'll dislike getting to the end of the book. Carry this book, your pride and joy, whenever, wherever -- at home, work, or on the go. Arguably, it's better than the joy of sex. You'll gain the advantage of being able to read these crafty jokes and relive the experiences over and over again. These "nuggets of funny" are permanent and real. That's so not funny (full of stuff).

When reading for spiritual formation and growth, you can also expect to be able to start your day off in faith; these enlightening jokes will give you the strength and happiness to make your day enjoyable. Like your favorite song or hymn, these inspiring jokes can help uplift and carry you through troubled times. Like a choir and music ministry, in effect, these edifying jokes help to usher in the Spirit now, stay connected and in the realm of God while still having fun.

When and Where to Go from Here

Before presenting these clean, safe jokes to make you laugh or maybe blush, I hope the introduction revealed what *I Like to Start with Something Funny* is all about. You "get it:" the sequential organization in telling a joke – framing, telling and responding. The pattern parallels the main parts to a speech and attendance at a church – "opening" (invitation to church), "body" (friend attends church), and "conclusion" (pastor seals the deal). These happy-go-lucky jokes will also help to provide an incredible first-time impression to your public where they live, work, play and pray.

All right, you're all set and ready to jump into this book. Jump for joy and dive in anywhere you like – the new book was penned to allow you to dive right in. But, if you want to get a head start on the quick-witted jokes, leap now to Chapter 1 – where all the rolling on the floor laughter starts! Happy reading ... as happy as a pig in mud or at the end of a workday on Friday! Laugh out Loud!

SECTION I

SPIRITUAL JOY

CHAPTER 1

Male Wisecracks

I like to start with something funny.
I heard about this man. He called the church office and said, "I want to speak to the 'head hog at the trough."

The secretary was offended. She said, "If you mean the pastor, you're going to have to call him Pastor, but you may not call him the head hog at the trough."

He said, "Well fine, I was thinking about making a five thousand dollar donation to your church." She said, "Hang on, Porky walked in."

I like to start with something funny.
I heard about this man. He came up to a Baptist pastor. He said, "Sir my dog passed away. I was wondering if you could come to my house and have a funeral for him."

The pastor seemed kind of annoyed and said "Naw, I can't do a funeral for a dog"

The man said, "That's too bad, I was thinking about making a five thousand dollar donation to your church." The pastor smiled and said, "Why didn't you tell me your dog was Baptist."

I like to start with something funny.

I heard about this minister driving down the road. He looked down and accidentally veered off and went through a ditch and ended up crashing into a telephone pole.

The man behind him pulled over and ran up to him, "Sir are you ok?"

The minister said, "Yes, I'm fine; the angel of the LORD was with me."

I like to start with something funny.

I heard about these three men out hiking through the wilderness. They came upon this violent, raging river and they needed to get to the other side. The first man prayed, "Please God give me the strength to make it across."

And Poof! God gave him big arms and strong legs and he was able to swim across in 2 hours. Seeing this, the next man said, "God please give me the strength and the tools I need to make it across." And Poof! God gave him a boat. He was able to row across in 30 minutes.

The next man said, "God give me the strength, the tools and the intelligence to make it across." And Poof! God turned him into a woman. She looked at the map, hiked 5 minutes upstream and walked across the bridge. The man shook his head and said, "you'd better let him ride with me; you're about to kill him."

I like to start with something funny.

I heard about this pastor. He decided to skip church one Sunday morning and go play golf.

He told his assistant he wasn't feeling well and he drove to a golf course in another city where nobody would know him.

He teed off on the first hole and suddenly the wind picked up his ball ... And carried it an extra 100 yards and blew it right into the hole ... for a 420-yard hole-in-one.

An angel looked at God and said, "What you do that for?"

God smiled and said, "Who is he going to tell."

I like to start with something funny.

I heard about this pastor. He was raising money for a new sanctuary.

He told his congregation one Sunday morning, "If anybody will give a thousand dollars, you can pick out the next three hymns."

A little old lady in the back raised her hand and said, "Pastor, I will do it."

He was so excited, he said, "Thank you so much. Go ahead and pick out the next three hymns."

She looked out over the congregation and said, "I take Him, Him and Him."

I like to start with something funny.

I heard about this minister. He brought a new horse.

He trained it to respond to 'Praise the LORD,' meaning 'giddy up' and 'Hallelujah,' meaning 'Whoa.'

Every time he said, "Praise the LORD," the horse took off running. When he said, "Whoa," it would quickly stop. One day he was out riding. The horse got spooked and took off straight toward the cliff... running full speed. In the panic, he couldn't remember what he trained the horse to respond to. He said, "Bless God," "Glory," "Amen"... Nothing happened. At the last second, he shouted "Hallelujah."

The horse came to a screeching halt ... inches before the edge of the cliff.

He breathed a sigh of relief and said, "Praise the LORD."

I like to start with something funny.

I heard about this atheist. He was spending a quiet day on the lake. When all of a sudden his boat was attacked by the Loch Ness Monster. One easy flip, it tossed him and his boat high into the air. It opened its mouth, waiting to swallow.

As the man tumbled head over heels. He cried out, "God help me."

All at once, time stood still. The whole picture froze.

God said, "But I didn't think you believed in me."

The atheist said, "God please give me a break. Two minutes ago I didn't believe in the Loch Ness Monster either."

I like to start with something funny.

I heard about this pastor. He found a small box hidden in his wife's closet.

He opened it up. There was six eggs and a 1000 one dollar bills.

He asked his wife about it. She explained how every time he preached a bad sermon, she put an egg in the box.

After 35 years of ministering, he felt pretty good about himself ... only six bad sermons.

"What the $1000 was?"

She said, "Every time I got a dozen of eggs, I sold them for a dollar."

I like to start with something funny.

I heard about this pastor. He parked in a 'No Parking' zone downtown in a large city.

He left a note on the windshield, saying, "Officer, I circled this block 10 times. If I don't park here, I'll miss my appointment."

In big letters, he wrote, "FORGIVE US OF OUR TREPASSES."

He returned to his car and had a ticket.

The officer had written him a note. It said, "Sir, I circled this block for 10 years. If I don't give you a ticket, I could lose my job."

In big letters, he wrote, "LEAD US NOT INTO TEMPTATIONS."

I like to start with something funny.

I heard about this pastor.

He was asked to inform a member of his congregation, who had a heart condition, he had inherited 10 million dollars.

They were concerned because of the shock he may have a heart attack.

The pastor said, "Sir, what would you do if you inherited 10 million dollars?"

The man said, "Pastor, first thing I'll do is give half of it to the church." At that point, the pastor fell over dead.

I like to start with something funny.

I heard about this minister. He was walking down the street. He came upon this group of young boys surrounding a small dog. He asked what they were doing. They explained they were having a contest ... and whoever could tell the biggest lie would get to keep the dog. The minister launched into a 10-minute sermon on lying, starting with don't you know lying is a sin ... And ending with when I was your age I never told a lie. There was complete silence. When he thought he had got through to them, the youngest boy spoke up and said, "Alright, give him the dog."

I like to start with something funny.

I heard about this minister. He was driving down the road when he got pulled over by a policeman.

The officer came up to the window and smelled alcohol.

He saw a thermos and said, "Sir, what are you drinking?"

The minister said, "Just water officer."

He asked to see the thermos and took one sniff and said, "Smells like wine to me."

The minister said, "What do you know, Jesus did it again."

I like to start with something funny.

I heard about these three pastors. They were in a boat on a lake fishing one day together.

One of them said, "We never get to let our hair down.

Let's each tell the area we struggle in the most ... our greatest sin so we can pray for each other."

The first man said, "I hate to admit this, but I have a problem with gambling. I sneak out a lot of nights and go gamble."

The second pastor said, "I'm ashamed to admit this, but I have a problem cheating. I hardly ever pay my taxes."

The third pastor sat their silently. They waited and waited. He wouldn't budge. They said, "We're not getting off this boat until you tell us your greatest sin."

He said, "Alright, my greatest sin is gossiping and I can't wait to get off this boat."

I like to start with something funny.

I heard about this pastor. He was raising money for a new sanctuary.

He told his congregation, "I got good news and I got bad news. The good news is we have plenty of money for our new sanctuary. The bad news is it's still in your pockets.

I like to start with something funny.

I heard about this Baptist man named Bill. He like to sneak out to the horse races and bet.

One day after losing almost all his money, he saw a Catholic priest step out onto the track and bless a horse.

Sure enough that horse won first place.

The next race he blessed another horse and that horse won again.

Seeing this Bill went down to the ATM machine and took out all his money.

This time he saw the priest not just touch the horse's forehead, but his eyes, his ears and all his legs.

Feeling confident he bet all his money. But on the middle of that race, the horse fell down dead.

He couldn't believe it. He said to the priest, "What in the world happened?"

He said, "That's the problem with you Protestants, you don't know the difference between a blessing and the Last Rites."

I like to start with something funny.

I heard about this minister. He was up on the pulpit preaching away one Sunday morning when he noticed a man on the front row sound asleep. That made him so aggravated, he started preaching louder and harder. But it seemed like the louder he got, the sounder he slept. So he finally stopped right in the middle of his sermon and he said to the man sitting next to him, "Would you please wake that man up?" The man said, "Wake him up yourself. You put him to sleep."

I like to start with something funny.

One Sunday morning, this man walked into church wearing blue jeans, t-shirt, and an old cowboy hat.

Some of the members were appalled. They sent notes to the Pastor expressing their concern.

Afterwards the Pastor told the man he needed to pray ... And ask God what he should wear when he came back to his church.

The next week the man came back wearing the exact same thing.

Pastor said, "I told you to ask God what you should wear before you come back to my church."

The man said, "I did ask God and He told me He didn't know what to wear because He has never been here before."

I like to start with something funny.

I heard about this pastor. He was in the lobby after service greeting people.

He saw this man he hadn't seen in a long, long time.

Pulled him over to the side and said, "Sir, you need to join the Army of the LORD."

The man said, "What are you talking about, I'm in the Army of the LORD."

The pastor said, "How come I only see you on Christmas and Easter?"

He whispered back, "I'm in the Secret Service."

I like to start with something funny.

I heard about this minister that died. He was standing in line at the Pearly Gates and in front of him was a man dressed in a loud shirt, wearing blue jeans and sunglasses. Saint Peter asked, "What's your name sir?" He said, "My name is Joe Cohen, taxicab driver, New York City." Peter checked his list and handed him a gold staff and a silk robe and said, "Welcome to Heaven." The minister stepped up and said, "I'm Reverend Joseph Snow, Pastor of Saint Mary's Cathedral." Peter checked his list and handed him a cotton robe and a wooden staff. He said, "Hey wait a minute. That's not fair. The taxicab driver got a gold staff and a silk robe. How could that be?"

Peter said, "Sir, up here we work by results. When you preached, people slept. But when he drove, people prayed."

I like to start with something funny.

I heard about this elderly minister. He was close to death.

He sent word for two of his members, an IRS agent and a lawyer, to come to his house. Upon arrival, he motioned for them to sit on each side of the bed. The men were moved they could be with the minister in his final moment. [At] one point, the lawyer asked sincerely, "Sir, why did you choose us?" The minister mustered up some strength and said, "Jesus died between two sinners. That's the way I want to go."

I like to start with something funny.

I heard about this wealthy man known for being eccentric. He was having a big party at this house and in his backyard he had a huge pool filled with alligators and sharks. He said to the guests, "Anyone will swim across my pool, I'll give you anything you want." In a few minutes there was a big splash and a man was in there going 90 to nothing … Dodging alligators, maneuvering around the sharks. He made it to the other side in the nick of time and got out as frantic as can be. The wealthy man said, "I can't believe you're the bravest person I've ever met. Now what is it you would want?" The man said, "What I want, more than anything else is the name of the person that pushed me in."

I like to start with something funny.

I heard about this man. He was driving through an intersection monitored by cameras. If you ran the light or broke the law in any way, it would take your picture and you would receive a ticket in the mail. So he made sure to go through it extra slowly and not break any laws. But he noticed the camera flashed and took his picture. He thought that's not right. He turned around and drove through it again … even more slowly. Once again it took his picture. He thought this thing is messed up; they cannot give me a ticket. Out of spite, he drove through it three more times … each time waving at the camera with a big smile. A week later, he received five tickets in the mail for not wearing his seatbelt.

I like to start with something funny.

I heard about these three men, a Baptist, Catholic, and a Charismatic. They died on the same day and went to Heaven. St Peter met them at the gates and said, 'I'm sorry men, your rooms are not available yet.' He didn't know what to do. He decided to call Satan and see if he would keep them for a little while. Satan reluctantly agreed. A few hours later, Satan called back and said, "Peter, you got to come get these guys. The Baptist man is saving everybody. The Catholic man is forgiving everybody and the Charismatic has already raised enough money for air conditioning."

I like to start with something funny.

I heard about this man that died and went to Heaven. St Peter escorted him down this long hallway filled with clocks. The hands on the clocks were all moving at different speeds. Peter explained every person has a clock. When they sin, the clock ticks.

The man saw a clock verily moving. It was Billy Graham's clock. There was another clock creeping along … Mother Teresa's clock.

He said curiously, "Can I see my clock?"

Peter said, "Yeah, we keep yours in the office and use it as a fan."

I like to start with something funny.

I heard about these two guys. They argued for years on whether Jesus was white or whether he was black. Archie was sure he was white. Jack was as sure he was black. As faith would have it, they both died on the same day.

They rushed to the Pearly Gates. Said St Peter, "Please tell us is Jesus white or black? We've been arguing our whole life over this." About that time Jesus walked up and said, "Buenas Dias."

I like to start with something funny.

I heard about this man who was out walking through the woods with a friend. All of a sudden they came up on this huge grizzly bear. They froze in their tracks. As the bear intently stared them down. They contemplated what they should do.

The man turned to his friend and said, "I think we should run."

His friend said, "Are you crazy, you can't outrun a grizzly bear."

He said, "I know that. I don't have to outrun him; I just have to outrun you."

I like to start with something funny.

I heard about this man walking on the beach. God said, "Son you've been so faithful, I'm going to grant you one special wish". He was so excited. He said, "God I always wanted to go to Hawaii, but I'm afraid to fly. So my wish is you would build me a bridge across the ocean". God said, "Son that is impossible. Think of the logistics. Now take some time and wish again". He said, "Okay God, I have been married four times. All my ex-wives say I am so insensitive. So my wish is I would be able to understand a woman. I want to know why they think like they think ... why they feel like they feel". It was a long pause ... God said, "Do you want two lanes or four lanes on that bridge?"

I like to start with something funny.

I heard about this elderly man. He had a serious hearing problem for years and years. He could hardly hear anything. One day he went to the doctor and he was fitted with a new type hearing aid to where he could hear 100 percent. A month later he went back for a checkup.

The doctor said, "Man, your family must be happy; your hearing is perfect."

He said, "No, I haven't told my family. I sit around and listen to the conversations and I've changed my will three times."

I like to start with something funny.

I heard about this man. He was sitting in a dark restaurant. He said to the lady sitting next to him, "Would you like to hear a 'Blond' joke."

She said, "Well before you tell me, you should know I'm blond, six foot tall, and a professional body builder. The lady next to me is blond, six foot two, and a professional wrestler. And the lady next to her is blond, six foot five, and the kickboxing champion of the world. Now do you still want to tell me?"

He thought about it a moment and said, "Naw, not if I'm going to have to explain it three times."

I like to start with something funny.

I heard about this 92-year old man. He wasn't feeling well one day and so he decided to go to the doctor and have a check-up.

A few days later the doctor saw him out walking down the street with a beautiful young lady by his side. And he seemed to be as happy as could be. The Doctor was kind of surprised. He said, "Wow, you sure are doing a lot better."

The man said, "Yes Doctor, I took your orders. You said get a hot momma and stay cheerful." The Doctor said, "I didn't say that! I said you got a heart murmur. Be careful!"

I like to start with something funny.

I heard about a young man who once asked God, "How long was a million years to Him?"

God said, "A million years to me was like a single second in your time."

The young man asked God, "What was a million dollars to Him?"

God said, "A million dollars to me was like a single penny to you."

The young man got his courage up and asked God, "Would you please give me a penny?" God said, "Sure, just a second."

I like to start with something funny.
I heard about this pastor. He was new in town. He was going to door to door inviting people to come to his church.

He knocked on this one door. He could tell someone was there but nobody would answer. He took his church card out and wrote on the back the Scripture reference, "REVELATION 3:20" and left it on the door. The next Sunday after service an usher handed him the same card under what he had written was the Scripture reference: "GENESIS 3:10." Here's what they say:

The pastor's word, Revelation 3:20, "Behold I stand at the door and knock. If anyone answers, I will come in." The reply was Genesis 3:10: "I heard your voice, but I was afraid because I was naked."

I like to start with something funny.
One day up in heaven, God said to the men, "I want you to form two lines. One line is for the men who are the head of the house. The other line is for the men who let the woman be the head of the house."

The line where the woman ran the house was 100 miles long. There was only one man in the other line. God said, "Men I'm ashamed of you. I created you to be the head, but only one man stood up to make me proud." He looked at him and said, "Son, tell them how did you manage to be the only one in this line?"

The man looked confused and said, "I don't know. My wife told me to stand here."

I like to start with something funny. *Somebody sent me these funny one liners about blonds. But since I'm a friend to a beautiful, smart intelligent blond, I'm going to change it from a blond lady to a blond man. He was so blond he tripped over a cordless phone. He was so blond he asked for a price check at the 'Dollar Store'. He was so blond it took him two hours to watch '60 Minutes'. He was so blond he thinks 'Taco Bell' is the Mexican phone company.*

I like to start with something funny.

I heard about this man. He was the only Protestant in a large Catholic neighborhood. Every Friday during Lent, while his neighbors were eating cold fish, he was grilling a steak in the backyard.

They couldn't stand the temptation and decided to try to convert him to Catholicism. He finally agreed. The priest sprinkled water over him and said, "You were born a Baptist; you were raised a Baptist. Now you're a Catholic." The next year when the first Friday of Lent, they smelled the same smell in the air.

They rushed to his house. He was in the backyard sprinkling water over this steak, saying "You were born a cow; you were raised a cow, but now you're a fish."

I like to start with something funny.

I heard about this man named Bubba. He lived way out in the country.

There was this stray dog that kept showing up at his house.

His wife said, "Bubba, you have to put the dog in the truck and take him out to the woods and drop him off. That's where he lives."

Bubba drove him a mile down the road [and] dropped him off. When he came back home, the dog was walking up the driveway … practically beat him back.

He did the same thing; it happened again.

His wife said, "Bubba, you have to take him way out, drive him around in circles [and] get him all mixed up."

Bubba drove him an hour away, crisscrossed country roads he never driven before [and] dropped the dog off.

Two hours later, Bubba called his wife from the truck and said, "Did that dog make it back home?"

She said, "Yeah, here he comes walking up."

He said, "Do me a favor, [and] put him on the phone. I need directions."

I like to start with something funny.

I heard about this 85-year old man. He was out fishing one day and he heard this voice saying, "Pick me up."

He looked all around and didn't see anything and he thought he was dreaming.

He heard it again, "Pick me up."

He looked down and saw a frog on the ground. He said in amazement, "Are you talking to me?"

The frog said, "Yes, pick me up and kiss me and I'll turn into a beautiful bride."

He quickly picked the frog up and put him in this front pocket.

The frog said, "Hey! What are you doing? I said kiss me and I'll turn into a beautiful bride."

The man said, "No thanks. At my age, I'd rather have a talking frog."

I like to start with something funny.

I heard about these three men traveling together, a Hindu priest, a Jewish Rabbi and a Televangelist.

They stopped at a farm house for lodging and the farmer said, "I only have room for two in the house. Someone's going to have to stay in the barn."

The Hindu priest said, "I'll do it." After a few minutes there was a knock on the door.

He said, "I can't stay out there. There's a cow, and cows are sacred in our religion."

The Jewish Rabbi said, "I'll do it." After a few minutes, there was a knock on the door.

He said, "I can't stay out there. There's a pig and that wouldn't be Kosher."

The Televangelist finally said, "Alright, I'll do it." In a few minutes, there was a knock on the door. It was the cow and the pig.

I like to start with something funny.

I heard about this man at the airline ticket counter, hollering and screaming at the agent … being so rude. As he continued to rant and rave, the agent was as calm and polite as could be. She treated him so respectfully, like it didn't even bother her. He left and the next man stepped up and said, "Wow! I am so impressed. You must be a Christian. How could you possibly be so kind to him?" She smiled and said, "Aww, it wasn't hard. See, he's going to Detroit, but his bags are going to Bangkok."

I like to start with something funny.

I heard about this single man. He had been living at home with his elderly father who was wealthy. He decided he needed to find a wife so he could enjoy the fortune he would inherit when his father died.

One evening at an investment meeting, he saw the most beautiful girl he had ever seen. She took his breath away.

He said to her, "I know I look like an ordinary guy. But in a few years when my father passes, I will inherit hundreds of millions of dollars." Impressed she took his business card. Three months later she married his father.

I like to start with something funny.

I heard about this senior citizen. He was driving down the freeway in his brand new Corvette with the top down going 80 miles hour when he saw flashing red lights from a state trooper in his rear view mirror. Without thinking about it, he floored it ... took off to a 100 miles an hour.

He heard the sirens behind him. He finally pulled over and said, "Officer I'm so sorry, I don't know what I was thinking."

The state trooper said, "Listen, it's Friday, 4 o'clock [and] my shift is over in 30 minutes. If you tell me a reason why you're speeding I've never heard it before, I'll let you go."

The man thought about it and said, "Officer, years ago my wife ran off with a state trooper and I thought you were bringing her back."

The officer said, "Have a great weekend!"

CHAPTER 2

Female Quips

I like to start with something funny.

I heard about this elderly lady. She came into church one Sunday morning. A friendly usher greeted her "Ma'am, where would you like to sit?"

She said, "I would like to sit on the front row."

"Oh No ma'am, you don't want to do that, our pastor is boring. He will put you to sleep; let me seat you somewhere else."

She was appalled. She said, "Sir, do you know who I am."

He said, "No."

She said, "I'm the pastor's mother."

He hung his head in embarrassment. Finally he looked up and said, "Ma'am, do you know who I am?"

She said, "No."

He said, "Thank God."

I like to start with something funny.

I heard about this elderly lady. She was at the store, she accidentally locked her keys in her car. She was using a coat hanger to try to get it open ... with no success. She prayed and asked God to help her.

About this time, this real rough looking guy drove up on a motorcycle ... wearing leather, tattoos, and a skull cap.

In 15 seconds, he had her car door open.

She hugged him and said, "LORD thank you for sending me this nice man."

He said, "Lady, I'm not a nice man. I got out of prison for auto theft."

She gave him a bigger hug and said, "LORD thank you, you even sent me a Professional."

I like to start with something funny.

I heard about this elderly lady close to death. She had never been married. She called her pastor over to talk about her funeral.

She said she only wanted female pallbearers.

The pastor looked at her kind of strange and asked, "Why?"

She said, "The men wouldn't take me out when I was alive, they're not going to take me out when I'm dead."

I like to start with something funny.

I heard about this group of elderly ladies. Way up in their eighties, they were driving down the freeway together when they got pulled up by a police officer.

The officer said to the woman driving, "Ma'am, Do you realize you're only going 35 miles an hour?"

She said, "Yes officer, I realize that."

He said, "Why are you going so slow?"

She said, "That's what the sign said."

He kind of laughed and said, "No ma'am, that's the number of the freeway. This is Highway 35."

By the way, "Why are these women so terrified?"

She smiled and said, "We just got off Highway 95."

I like to start with something funny.

I heard about this 84-year old woman. She went on a blind date with a 93-year old man. When she returned home to her daughter's house, she seemed kind of upset. Her daughter asked her, "What was wrong?" She said, "I had to slap him three times."

She said, "You mean he tried to get fresh." She said, "Naw, I thought he was dead."

I like to start with something funny.

I heard about this 84-year old woman. She'd gotten out of shape and knew she needed to start exercising. So she decided to join an aerobics class for seniors.

And the first day, she bent and twisted and gyrated back and forth, jumped up and down, perspired for over an hour. But she said by the time she got her leotards on, the class was over.

I like to start with something funny.

I heard about these three sisters ... ages 96, 94, and 92 living together.

One day the 96-year old draws a bath. She puts one foot in and stops. She hollers downstairs, "I can't remember if I was getting in or getting out."

The 94-year old said, "Just a second, I will come up and help you."

She gets half way up the stairs and stops. She said, "I can't remember if I was going up or coming down."

The 92-year old shook her head and said, "Boy, I hope I never get that forgetful."

She knocked on wood for good luck. [... sound of knocking on wood]. She said, "Hang on, I'll come help both of you as soon as I see who's at the door."

I like to start with something funny.

I heard about this 85-year old woman.

She went on a blind date with a 92-year old man.

She came home frustrated and her daughter said, "Mom, what's wrong?"

She said, "I had to slap him three times."

The daughter said, "You mean he tried to get fresh?"

She said, "No, I thought he was dead."

I like to start with something funny.

I heard about this country grandmother. She'll go out on her front porch every morning and thank the LORD for another day.

Her neighbor didn't believe in God. He'll shout back: "There's no such thing as the LORD." One day he overheard asking the God to give her groceries for the week. He snuck over the next morning and put some groceries on her front porch. She got up and said, "Thank you LORD, you did it again!" He laughed and laughed and said, "God didn't give you those groceries, I put them there." She said, "Thank you LORD! You not only gave me the groceries, but you made the Devil pay for it."

I like to start with something funny.

I heard about this Mother. One Sunday morning, she went into her son's bedroom and she said, "Son, wake up. It's time to go to church." He kind of groaned and rolled over and said, "No Mom, I'm not going to church today." She said, "What do you mean you're not going? Why not?" He said, "Mom, I'll give you two good reasons. Number one, I don't like those people. And number two, they don't like me." She said, "Son, that's no excuse. I'll give you two better reasons why you SHOULD too. Number one, you're 59 years old and number two, you're the Pastor."

I like to start with something funny.

I heard about this middle age woman. She had heart attack.

On the operating table, she asked God, "If this was it?"

God said, "No, you have 40 more years." Upon recovery, she decided to stay in the hospital ... have a face lift, tummy tuck, and liposuction ...extreme makeover. Two months later as she was leaving the hospital. She was hit by a car and killed. She got to heaven and said, "God, I thought you said I had 40 more years." God said, "I'm sorry. I didn't recognize you."

I like to start with something funny.

I heard about these four Catholic ladies. They were bragging on their sons. The first one said, "My son is a Priest. When he walks in the room everyone calls him 'Father'."

The second one said, "My son is a Bishop. When he walks in the room, everyone calls him 'Your Grace'."

The third one said, "My son is a Cardinal. When he walks in the room, everyone calls him 'Your Eminence'."

The fourth lady said, "My son is 6 foot 3, has broad shoulders, is incredibly good looking, and dresses impeccably well. When he 'walks into the room, all the ladies say, 'Oh, My God!'"

I like to start with something funny.

I heard about this lady. She was on the airplane reading her Bible.

The man next to her said, "You don't believe all that stuff in there do you?" She said, "Of course I do, it's the Bible."

He said, "What about that guy that got swallowed by the whale?"

She said, "You mean Jonah. Yes, I believe that too."

He said, "How could he possibly live that long inside a fish?"

She thought about it moment and said, "I don't know. When I get to heaven, I'll have to ask him." He said sarcastically, "What if he is not in heaven?" She said, "You will have to ask him."

I like to start with something funny.

I heard about this lady. She surprised a burglar in her kitchen late one night. She was home alone ... didn't have any weapon ... didn't know what she would do. Finally she thought I will say a Scripture verse. She shouted out, "Acts 2:38." The burglar suddenly froze in his tracks ... wouldn't move. Soon the police arrived. They were amazed a woman with no weapon could do this. They said to the burglar, "What was it about that Scripture that had such an effect on you?" He said, "Scripture. What Scripture? I thought she said she had an axe and two thirty eights (.38s)."

I like to start with something funny.

I heard about these two ladies that died and went to Heaven.

Peter met them at the gate and said, "You will be happy here if you follow one main rule: don't step on a duck.

If you step on a duck they make a terrible racket."

A week later one of the ladies accidentally stepped on a duck.

Peter came up to her with this extremely unattractive man.

Nothing appealing about him whatsoever. [Peter] said, "As your punishment you're going to be chained to this man."

Seeing this, the other lady was careful.

A month later, Peter came up to her with this incredibly handsome man.

Amazing physique, looked like a movie star ... chained them together.

The lady was thrilled. She said to him, "I don't know what I did to get chained to you."

He said, "I don't know what you did ma'am, but I stepped on a duck."

New Day, New Life

I like to start with something funny.

I heard about this lady. She saw this little old man sitting on his front porch, rocking in his rocking chair.

... always seemed to be so happy.

She finally went over to him and said, "I can't help but notice. You're always smiling ... always in a good mood. Tell me what is your secret for such a long, happy life?"

He said, "That's easy. I smoke three packs of cigarettes every day. I eat nothing but junk food, and I never exercise."

She said, "That's amazing! How old are you?"

He said, "26."

I like to start with something funny.

I heard about this Sunday morning church service. It was going fine. All of sudden, this lightning bolt hit. When the smoke cleared, Satan himself was standing behind the podium.

People panicked and ran out of the building as fast as they could. Satan stood there with glee. But suddenly his mood changed when he noticed a woman sitting on the front row as calm as can be.

He said, "Lady, do you know who I am?"

She said, "I sure do."

He said, "Aren't you afraid of me?"

She said. "No, I'm not."

He said, "Why not?"

She said, "Why should I be ... For 30 years I have been married to your brother."

I like to start with something funny.

I heard about this blonde lady … and you know I'm a close friend with a beautiful, smart, intelligent blonde. But this blonde was at Target and she saw this thermos up on the shelf. She asked the clerk what it was.

He said, "That's a thermos. You've never used one of those?"

She said, "No. What does it do?"

He said, "It keeps things hot and it keeps things cold."

The next day she showed up at work with it. Her boss said, "I've never seen you with a thermos. What do you have in there?"

She said, "Two popsicles and some coffee."

I like to start with something funny.

I heard about three people … a Russian, an American and a blonde. They were talking one day. The Russian said, "Well we were the first ones on the moon." The blonde said, "That's nothing. We're going to be the first ones on the sun." The Russian and the American, they laughed and said, "What are you talking about? You can't go the sun. It's too hot. You'll burn up." The blonde said, "We're not dumb; we're going to go at night."

CHAPTER 3

Marital Jests

I like to start with something funny.

I heard about this lady who was shopping with her husband. He asked her not to buy any new clothes.

Well, she saw this dress in the window and decided to try it on; she liked it so much, she bought it in secret. A couple of days the later, the husband discovered it. He was so upset.

She explained to him when she tried it on, it looked so good, Satan tempted her to buy it and she couldn't resist it.

He said, "Why didn't you do what the Scriptures said and say, 'Get behind me Satan!'"

She said, "I did and he told me it looked even better from a distance."

I like to start with something funny.

I heard about this wife. She was taking a nap on Valentine's Day during the afternoon. When she woke up, she called her husband and said, "Honey, I had a dream you brought me a beautiful diamond ring for Valentine's Day. What do you think this dream means?" He said, "You will find out tonight." That evening he brought home a beautifully wrapped, small package. She opened it up so excited. It was a book entitled, "The Meaning of Dreams."

I like to start with something funny.

I heard about this lady that died and she found herself standing at the Pearly Gates. Saint Peter said, "You can't come in unless you correctly spell a word."

She said, "What word?" He said, "Any word." So she spelled the word, "L-O-V-E." Peter said, "Welcome to heaven." Peter asked her if she would take his place. He instructed her, "If anybody comes, follow the same procedure." Well, in a few minutes the lady sees her ex-husband coming up. She said, "What are you doing here?" He said, "I had a heart attack. Did I make it to heaven?" She said, "Not yet. You have to correctly spell a word." He said, "What word?" After a long pause, she said, "Czechoslovakia."

I like to start with something funny.

I heard about this husband. He was quietly reading his newspaper when his wife snuck up behind him and hit him in the head with a frying pan.

He said, "What was that for?"

She said, "That was for the piece of paper I found in your pocket with the name Mary Lou on it."

He said, "Aw honey, that's one of the horses that I bet on at the race track last week."

She apologized and went about her business.

Two days later, she hit him on the head with a bigger frying pan. When he came to, he said, "What in the world was that for?"

She said, "Your horse just called."

I like to start with something funny.

I heard about this husband that died. He left his wife $20,000. After the funeral his wife told a friend she was broke. The friend said, "What do you mean you're broke? I thought you said you had $20,000". She said, "Well, I spent $5,000 on the funeral and $15,000 on the Memorial Stone". The friend said, "Wow, that's some kind of stone. How big was it"? She held up her finger and said, "Three and half karats."

I like to start with something funny.

I heard about this groom. At the wedding rehearsal, he said to the minister, "I'll make a deal with you. If during the vows, you'll leave out all love, honor and obey stuff, I'll give you $100."

He slipped a $100 bill in the minister's hand and walked away with a smile.

The next day during the ceremony, the minister said to him, "Do you promise to bow down before your wife, take her breakfast in bed, to fulfill her every desire?"

He gulped in astonishment and said in a weak voice, "I do."

He whispered in the minister's ear, "I thought we had a deal."

The minister handed him his money back and said, "Your wife made me a much better offer."

I like to start with something funny.

I heard about this husband and wife. They were celebrating their 60th birthdays together. An angel suddenly appeared and said, "God was going to grant them each one special request." They were so excited.

The wife said, "My request is we would be able to travel all over the world." Poof, when the smoke cleared, "She had tickets in their hand."

The husband hung his head in shame. He said, "My request is I will be married to a woman 30 years younger than me."

Poof, when the smoke cleared, he was 90 years old.

I like to start with something funny.

I heard about this elderly couple. They'd been married for over 60 years. They were at a church fellowship and someone asked them the secret of their success. The man told how he always treated his wife with respect and took her on trips all over the world. He said, "In fact, for our 25 wedding anniversary, I took her to Beijing, China." Everyone politely applauded and someone asked, "What did you do for your 50th wedding anniversary?" He said, "I went back and picked her up."

I like to start with something funny.

I heard about this husband and wife. They had been arguing.

Now they were giving each other the silent treatment.

The man had to get up early the next day and catch a flight. He needed his wife to wake him up.

Not wanting to break the silence, he left a note on her bed saying, "Please wake me up at 5AM."

The next day he got up at 8 o'clock and missed his flight.

He was so upset and thought I am going to go and find out why she didn't wake me up. There was a note on his side of the bed; it said, "Wake up, it's 5."

I like to start with something funny.

I heard about this man and his wife. They argued for months over who should make the coffee in the morning. The man thought it was the wife's job and she didn't agree. After several heated debates she finally said, "I can prove from the Bible it's your job."

He said, "There's nothing in the Bible about making coffee." She said, "Sure there is." She called him over and opened her Bible and pointed to the book of "Hebrews."

I like to start with something funny.

I heard about this country couple. They were celebrating their 50th wedding anniversary. They'd never had an argument before. Someone asked them the secret of their success. The husband explained as they were leaving the church going on their honeymoon, the wife's horse refused to go. She got off and looked at the horse in the eyes and said, "That's one." He went a little bit further ... stopped again. She got off and looked at the horse in the eyes and said, "That's two." He went a little bit more, but once again, he stopped. This time, she got off, pulled out her revolver and shot the horse dead. The husband said, "What in the world are you doing? You can't shoot an animal." She looked at him and said, "That's one."

I like to start with something funny.

I heard about this man. Somebody had stolen his wife's credit card. A couple of months later, the company called him and said, "Sir, we got good news; we found the credit card." The man said, "Tell the thief to keep it. He spends less than my wife."

I like to start with something funny.

I heard about this guy. He was late to work for the third day in a row. His boss said sarcastically, "Okay, What's your excuse this time."

He said, "I'm so sorry, but my wife asked to drive me to work. And I told her she didn't need to, but she insisted and said she could be ready in 10 minutes. But when we left, the drawbridge was up and I had to swim across the river, fighting off alligators. A helicopter picked me up, [and] put me on top of a building. I ran down 60 flights of stairs and got here as quickly as I could." His boss shook his head and said, "You expect me to believe that? No woman can get dressed in 10 minutes."

I like to start with something funny.

I heard about this man that was stingy with his money.

Before his death, he made his wife promise him she would have him buried with the $50,000 he had saved. His wife reluctantly agreed. At the funeral, before they closed the casket, she snuck in this small wooden box. Her friend said, "Surely, you didn't bury the money did you?" The wife said, "Of course I did. I'm a Christian, I can't lie." She said, "You mean you buried $50,000?"

Wife said, "Yes, I did. I wrote a check."

CHAPTER 4

Family Witticisms

I like to start with something funny.
I heard about this old country farmer. He was taking his nephew camping for the first time. His nephew had five degrees, was one of the smartest men alive; they set their tent up and quickly fell asleep.

The middle of the night, the farmer woke his nephew up and said, "Look up, what do you see?"

He said, "I see millions of stars."

The farmer said, "I know that, but what does it tell you?"

He said, "Astronomically, tells me there are billions of galaxies, meteorologically, it tells me it's going to be a beautiful day, theologically, it tells me God is a great Creator. What does it tell you?"

Old farmer shook his head, and said, "Tells me, somebody stole our tent."

I like to start with something funny.
I heard about this man. He was on vacation in Jerusalem with his family when his mother-in law suddenly died. He went to make arrangements to get her body back home. The consulate said, "It would cost $5,000 to have her shipped. But he could have her buried right there in Jerusalem for $150." The man thought about it a moment and said, "I like to have her body shipped home." The consulate said, "Wow, you must have loved your mother-in-law." The man said, "Naw, it's not so much that. I remember this case many years ago when they buried somebody and on the third day they arose. I can't take that chance."

I like to start with something funny.

I heard about these three sons that left home and went out and prospered. They got back together to talk about the gifts they brought their elderly mother. The first son said, "I built mom a big house." The second one said, "I got her a fancy car." The third son said, "Since mom loves to read the Bible, but she can barely see anymore, I got her a specially trained parrot that can quote the entire Bible." A few months later, they received a letter from their mother. It said, "Milton the house you built me is way too big. Gerald, the car you bought me is way too small. But, my dearest Donald, your simple gift is my favorite. The chicken is delicious."

I like to start with something funny.

I heard about these two evil brothers. They were extremely rich.

They attended the same church and on the surface appeared to be good Christians.

One of the brothers suddenly died. The remaining brother sought out the pastor and handed him a large donation.

He said, "I only have one condition. At the funeral, you must say my brother was a saint."

The pastor agreed and deposited the check.

At the funeral, the pastor said, "This man was an evil man. He lied, he stole, [and] he cheated people."

After going on and on for several minutes, he finally said, "But compared to his brother, he was a saint."

CHAPTER 5

Children Rib-Ticklers

I like to start with something funny.
I heard about these two little boys, ages 4 and 6; they were brothers. They were spending the night at their grandmother's house.

She told them to make sure they said their prayers before they went to bed.

They went in the bedroom, got on their needs. The youngest boy started praying at the top of his lungs, "God, I pray for a new bicycle; I pray for a new PlayStation; I pray for a new DVD."

His brother punched him and said, "Why are you screaming, God isn't deaf."

He said, "I know, but grandmother is."

I like to start with something funny.
I heard about this little girl. She was sitting on her grandfather's lap. She noticed how wrinkled his face was. As she contemplated the difference between hers and his. She said, "Granddaddy, Did God make you?" He laughed and said, "Yes honey, God made me long time ago." Well she said, "Did God make me?"

He said, "Yes, God made you a little while ago."

She thought about it a moment and said, "Granddaddy, God's getting better, isn't he?"

I like to start with something funny.

I heard about a mother invited some people for dinner. At the table she turned to her five-year old daughter and asked, "Honey, would you like to say the blessings?"

The little girl replied, "I don't what to say."

The mom answered back, "Say what you hear mommy say."

The little girl bowed her head and said, "Oh LORD, Why did I invite these people to dinner?"

I like to start with something funny.

I heard about this little girl. She was attending a wedding for the first time.

She asked her mom, "Why is the bride wearing all white?"

The mom smiled and said, "Oh, white is the color of happiness. Today is the happiest day of her life."

The little girl thought about it, "Why is the groom wearing all black?"

I like to start with something funny.

I heard about this little boy. He was out in his front yard playing.

This man came walking down the street kind of frustrated.

He said, "Son I'm lost. Can you tell me how to get to the post office?"

The little boy said, "Yeah, go to the stop sign and turn left; it's right around the corner."

He thanked him. He said, "By the way, I'm the new pastor here in town. If you'd come to my church this Sunday, I'll tell you how to get to heaven."

The little boy said, "No thanks. You don't even know how to get to the post office."

I like to start with something funny.

I heard about this little girl. She asked her mother how the human race got started. The mother explained how God made Adam and Eve and they had children and on and on and here we are today. A few days later she asked her father the same question. He explained how many years ago there were monkeys. Little by little, they became more like people and now here we are.

Confused, she went back to her mom and said, "Mom, you said God created people. Dad said we came from monkeys. How can that be?"

She said, "Oh honey, that's easy. I told you about my side of the family. Dad told you about his."

I like to start with something funny.

I heard about this little 3-year old boy. He had a sore throat. His mom took him to the Doctor and the Doctor put his stethoscope on his chest to listen to his lungs and he said to the little boy, "Okay, be still buddy. I'm going to check to see if Barney's in here." The little boy said, "Jesus is in my heart, but Barney's on my underwear."

SECTION II
NON-SPIRITUAL HUMOR

CHAPTER 6

Animal Bits

I like to start with something funny.
I heard about this cat and mouse. They died on the same day and went to heaven. After a couple of weeks, Peter asked the mouse, "How he liked it so far?" He said, "Ah Peter, it's great … But it's so big, do you think I can get some roller skates?" Peter said, "No problem, got the mouse some roller skates." A couple of weeks later, he saw the cat and asked him, "How he liked it?" He said, "Ah Peter, I love it. And when I thought it couldn't get any better, I discovered the Meals on Wheels."

I like to start with something funny.
I heard about a man was being chased by a bear. The bear cornered the man and the man prayed, "Dear God, please make this bear a Christian bear." So God did as he said. And the bear said, "Dear God, please bless this food I'm about to eat."

I like to start with something funny.

I heard about this minister that was out bear hunting. He searched and searched all through the woods but didn't see any sign of a bear. Finally in frustration, he threw his gun down and went down to the stream to cool off. About time he saw this huge grizzly bear racing toward him. He fell on his knees and said, "Please God protect me. I'm asking You God to convert this bear into a Christian." Miraculously the bear froze in its tracks, put up both paws toward the Heavens and said, "Thank You LORD for this food I'm about to eat."

I like to start with something funny.

I heard about this blond lady. She was out in the yard doing some work with the weed eater when she accidentally cut off her cat's tail.

He was in the bushes and she didn't see him.

She felt so bad. She grabbed the cat, grabbed the tail and told her friend she was going to Walmart.

She said, "Walmart? Why Walmart?"

She said, "Hello. They're the largest 'Retailer' in the world."

I like to start with something funny.

I'll preface this by saying this was sent to me by a woman.

Accordingly to the Alaskan Department of Fish and Game. While both male and female reindeer grow antlers in the summer, male reindeer lose their antlers at the start of winter in early November.

Female reindeer keep theirs until the spring.

This means all of Santa's reindeer, from Rudolph to Blixen, had to be female.

We should have known only women can drag around a fat man, wearing a red velvet suit all around the world in one night, and not get lost.

I like to start with something funny.

I heard about this blond lady. She was trying to get to sleep one night. But her next door neighbor's dogs were barking so loud, she couldn't.

She finally had had enough. She got up and told her husband she was going to do something about it. She came back a few minutes later and the dogs were barking louder than ever.

He said, "What did you do?" She said, "I put the dogs in our backyard. Let's see how they like it."

I like to start with something funny.

I heard about this burglar that broke into a home one night. As he was stealing the stereo, he heard a voice saying, "Jesus is watching you." He froze in his tracks and he shined the flashlight around the room. And he saw a parrot over in the corner. He said, "Did you say that to me?" The parrot said, "Yes, I'm trying to warn you."

He said, "Warn me, what are you talking about? Who are you?"

The parrot said, "My name is Moses." The burglar laughed and said, "What kind of crazy people would name a parrot Moses?"

The parrot said, "The same kind of people that would name a 150-pound Rottweiler Jesus."

I like to start with something funny.

I heard about this man. He was walking up to a country store.

There was a little boy sitting on the front porch with a huge dog sitting next to him.

The man said, "Son, does your dog bite?"

He said, "No sir, my dog doesn't bite."

The man reached down to pet the dog and the dog took about half his arm off.

He pulled it back and said, "Son, I thought you said your dog didn't bite." The little boy said, "That's not my dog."

CHAPTER 7

Sports Antics

I like to start with something funny.

I heard about these two professional baseball players. They were discussing whether or not there would be baseball up in heaven.

They made an agreement whoever died first would come back and tell the other one if indeed there was baseball in heaven.

A few months later one the men died ... like he promised he came back.

He said to his friend, "I got good news and I got bad news.

The good news is there is baseball up in heaven; the bad news is you're scheduled to pitch next Thursday."

I like to start with something funny.

I heard about this professor. He was going to prove to his students there is no God.

He said, "God if you're real, knock me off this platform. I'm giving you 15 minutes to do it."

With every minute that went by, he taunted God, "God I'm still waiting. I'm still here."

The last minute, [a] 300-pound football player walking down the hallway overheard what he was saying.

He took off running toward him full blast, put his shoulders down and sent him flying off the platform.

The professor got up in a daze and said, "What did you do that for?"

[The] Football player replied, "God said He was busy, so he sent me."

CHAPTER 8

Occupational Laughs

I like to start with something funny.
I heard about this blond lady, she was driving down the freeway when she got pulled over by a female police officer, who also happened to be blond.

The officer asked for a driver's license.

She dug and dug in her purse, getting more and more agitated and couldn't find it. Finally [she] asked the officer, "What does it look like?"

She said, "It's a little square that has your picture on it."

The lady found her mirror, saw herself and said "O"' and handed it to the officer.

The officer looked in the mirror and saw herself, handed it back, and said, "You can go, I didn't realize you were a police officer."

I like to start with something funny.
I heard about this new police recruit. He was taking his final exam. He was in front of a large classroom. The sergeant asked him, "What would you do if you had to arrest your own mother-in-law?" Without missing a beat, he said, "Call for backup."

I like to start with something funny.

I heard about this man that lived in the country. One night he heard some noise and he saw some burglars stealing things from his barn. He ran to the phone and dialed 9-1-1. But, the dispatcher said, "I'm sorry sir. There are no patrols cars available. You need to lock your doors and we will get somebody there as soon as possible."

He hung up so frustrated.

About 30 seconds he called back and said, "Ma'am, don't worry about it, you don't need to send anybody. I shot all the burglars."

Ninety seconds later ... three patrol cars, one sheriff and two ambulances showed up and they caught the burglars red-handed.

The sheriff went over afterwards and said, "I thought you said you shot the burglars."

The man said, "I thought you said nobody was available."

I like to start with something funny.

I heard about this kindergarten teacher. She was walking around her classroom as her students drew pictures. She noticed this one little girl drawing so intently. She asked her, "What she was drawing."

The little girl said, "She was drawing a picture of God."

The teacher kind of laughed, she said, "Aw honey, nobody knows what God looks like."

The little girl without missing a beat, "They will in a minute."

I like to start with something funny.

I heard about this kindergarten teacher. She was teaching her students about self-esteem. She said to the class, "Anyone that felt dumb, she asked them to stand up." She didn't think anybody would stand. She'll make the point how no one is dumb.

About that time little Johnny stood up.

She thought, "Oh no, now what am I going to do?"

She said, "Now Johnny, Do you feel like you're dumb?"

He said, "No ma'am, I hate to see you standing there all by yourself."

I like to start with something funny.

I heard about this airplane that was about to crash. There were four passengers, but only three parachutes. The first passenger said, "I'm a leading heart surgeon; my patients need me." He grabbed the first parachute and jumped. The second passenger said, "I'm a rocket scientist, one of the smartest men in the world; my country needs me." He took the second parachute and jumped. The third passenger was Pope John Paul. He said to the fourth passenger, a 10-year old boy scout, "Son, I'm old and frail, you take the last parachute." The Boy Scout said, "That's okay sir, there's still two parachutes left. The world's smartest man jumped out with my backpack."

I like to start with something funny.

I heard about this scientist. He said to God, "We decided we no longer need you." We can clone people ... transplant ... harvest ... do all kinds of things once considered miraculous." God said, "That's fine. To prove you don't need me, let's have a man-making contest. The only requirement is you have to make man out of dirt."

The scientist said, "Great." He reached down quickly for a hand full of dirt. God said, "Not so quick. Go get your own dirt."

I like to start with something funny.

I heard about this archeologist in New York. He dug down 10 feet and found traces of copper wiring dating back 100 years.

He concluded New Yorkers had a telephone network over 100 years ago. Not to be out done, an archeologist from California dug down 20 feet and found copper wiring dating back 200 years.

He concluded Californians had a massive communications networks 100 years earlier than New Yorkers.

Upon hearing this, Bubba from Texas dug down 30 feet on his farm and found nothing. He concluded 300 years ago Texans had already gone wireless.

I like to start with something funny.

I heard about this airplane; it was about to land. The flight attendant came over the loudspeaker and said, "We'd like for you to help welcome our new copilot. He's about to make his first commercial landing. So when the plane stops, give him a big round of applause." A few minutes later the plane made an extremely bumpy landing ... bouncing up and down. She came back on and said, "Thanks for flying with us today. Don't forget to tell our new copilot which one of his three landings you liked best."

I like to start with something funny.

I heard about this reporter. He was visiting churches all across the country.

While in New York, he noticed this golden telephone on the wall and a sign that said, "Calls, 10 thousand dollars per minute."

He asked the pastor what it meant.

The pastor explained, "That was a direct line to heaven. If you were willing to pay the price, you could talk directly to God."

He continued to visit different churches, saw the same phone with the same sign.

When he finally made it to Texas, he saw the phone. But the sign said, "Calls, 25 cents per minute."

Intrigued, he asked the pastor, "Why it was so much cheaper?"

The pastor said, "You're in Texas. Now, it's a local call."

CONCLUSION

Take Charge of Your Own Joy

These clean, funny jokes were to make you laugh, whether reading for yourself or telling them to your audience. Feeling blue or have the blues? Living uptight and on edge? All work and no play?

> Laughter can conceal a heavy heart, but when the laughter ends, the grief remains. *(*Proverbs 14:13 NLT)

Consider what you are going through as a matter of joy. With no strings attached, believe trials can suddenly work patience as well.

Every day people let their happiness depend on other people and situations, when in reality, God wants you to find joy in him. To help people instantly open up to the amazing Gospel and come to faith in Jesus now when reading or telling a joke, framing, telling and responding were promoted to conceptually parallel the main parts of a speech and attendance at a church.

Framing, similar to the opening of a speech and invitation to church, keys the audience's expectations. Telling is like the body of a speech or the friend attending church, which is the pivot or comparable to the punchline. Responding to a joke is laughter and akin to the conclusion of a speech and the pastor closing the deal by making an "invitation" to accept Christ. Be one of the few, God wants you to look to him first and rely on him for your joy.

So, are you ready for it? You cannot count on someone else to make you joyful. God has given you the ability to take responsibility for your own joy. For this reason, be beside yourself with joy. These jovial jokes, which foretell a feel good factor, are to make you giggle and laugh, whether reading for yourself or telling them to your listeners --Happy happy joy joy!

They'll immediately hit the spot and your hot audience and you will get guaranteed satisfaction. Now's your sensational opportunity to also read or tell these unprecedented compilation of over 100 tested, short clean jokes reminding us to be joyful and encourage laughter.

> A joyful heart is good medicine, but a crushed spirit dries up the bones. Proverbs 17:22 (ESV)

Discover when the joy in your life is obvious and on display, it remarkably rubs off on others. Accordingly, your laughter, smile and joy makes people feel good quick and easy. It instantly creates joy and comfort to those who receive it. Thus, your expression of joy can suddenly help change circumstances and, perhaps, the lives of others now instead of having regrets of not reaching them earlier. Hurry, share your contagious joy now!

PART III
LOVE

WHAT LOVE REALLY MEANS

Love God, Love People

In the Parable of the Good Samaritan (Luke 10:25-37 NLT), Jesus focuses on our relationships and what it means to love. He is telling us to follow the Samaritan's example in our own behavior. Let's show compassion and love for those we come across in our daily activities.

Let's love others regardless of their race or religion; the standard is need. If fellow humans need and we have the means, generously and freely give without any expectation of return. Let this Scripture change your thoughts and actions towards people who are not like you! God tells us to love everyone without judgment!

25_ One day an expert in religious law stood up to test Jesus by asking him this question: "Teacher, what should I do to inherit eternal life?"

26_ Jesus replied, "What does the law of Moses say? How do you read it?"

27_ The man answered, "You must love the Lord your God with all your heart, all your soul, all your strength, and all your mind.' And, 'Love your neighbor as yourself.'"

28_"Right!" Jesus told him. "Do this and you will live!"

29_ The man wanted to justify his actions, so he asked Jesus, "And who is my neighbor?"

Parable of the Good Samaritan

30_ Jesus replied with a story: "A Jewish man was traveling from Jerusalem down to Jericho, and he was attacked by bandits. They stripped him of his clothes, beat him up, and left him half dead beside the road.

31_"By chance a priest came along. But when he saw the man lying there, he crossed to the other side of the road and passed him by.

32_A Temple assistant walked over and looked at him lying there, but he also passed by on the other side.

33_"Then a despised Samaritan came along, and when he saw the man, he felt compassion for him.

34_ Going over to him, the Samaritan soothed his wounds with olive oil and wine and bandaged them. Then he put the man on his own donkey and took him to an inn, where he took care of him.

35_ The next day he handed the innkeeper two silver coins, telling him, 'Take care of this man. If his bill runs higher than this, I'll pay you the next time I'm here.'

36_ "Now which of these three would you say was a neighbor to the man who was attacked by bandits?" Jesus asked.

37_ The man replied, "The one who showed him mercy." Then Jesus said, "Yes, now go and do the same."

CONTENTS

Introduction: What's Love Got To Do With It?............. 191

Chapter 1. Do You Love Me? 200
Chapter 2. What Do You Read There? 210
Chapter 3. Won't You Be My Neighbor? 216
Chapter 4. Am I My Brother's Keeper? 226

Conclusion: Like A Good Neighbor?.................... 232

INTRODUCTION

What's Love Got to do With It?

Marah was a caring, compassionate, well-loved woman. Some people were selfish in how they treated her; they loved her the wrong way. Scripture tells us to Love God, Love People. Like the 'Good Samaritan,' love your neighbor as yourself.

Discover whether you will choose to be a good neighbor.

"Self is the worst enemy a Christian has," advocated Charles Spurgeon, known as the "Prince of Preachers." Many folk exhibit selfishness; they're all about putting a feather in their cap above the interests of others. Because Cain was selfish and jealous, he hated and killed Abel, his brother (Genesis 4).

King Ahab coveted Naboth's vineyard now and went postal when Naboth refused to give the king the inheritance of his ancestors (1 Kings 21). His wicked wife Jezebel killed Naboth. Accordingly, she gave Naboth's vineyard to her husband as a gift.

Because of David's quest for instant pleasure, he sinned with Bathsheba (2 Samuel 11). His selfishness suddenly led to a love, lies and murder true story. Therefore, he had no regard his action cost others an arm and a leg.

The prodigal son's older brother gave the impression of loving his father; yet, he showed an amazing lack of love for his brother. Likewise, it's remarkable one may claim to love God. If out of selfishness, you don't love your brother, you don't love God as a matter of fact (1 John 4:20-21).

Let's face it—you can quash out your love for others due to love of self. I've got something for you. In this book, through Marah's trip to overcome her own struggles, you will learn how to love others more.

You'll love God and love people more and think less of yourself than you should. How does that sound to you?

While taking a road trip to Florida to celebrate her fortieth birthday, drop-dead gorgeous Marah pondered this problem and reflected on how far she'd come to be the person she is now. Driving while black and taking the road less travelled, she revealed her expectations as a little girl of a fairy-tale ending relationship and happily-ever-after marriage. Her thoughts also returned to a young girl playing with child hood friends.

While residing in the local community as a military family stationed overseas, they cherished the opportunity and fun to visit the military base. From sea to shining sea, many people see military bases as sensational installations to visit. Besides the natural beaches nearby, they had such an enjoyable time making a bee-line for the community center, library, and movies at the base theater; they also had access to the base exchange (e.g., similar to Wal-Mart or Target), commissary (i.e., American grocery store), and chain restaurants like Burger King, Subway, or Baskin Robins to name a few.

Once when visiting the base's community center, she remembers viewing the American Forces Network, the US military's radio and TV network for American servicemen and women serving overseas. Breaking news interrupted regular programming. The news report announced the Syrian refugee crisis and the U.S. plans to provide shelter and hope for families fleeing conflict in the Middle East.

Marah's dad would be a part of service members' efforts at an air base in Southern Turkey where American military were assigned to build up U.S. processing facilities on the base. Daddy's little girl may have the opportunity to see first-hand the U.S. military securing the operation and providing logistical and medical support on the base. Government employees processed and transported vetted Syrian refugees from the air base and helped further screen and resettle into American cities.

As Marah thought about her past, present day citizens debated and vented over whether the U.S. should take any additional refugees in the wake of terrorist attacks at home and abroad. Political spin doctors declared the security of American citizens must prevail over America's time-honored traditions to resettle refugees. One official came up trumps and blew his own trumpet:

- "[I'm] calling for a total and complete shutdown of Muslims entering the United States until our country's representatives can figure out what is going on."
- "I will build a great wall – and nobody builds walls better than me, believe me – and I'll build them very inexpensively. I will build a great, great wall on our southern border, and I will make Mexico pay for that wall. Mark my words."
- "When Mexico sends its people, they're not sending the best. They're not sending you, they're sending people that have lots of problems and they're bringing those problems with us. They're bringing drugs. They're bring crime. They're rapists… And some, I assume, are good people." And later declared, "I love the Mexican people."
- "Why are we having all these people from shithole countries [African nations and Haiti] come here? Haitians immigrants 'all have AIDS. They give us their worst people; put them in a bin. They're picking the worst of the worst; congratulations you're going to the U.S."
- "Nigerians will 'never go back to their huts. Syrian refugees could be ISIS [Islamic State in Iraq and Syria} -affiliated." When the powers that be gets too big for their breeches, people can be rubbed the wrong way. So, there are two Americas. It's the real McCoy we have a bitterly divided nation. We have a divided nation based along race, class and political lines to name a few.

It's a foregone conclusion, a house divided against itself cannot stand. And like our nation's divisive discourse, Marah's current situation was also polarized. Her parents had broken apart; their relationship was broke and needed fixing. She had an unhealthy relationship with her mother and good-natured relationship with her father. Her parents loved her in different ways.

Love is the purpose of human existence and the strongest emotion; the most important part of our lives is to love one another. Everyone values love and recognizes love shapes what is true and good. Every human being is wired either to receive love or to give love. The course of true love sometimes never does run smooth. I've been through this, too.

Many have said much about love, but few show love. A lot of people use the term "love" so broadly to describe a hot, erotic attraction between two or more people; most people are head over heels with the emotional feeling and state of being *in love,* an *Eros* or passionate and sexual type of love. However, the Bible speaks of two types of love: *Agape* and *Phileo.*

Agape speaks of the most powerful, moral type of love: sacrificial love. *Agape* love is more than a feeling—it is an act of the will. This is the love God has for his people and prompted Jesus' sacrifice as the Lamb to the slaughter for our sins. As a believer, you are to love one another with *Agape* love, as seen in Jesus' Parable of the Good Samaritan.

Phileo or *Philia* refers to brotherly love; you see *Phileo* love most often exhibited in a close quarter's friendship. You display this shared goodwill for your best friend as you each seek to make the other feel on cloud nine (e.g., Jonathan made a covenant with David because he loved him as himself" (1 Samuel 18:1-3 NIV). Many Christians tend to practice this kind of love towards one another.

Storge, like *Eros* love, doesn't expressly appear in the Bible. *Storge* is the type of affectionate love you have for family or a spouse. It naturally occurs and is voluntary. You may find examples of *Storge* love in the stories of Noah, Jacob, and siblings Mary, Martha, and Lazarus.

In a society that by and large places a lot of weight on the *Eros* feeling of love, it seems there is barely a trace left of what love means for real – love God, love people. We can sometimes deny what life and relationships are all about. We want to justify ourselves. Love is a gift we are able to give as well as receive. Are we – and a part of Marah's setting – headed in the right direction or can we bridge the divide? What's your reaction to this course of action?

If we change directions, we may not end up where we are heading. While tingly feelings of being "in love" are a crown jewel, this devotional can help you become more successful by inspiring a framework to live a different standard of love – and less selfishness. Will that work for you?

Like the Parable of the Good Samaritan, a clear and present answer for you and I is the "law of love:" Love the Lord your God with all your heart, all your soul, and all your mind. This is the first and greatest commandment. A second is equally important: 'Love your neighbor as yourself.' (Matthew 22:37-39) -- Love God, Love People.

Pretty straightforward, isn't it? Have I been helpful? Yet, keeping it real, anything dealing with God is unappealing to some people; I admire people who have had different life experiences than I. Some people are turned off by a reference to him; they're not interested in reading about him. By God being mentioned in the sub-title, it's automatically perceived as preachy and definitely a turn off for these folk.

Real talk, they're not into God stuff; they're not interested in him. These beliefs interest me. But, that's not all folks! Don't settle or rely on what you perceive or assume. Start small and just get your foot in the door – love God, then love people. You stop growing because you stop learning. Keep growing, improving, getting better, and increasing your skills and gifts with this book. You're empowered to decide; winners never stop growing!

In loving God, you hold nothing back. Thus, you love him with an all-out love that affects everything you do. In essence, you focus 100 percent of your time, energy, strength, and actions on loving him. To love the Lord is to follow him wherever he leads, to obey him whatever he asks, and to trust him whatever the test. To love him is to reflect the love he has for us, for "This is real love—not that we loved God, but that he loved us and sent his Son as a sacrifice to take away our sins." (1 John 4:10). And to care for the ones he loves (i.e., to take care of his sheep) (John 21:16).

'Love God with all your heart, and with all your soul and with all your mind' isn't a checklist of rules. Being in love with him is a passionate relationship – and according to Jesus the first and greatest commandment. You're going to have to decide what 'all' means for you. And the second is like it: *'Love your neighbor as yourself.'* The first commandment is genuine, all-out love for him. The second commandment is also about love – loving others as much as you love yourself. It can't be underestimated you can sum up the two commandments with four words: Love God, Love People.

Because the "law of love" is backed up with Scripture, you can claim these commandments as your own. Far be it from me, it's not a generality to say you can condense the entire Gospel in those four words: Love God, Love People. You can hang your hat on who speaks this parable and who urges us to immediately apply the law of love to the situations of our day and our time, right now. It isn't at the beck and call of any policymaker or legislator. Doubtful of fake news or alternative facts?

Skeptical of receiving a friend request from God? Like opening an e-mail from an encrypted source or knowing the certainty of death and taxes, you can trust the sender and profit from his message of hope. So faith cometh by hearing, and hearing by the word of God (Romans 10:17 KJV). Make no bones about it, Jesus is the one who is speaking in this engaging devotional.

In unpacking the stories behind the story and interplay of Marah's internal and external world, you'll know these two roads or dynamics diverge; they apply for what's happening in your situation today. Each chapter is structured into the framework that lightly mirrors the powerful Parable of the Good Samaritan. And the chapter title, formed as a question, enables you to create how you'd answer and evaluate the question. What would Jesus do? What would you do? The action steps "wrap up" at the end of the chapter also motivates and encourages you to take action; create the law of love change put forth in this book.

In both tales, you can have a new enthusiasm about the law of love and internalize within your heart. These ironclad decrees are something near to you; they're already on your mind and in your heart. These charges are not far off; you don't have to go to a far, distant land, on the other side of the sea, nor a million miles away. They're near you.

These commandments are neither too high; they are not in heaven. The authentic law of love is in your heart and you can put them into practice in the nick of time. God is securely living in your heart. And you can seek out a new kind of inward 'Love God, Love People' feeling. Go within the depths of your heart and listen to him speaking to you now. Humble yourself and put others before yourself.

When I served in the U.S. Air Force, one of our core values was Service before self. *Service before self* tells us professional duties take precedence over personal desires; it includes behaviors like: rule following, respect for others, discipline and self-control, and faith in the system. As a leader, you place others ahead of your personal desires.

The Bible also tells us to treat others how we would like them to treat us; so if you want people to put you before themselves, you should do the same with no strings attached. You can find great joy when putting others before yourself. What do I mean? You put others first and me last but not least as the starting place. Paul wrote: *"Honor one another above yourselves."* (Romans 12:10 NIV). Others increase and you decrease.

If you can do this, you will radically standout from your family, friends, co-workers and other students in your school. Clearly, you'll live by a different standard. Putting others first or loving your neighbor as yourself doesn't sync up with 'what's in it for me'? I know, it's counter-cultural and revolutionary.

Everything in our culture – from the moment we're born – tends to train us to think 'me first.' It's our nature to seek the good of own than our neighbor. Putting others first sounds easy until you have to do it; it's a challenge. If you put others first, you're not first – unless you're captured by a four-letter word: LOVE.

At first blush, selfless love sounds awfully like "doormat". But it's not. Because a person on the receiving end of "true love" can't help but respond positively to it. When you put others before yourself and love your neighbor as yourself, you benefit the person who is the object of your love over yourself. Now if we all practiced a love that would affect others like that, wouldn't we make the world a better place?

This book is for you because you are a person of vision and empire dreams; it'll support your success or being successful. You want something special and better from your life as good as gold. You can excel and grow; put your best foot forward. Most of all, if you take a back seat and demonstrate less selfishness in your life, you will benefit from receiving the guaranteed advantage of God's miracle blessings in your life. Right?

Seek him and his righteousness first and he'll add all you need. Consider the verses in the Bible saying "It is more blessed to give than to receive" (Acts 20:35) and "Don't be selfish; don't try to impress others. Be humble, thinking of others as better than yourselves. Don't look out only for your own interests, but take an interest in others, too." (Philippians 2:3-4).

You want a perfect, amazing day? Bear with one another in love and imagine a new story for your life and quickly and easily live it ... and not to please yourself. Isaiah 1:19 (NIV) reassures us: "If you are willing and obedient, you will eat the good things of the land."

By opening this book, you've shown interest in where you are and desire to be now. My prayer is you'll listen deeply to the word of God today. As you read more, some stories may not exactly fit your situation; however, hear what he is telling you. Listen in the depths of your heart, where his law – the law of love – is placed and respond to it before you can say Jackie Robinson.

He'll love on you and live in you. I bet the farm if you suddenly give up your difference or dislike and turn to your brothers and sisters with love, as a result you'll be motivated to satisfy what he intends for this parable to mean. You'll be as pleased as punch. It's also my hope this devotional will inspire you to love!

Well, enough of waiting for you to make a daily, non-natural lifestyle decision. Leap without looking and avoid wasting a lot of time hemming and hawing. Selfishness impedes your progress. This motive lacks consideration for others and is chiefly concerned with one's own personal profit or pleasure. Overachieve and take this book as your guide to uplift and love your neighbors as yourself; make others your priority. That sounds like Love God, Love People.

You might say, "That's too high of a standard. No way, Jose I can do this. I think I can love God with all my heart, soul and mind. But, this loving others is too difficult. You have another thing coming; there's no way I can do it. The bar is so high." Will Rogers, an American actor, harped, "Even if you're on the right track, you'll get run over if you sit there." You're headed in the wrong direction. It's better late than never to stop driving this train down that track. Because there is a cliff at the end of the line. The train has left the station. Hurry and get on board now.

Many people are in the same boat and you're not alone on this train. All right, you're all set and ready to jump into this book now. Jump for what love means for real and dive in anywhere you like; you can bet your bottom dollar the book was penned to allow you to do that. You want to standout and you want improvement? Be one of the few and turn your heart outwards toward others instead of inward upon self.

If you want to discover and live a new standard of love, the law of love is a great place to start. And if you want to get a head start on your love for God and love for people, let's begin. Leap now to Chapter 1 – where all the loving others start. If you love him with an all-out love, you will love people for this reason. When you love people, it demonstrates his love! For many people, their image of him is shaped by their kinship with other people, not other people's image of him. Life is all about love.

Love all started with God. He loved us first and he certifies our ability to love others. And he showed his amazing love by sending his Son to earth to die for us. He showed love by creating you. He showed love by everything you have in life; it's all a fancy free gift of his complete and unconditional love. I love you Lord, I love you. Thank your Lord for saving me!

Friends, I urge you to love God with all your heart, soul and mind and love your neighbor as yourself – Love God, Love People. When you live according to these two commandments, the law of love, you can change the world. What am I driving at? Belt up and get ready for the journey of your life. It's my hope you won't just curl up in your easy chair with this new book and enjoy the ride, but you'll experience a transformation that'll inspire you to love and create the life-changing influence and growth this book offers – Love God, Love People!

CHAPTER 1

Do You Love Me?

Does the erection of a wall signify putting others first? You may agree to disagree. Other people climb on the bandwagon and say "tear down those walls" or "that wall must fall." For them, a wall is a symbol used to promote imprisonment or create division or a state of mind. Does this expression inspire Love of God and Love of People? Does this action increase love of your neighbor? Does this motive speak volumes concerning value, a sense of belonging, significance, and acceptance? You do not want to share with others nor cut and run from your preferences and desires.

As different as chalk and cheese, another perspective is movers and shakers can use a physical wall to protect or all of a sudden give its citizens a sense of security from anxieties and fears. One axe to grind during the 2016 general election was to build a wall along the whole length of the US-Mexico border, accordingly to address the issue of undocumented migration. That effort hit a lot of red tape and backed up Isaac Newton spilling the beans, "We build too many walls and not enough bridges."

After motorway madness, Marah rode like the wind and thought over the high walls family members had built in their relationships. When a family is in trouble, suffering often shows up in the children as a result.

"Did her mom love her?" Her mother had split in order to become independent and earn a living because of a marriage that didn't have fair play. That fall from grace left Marah's siblings and her with their father. They were alike as peas in a pod and through thick and thin. Her dad had loved her in an inappropriate way like a wolf in sheep's clothing; he nagged and persuaded her under the pretext of "Do you love me?"

For all intents and purposes, her siblings were consequently traumatized from what took place. And as a result, the separation instantly created division and walled off communications. After her dad left to work a distant job, Marah's mother took her children back; they had lived with her parents. Marah perceived she was unwanted as a baby coming into the world, which caused her to feel unloved.

Young children naturally believe what their parents say about them. At that time in her life, her mother had no help. Thus, she had done the best she could with what resources she had at the time. Each sibling went off to college and the military under not so great circumstances. Such is life; it was hard and challenging for them.

By and large, an adversarial relationship remained a complete shamble years later. For this reason, mother and daughter lingered at odds. They found unpleasant family disagreements hard to unravel, which resulted in knee-jerk reactions, anger, mistrust, hissy fits, frustration and temporarily alienation. Marah allegedly exhibited a fierce loyalty, protection and closeness with her dad, which caused deep issues and discord with her mother.

Marah's offspring grew up seeing both mothers' moving the goalposts during berserk in-fighting – an intergenerational transfer and much ado about nothing.

Both sides are needed for a healthy family. As was the case with Marah's father and mom, some children child may align with one side, and other children with the other side. When parents sling mud and hit below the belt, it may follow the children will also lose ground and not get along. You can't change a blast from the past, but you can change the future. Exodus 20:12 tells us to "Honor your father and mother" period.

All things must pass and Marah announced this skeleton in the closet; she forgave her father who sexually abused her. Her willingness to forgive honored both God and her parent. To err is human and to forgive divine. Such is life and she trusted Jesus; he desires only our good and never to harm us.

Parents can bring up a child and supply all needs. Yet, love, regard, approval, appreciation and value are also important needs. It's beyond belief someone who professes to love you can go on to abuse you. Marah felt crippled inside by the indifference of her parents and broke free from dysfunction. These walls imprisoned and created a severed family from truly showing love with each other.

Folk today may feel walled off or left out by our country's split identity. There's a lot of division lately; we seem to divide ourselves into different groups: social class, race, political affiliation, generation or denomination. Beyond belief, one leader in recent times sang his own praises and disrespected and threw shade at women and how others may see them:

- "You know, I'm automatically attracted to beautiful — I just start kissing them. It's like a magnet. Just kiss. I don't even wait. And when you're a star, they let you do it. You can do anything… Grab them by the pussy. You can do anything."
- "You could see there was blood coming out of her eyes, blood coming out of her wherever."

On the other hand, accepting the pain and discomfort that comes with a sexual abuse problem's awareness, the Me Too movement appears it moved the bar upwards. For a long time, women largely tolerated obvious inequities. Though it didn't feel right, many women branded their own sexual harassment and assault as unspoken, private, or shameful to admit. Their story was also dismissed or overlooked.

The Me Too era's progress is impacted or slowed by partisanship and a divided nation. While against the grain, social media mushroomed its goals to give people a sense of the issue's magnitude and commonness in society. When things are uncertain, or things look like the ends of the earth with Rape Abuse & Incest National Network statistics like "Every 98 seconds, an American is sexually assaulted," we can always find a bright spot somewhere.

The Me Too's momentum prompted a remarkable turning point in the ways people are fed up with sexual misconduct. But sexual violence is not only an albatross around America's neck. In fact, the United Nations says, "1.3 billion people are sexual assault survivors worldwide." Had enough? Ready to nip it in the bud? Me, too.

Even in the face of trying, difficult times, America still holds its place as the greatest country in the world – from sea to shining sea. We've accomplished sensational achievements as a nation: from the extraordinary rendition of the first moon landing; first controlled powered, manned flight; first mass-produced practical, and affordable car; to the cell phone and the American concept of the Internet.

Similarly, focusing on the gains of the Me Too movement gives us the motivation to lead the way and keep pressing forward, especially within the social media circle of influence and women telling or adding to their story. While we as a nation have come a long way, we can't act as a lame duck and stop now. Cutting to the chase, we as Americans still have bumpy roads and detours ahead of us. These long and winding roads are full of potholes and work improvements. We must face the music and keep leaning and moving forward, knowing tough times won't last forever. We can also see the pothole of sexual abuse as an opportunity to overcome – a valued future state.

Houston, we have a problem; many core problems divide us. A house divided against itself cannot stand. We can bridge the major gap between red, white, and rural working class America and blue, black, and urban educated America. These are different group identities (e.g., skin color, shared interest, etc.). They don't go together because they see different things, feel different things, and hope for different things.

Like birds of a feather flocking together, you may like people who are like you. Most people hang around members of their own group; you may like people who share your identity, who think the way you do, and value what you do. Though Jesus created a group whose identifying factor is dipped in love for each other, we've differently grouped ourselves together to the bitter end.

As Marah rode into the sunset, her inner monologue reasoned this truth is as basic as the nose on her face. A rose is a rose is a rose. So, as a nation, we're currently not united nor stand together.

Comparably, the Jewish-Samaritan relations (Luke 10: 25-37 and John 4:1-26) was also polarized; they had an "un-neighborly" relationship. Strained relationships possibly trace back to when the Assyrians' invaded, defeated, and intermarried with Jews who were living in Samaria. Due to this intermarriage and Samaritans' worship practices, folk viewed Samaritans as unalike from Jews in Judea. Though related through a common heritage of Abraham, Isaac and Jacob, each ethnic group could not bury the hatchet and mend fences as neighbors.

America faced a hot crisis of coming apart with slavery in 1860 and a similar crises related to the broader civil rights struggles in the 1960s. We confronted social, cultural and political division in the election year of 1968, one of the most doom and gloom and consequential years in history. As folk looked at America, they saw premiere cities enveloped in smoke and flames, they heard sirens in the night, they saw Americans dying on distant battle fields abroad, and they saw Americans hating each other, fending off each other, and killing each other at home. As affirmed by Martin Luther King's 1968 "I've Been to the Mountaintop" speech, "We got some difficult days ahead."

But, like the Apollo 8 lunar orbit around the moon on Christmas 1968, we took one small step for man and triumphed big. The mighty hadn't fallen and our darkest hours didn't last. And today, we face a third moment of imminent division: a campaign of blaming "others," primarily minority groups for America's decline. It's a new cultural civil war of "us" against "them" or "neighbor" and "non-neighbor." This is us now. We need to reset the tone. The government must represent all people, not just political party – E Pluribus Unum (Out of many, one, the motto of the US). And like Marah, Me Too, and group identities walled off, "others" may ask, "Do you love me?"

Now, if we shift our outlook and look at things from the point of view of those who have been "left out" (e.g., double whammy of race and immigration walled off), we can quickly and easily go back to the drawing board; we can learn and profit from an ongoing honest conversation about where we can go. Wrong attitudes, past experiences, and irrational fear lead to new areas for improvement.

Racial segregation's origin story remains firmly rooted in colonial slavery. Plus, America can confront slavery's violent legacy and move the goalposts as to its continued impact. Instead of letting bygones be bygones or feel one is playing the race card, we can suddenly come to terms with this ball and chain's past and craft ultimate resolutions to present-day struggles. And love is necessary for our way ahead. Martin Luther King Jr. encouraged, "Darkness cannot drive out darkness; only light can do that. Hate cannot drive out hate; only love can do that."

In 1619, the Dutch introduced the first captured Africans to America, planting the new seeds of a horrific, abusive slavery system that divided the nation in the long run. Discover why slavery, and its ensuing racial breakdown of groups of people, is at the core of our national identity and its Achilles' heel. Once you get this, our present conditions instantly become much clearer. For example, "one in three black men can expect to go to prison in their lifetime" according to 2012 Bureau of Justice Statistics. And "the incarceration rates also unduly impact men of color: 1 in every 15 African American men and 1 in every 36 Hispanic men are locked up in comparison to 1 in every 106 white men." Naysayers may say lies, damned lies, and statistics.

African Americans are largely the descendants of slaves—people who were brought from their African homelands by force to work in the New World. The struggles over slavery gave us a revolutionary Civil War, Reconstruction, segregation, Jim Crow laws, and in the end a civil rights movement. Let's come clean; racism was created, at least in large part, to justify slavery. Therefore, slavery bore the seeds for racism today. It is a direct outcome of one race's perception the other race can't hold a candle to their superiority; slavery helped draw the lines between black and white.

To maintain the upper hand, beliefs in Black inferiority and white superiority began under slavery. And the Jewish community also had similar beliefs. They were ticked off by the Samaritans' worship practices. And they saw the Samaritans as outsiders with an inferior lifestyle. Jesus' amazing Parable of the Good Samaritan outright destroyed this label of "inferiority."

Hot on the heels of race, anti-immigrant feelings comparably is an ongoing cause of strain in the world and echo all through American history. One would be at their wit's end to separate American history from the history of immigration. These are the same divisive issues our adversaries' propaganda attempted to stir up discord, disdain, and disorder during the 2016 general elections and beyond. Are we living in interesting times? Like race, we also can't let sleeping dogs lie. Let's batten down the hatches and increase our awareness of immigration's history to know its implication in America. We're can't truly move forward with hope for the future without acknowledging our heritage from the past. Let's transform despair into hope; sorrow into joy; and defeat into victory.

A part of America's identity is a "nation of immigrants." America was founded on immigration. According to the Institute for Human Sciences, "Almost 60 million people – more than one-fifth of the total population of the United States – are immigrants or the children of immigrants." They're part of the "American dream." They have improved American society in many positive ways. Immigrants don't represent America's "worst;" they offer some of our "best!"

Like big wigs wanting to create a physical wall to keep at bay or give a sense of security, many people are barking mad about perpetual immigration. Immigration to North America began with Spanish settlers in the sixteenth century, and French and English settlers in the seventeenth century. The century before the American Revolution introduced a major wave of free and indentured labor from England and other parts of Europe. Africa and the Caribbean also imported a large quantity of slaves.

During the course of American history, immigrants continuously arrived. Two notable eras were: primarily from southern and eastern Europe's mass migration (1880 to 1924) and Latin America and Asia's immigration wave (post-1965). Each period suddenly added more than 25 million immigrants. The U.S. immigrant population increased to more than 42.4 million, or 13.3 percent, of the total U.S. population of 318.9 million in 2014, according to the U.S. Census Bureau's 2014 American Community Survey official data. In one fell swoop between 2013 and 2014, the foreign-born population extraordinary increased by 1 million, or 2.5 percent.

The above-mentioned offensive comments (i.e., "people from shithole countries," "Nigerians will 'never go back to their huts,' etc.) also barked up the wrong tree and focused on immigrant "origins" – where they came from. Unchecked immigration is the last straw for many baby boomers; they are die-hard about wanting to protect the country's "Anglo-centric" heritage chiefly made up of European descendants. They desire to "to make America great again!" Immigrants are a part of and enrich the "American way of life." They also may ask, "Do you love me?"

Scripture tells us Jesus asked Peter three times, "Do you love me?" when having breakfast with his disciples soon after he was born again (John 21: 15-17). Likewise, he encourages and exhorts you about your important responsibilities to love others as much as you love yourself. Love God, Love People.

Like Peter, you have a role too; you can help influence and change the world. Similarly to the reason for the three-fold "do you love me?" question, Jesus is teaching the importance of your new role in loving others as much as you love yourself. Will you heed or deny his guaranteed instructions? I've heard it through the grapevine, "You cannot love your brother across the world if you do not love your neighbor across the street." It's my hope you trust and accept this vital charge – Love God, Love People.

As Marah makes a pit stop at the next service station, I'm glad you're along for the 'Love God, Love People' ride. You're more than a backseat driver; you're a driving force that enables unconditional, lifetime love to take over. Love and lose control. Love others as much as you love yourself. Love God, Love People.

Go and Do Likewise

You can take action now. By getting involved in the journey, you can help implement indicated changes and the subsequent action steps promised in this book right away:

1. **Comprehend God loves you.** To begin with, God created mankind in his own image. He is God in human form (John 1:14). Suddenly, there's an intimacy between him and mankind. With the rest of creation, he merely spoke and instantly it was. Yet he took time in forming man and woman. Discover a great image of his love in Jesus' passion and crucifixion. "For God so loved the world that He gave His only Son. Whoever puts his trust in God's Son will not be lost but will have life that lasts forever." (John 3:16). Romans 5:8 also says, "But God showed His love to us. While we were still sinners, Christ died for us."

Jesus' work on the cross was a remarkable declaration of love and poetic justice; his salvation made true life possible.

Turning to Jesus, one of the men the Roman centurions were crucifying, said, "Jesus, remember me when you come into your Kingdom." And Jesus replied, "I assure you, today you will be with me in paradise" (Luke 23:42–43). Hallelujah! His assurance wasn't a fool's paradise. Despite this criminal's sins, Jesus accepted his heartfelt act of faith and promised him eternity in heaven. Jesus gave his life to give us new life. Additionally, Scripture tells us "God is love" and one of his sensational statements of love is this:

"What shall we say about such wonderful things as these? If God is for us, who can ever be against us? Since he did not spare even his own Son but gave him up for us all, won't he also give us everything else? Can anything ever separate us from Christ's love? Does it mean he no longer loves us if we have trouble or calamity, or are persecuted, or hungry, or destitute, or in danger, or threatened with death? (As the Scriptures say, "For your sake we are killed every day; we are being slaughtered like sheep.") No, despite all these things, overwhelming victory is ours through Christ, who loved us. And I am convinced that nothing can ever separate us from God's love. Neither death nor life, neither angels nor demons, neither our fears for today nor our worries about tomorrow—not even the powers of hell can separate us from God's love. No power in the sky above or in the earth below— indeed, nothing in all creation will ever be able to separate us from the love of God that is revealed in Christ Jesus our Lord" (Romans 8:31-32, 35-39).

2. **Love the Lord and follow his words.** "Those who accept my commandments and obey them are the ones who love me. And because they love me, my Father will love them. And I will love them and reveal myself to each of them" (John 14:21). Obedience is tough. It becomes a contest when we feel lured to believe we stand to lose more through our obedience than we might gain. You may have to be dutiful to a boss, parent, crack troop, or

traffic law. Joined at the hip, obedience is a part of your faith that comes from your submission, surrender, and compliance to God's will; you continually apply your faith. Living out faith, requires "giving up something." In obedience, you give up your will, control, and trust; your life becomes Christ-centered versus self-centered.

3. **Love one another.** In John 13:34 Jesus taught, "So now I am giving you a new commandment: Love each other. Just as I have loved you, you should love each other." Then he added, "Your love for one another will prove to the world that you are my disciples" (verse 35). Followers of Christ display a deep, sincere love for brothers and sisters in Christ. Point-blank, they are identified by their love for each other. "And he has given us this command: Those who love God must also love their fellow believers" (1 John 4:21).

    Pounds of flesh creates selfish, unforgiving, and insincere "love." Jesus loves unconditionally, sacrificially, and everlastingly. His love is also holy. Preaching to the choir, we are to love each other like that. By obeying the Holy Spirit, through his Word, you can love like he does. You can push the envelope and show his love to friends, to family members, to coworkers, etc. Even enemies are the recipients of Christ's love (see Matthew 5:43–48). You also must put your best foot forward and have a change of heart to love like Christ. You must realize you must spruce up your behavior before him and understand Christ died on the cross and rose again; then you must rise and shine and make the decision to accept him as your personal Savior. At that point, you're forgiven by him and receive his gift of eternal life. Yes and amen! In Christ, you receive a shot in the arm to love like he loves.

CHAPTER 2

What Do You Read There?

As Marah gets underway and heads to her destination, it's no hit or miss she loves God and loves people. She puts love in action: always smiling; complimenting strangers; encouraging and building up people; volunteering; and giving gifts of her time, talents, finances, and hugs. As she thought about her everyday compassion, she safely changed lanes on an access road. Before heading down the highway, someone suddenly slammed on their brakes and sped – a hit and run. There's no rhyme nor reason for people drag racing on city streets. Everybody, buckle up please; it's important to follow traffic laws when driving.

Likewise, standards all have the same basic purpose of setting out agreed principles or criteria. We also adhere to many types of standards -- from job performance, fitness, behavior, or cultural to standards of care, living, or practice. To meet someone's standards or expectations means you're good enough for them.

In the military, standards are higher than those in our society at large because service members defend our nation. They are held to a higher zero tolerance standard and in high regard by the public; they demonstrate integrity by holding themselves accountable and others accountable for their actions – by the book standards and accountability.

When I served in the military, one key to success received from military supervisors was "to keep your nose clean." Due to you meeting expectations and staying out of trouble, you were eligible for promotion; you win! This 18th century English phrase derived from 'keeping one's hands clean', which referred specifically to the avoidance of corruption.

About face! You're expected to comply with standards of conduct relating not only to the performance of military duties, but also to accomplishment of your extra responsibilities and your relations with other members of the military community too. As a federal employee, you also undergo a "probationary period" before your supervisor determines she has hired the right person and declared you a "regular" employee. It's important you immediately abide with job standards and expectations at all times, not only during this "trial period".

Thinking about standards, Marah reflected on how military sexual assault hadn't lived up to its "zero tolerance" policy back in the day. Even now, the Defense Department's annual report on sexual assault in the military showed service members' reporting of sexual assault increased by about 10 percent in fiscal year 2017. The department remarkably discovered 6,769 reports of sexual assault involving service members as either victims or subjects of criminal investigation across all four military services. That's a sorry sight.

Marah also mulled over about being a victim of date rape sexual assault while in the military technical school. The military and society continues to strive for obedience and accountability to end violence against women and girls. This improvement truly leaves no one left behind. When one falls, another brings them home. In Jesus Christ, we find the perfect model of obedience. He lived a sinless life. Our chains are gone and he set us free and ransomed us. Thank God for your real, unending love and amazing grace!

One may reason, "If I do this, God will do this for me. Or am I allowed in heaven on the basis of the good things I have done?" For most people, religions, and philosophies, a common teaching of getting to heaven is a matter of being a good person; the person follows the Ten Commandments and the precepts of the Golden Rule, the biblical rule of "Do to others whatever you would like them to do to you" (Matthew 7:12).

Also, one of altruism's greatest foundations is love. For this reason, your love can suddenly help you to conquer the selfishness in your soul. Your love can amazingly push you to continue to give and to share and to care so others may live better lives. Real time, we must nurture and strengthen love in all of our relationships as 'humans.'

Jesus knew the human heart and its selfishness. In fact, in the preceding verse, he describes human beings as naturally "sinful" (verse 11). His Golden Rule promotes a remarkable standard by which naturally selfish people can gauge their actions: actively treat others the way they themselves like to be treated. He brilliantly condenses the entire Old Testament into this single principle, taken from Leviticus 19:18 (NIV): "Do not seek revenge or bear a grudge against anyone among your people, but love your neighbor as yourself. I am the LORD."

Back to basics, you can see the implication people are naturally lovers of self; the command to love others takes that human flaw as a place to start in how to treat others. Do you want others to suddenly show you regard? Regard others. Do you instantly expect a kind word? Share kind words to others. "It is more blessed to give than to receive" (Acts 20:35).

The Golden Rule is also part of the second greatest commandment, preceded only by the command to love God himself (Matthew 22:37–39). Discover how the Golden Rule depends on what went before—on your relationship to God as your Father who loves you. Therefore, however you want people to treat you, so treat them. Scripture tells us "Don't pretend to love others. Really love them. Hate what is wrong. Hold tightly to what is good. Love each other with genuine affection, and take delight in honoring each other" (Romans 12: 9-10).

If you wish others to magically love you, you must give love. If you desire others to miraculously respect you, you must respect all persons - even those you dislike. If you want others to easily forgive you, forgive them for they know not what they do. If you want solid marriage results, you must authentically show faithfulness to your spouse. If you wish to reap the rewards of our Heavenly Father's love now, you must truly love all his people.

If you do not want others to harshly judge you, you must not harshly judge others. Often others may perceive your behavior as holier than thou or high and mighty. However, you're called to correct the faults within yourself, instead of finding fault with others. "Do not judge, or you too will be judged. For in the same way you judge others, you will be judged, and with the measure you use, it will be measured to you.

"Why do you look at the speck of sawdust in your brother's eye and pay no attention to the plank in your own eye? How can you say to your brother, 'Let me take the speck out of your eye,' when all the time there is a plank in your own eye? You hypocrite, first take the plank out of your own eye, and you will see clearly to remove the speck from your brother's eye. (Matthew 7:1-5 NIV)

The Bible also tells us: "By this all people will know that you are my disciples, if you have love for one another." (John 13:35 ESV). "If anyone says, "I love God," and hates his brother, he is a liar; for he who does not love his brother whom he has seen cannot love God whom he has not seen." (1 John 4:20 ESV)

In addition the Bible tells us of a young ruler's unwillingness to spare all his goods to help the poor; he brings into question whether he loves his neighbor as himself. It's all good the man showed his fidelity toward God's guaranteed promises by obeying his laws. The young man is convinced he has kept them, as many of us have avoided breaking the society's laws. However, he showed lack in his readiness to enter God's kingdom and follow him. (Matthew 19: 18-28).

You may also know the well-known story of the Good Samaritan (Luke 10:25-37 NLT), viewed in this book's Front Matter. Thus, be one of the few and let this Scripture change your thoughts and actions towards people who are not like you today! God tells us to love everyone without discrimination – to Love God, Love People.

Go and Do Likewise

You can instantly get a piece of the action. By getting involved in the journey, you can help fulfill the foreshadowed changes and action steps conveyed in this book for good measure:

1. "**Never stop reading this Book [of the Law]**. Day and night you must think about what it says; Make sure you do everything written in it. Then things will go well with you. And you will have great success" (Joshua 1:8 NIRV). Read between the lines; you'll be exceedingly well read. When you're off at the start and travel that path, you can be off by miles later. "Trust in the Lord

with all your heart. Do not depend on your own understanding. In all your ways obey him. Then he will make your paths smooth and straight" (Proverbs 3:5-6 NIRV).

Read through this book chapter by chapter; reading it out loud brings the Word of God to life. His words are alive, active, powerful, and inspiring. His Word will help defend you when you're tempted or tested; he will carry you through severe trials._ Read it, use it, and you'll love it.

2. **"Do to others whatever you would like them to do to you"** (Matthew 7:12); actively treat others the way you yourself to be treated. The Golden Rule tells us whatever you wish others would do to you, do also to them. "Do not seek revenge or bear a grudge against anyone among your people, but love your neighbor as yourself." (Leviticus 19:18 NIV). Obeying the Christian necessity to love others is a mark of a true believer. In fact, followers cannot claim to love God if they don't actively love other people as well. "If someone says, "I love God," but hates a fellow believer, that person is a liar; for if we don't love people we can see, how can we love God, whom we cannot see?" (1 John 4:20).

3. **Have empathy for others**. In humility, die to self. Like Jesus' petition on the cross, we should forgive one another as he has forgiven us. Revenge is a dish best served cold. He also said we are to forgive others "seventy times seven" in response to Peter's question, "Lord, how often should I forgive someone who sins against me? Seven times?" (Matthew 18:21-22). Folk can have bitterness or ill will toward you or offend, hurt, lie to, or reject you. We also offend him every time we raise Cain. So, it's a lot easier to forgive when you remember you need forgiveness too. I'm so glad his grace covers us!

4. **Live in such a way as to please God**. Godliness is an attitude of seeking to please the Lord. Scripture tells us to live as children of light and find out what pleases him (Ephesians 4:17). Godliness is not just circumventing others catching you

red-handed in order to escape punishment. It is avoiding things which you know don't please him because you love him more than you love sin or your own way. Godliness fulfills the first great commandment: "And you must love the L___ your God with all your heart, all your soul, all your mind, and all your strength" (Mark 12:30). Trust in him and his promises and grow in godliness.

CHAPTER 3

Won't You Be My Neighbor?

As Marah draws near to her destination, she is saved by the bell from more road rage. She had seen better days growing up in her hood in a small Northeastern town. The city provided a strong quality of life without the typical problems associated with urban growth and development. Marah got solid values to last a lifetime; she also born again at an early age. When going to the store for neighbors, they gave you just enough money to buy the item with spare change for a treat. Everyone treated each other like family and neighbors were 'extended' parents, which reminded her of watching Mister Rogers' Neighborhood, an educational children's TV series.

While the "Neighborhood Trolley" crossed streets, Mister [Fred] Rogers talked the talk about various issues; he took viewers on tours of factories, demonstrating experiments, crafts, and music, and interacting with his friends. He sang, "It's Such a Good Feeling" to know your neighbor. His television neighborhood was a fantasy, myth and make-believe; your neighborhood is the real place. And knowing your neighbor is your realistic world.

We commonly think of neighbors as the people who lives nearby, normally in a house or apartment that is next door or, in the case of houses, across the street. Some people form friendships with their neighbors, and help them by sharing their tools and helping with gardening tasks.

Being a good neighbor commonly refers to living with others in a social community called a "neighborhood." Welcome to the block; welcome to the hood. People talking in their front yards, children playing on the sidewalk, people mowing lawns, and similar activities are all part of being neighbors. A good neighbor is normally someone who is nice and approachable – "How do you do?" or "How are you?" are general greetings. You don't have to be best friends with the person, but you should at least be able to smile and say hello to the person. You should expect to receive some sort of friendly response, as opposed to a glare or simply being ignored – "Yo, what's up?", "Ay gurl whasup", or "Howdie!"

Good neighbors usually introduce themselves—"Hey, we're your new neighbors, the Johnson's." As a new kid on the block, you make an effort to introduce yourself to your neighbors once you have moved into your new place. Pitch your tent and go meet the new neighbors yourself. You also keep your place clean; be considerate of neighbors; obey parking laws; keep noise down; party responsibly; and handle problems maturely. That's so not keeping up with the Joneses.

I heard about these good neighbors that looked out for each other with a labor of love when one was sick and shut in; they recognized when the lights were on, when the garage door was opened or not, etc. They were your 'Neighborhood Watch' or security monitoring service. You may consider good neighbors before purchasing home security cameras!

After a neighbor's passing, the funeral home staff suddenly stopped by undisturbed to pick up loaner chairs and a lectern residents had placed in the garage. The workers didn't knock on the door, ring the doorbell, or leave a message. It seemed kind of sneaky. Yet, the good neighbors knew the crew was there; they called and notified the family the funeral service employees had quietly picked up the loaner items – lots of laughs!

Some neighbors are not so well-behaved. I heard about this blond lady. She was trying to get to sleep one night. But her next door neighbor's dogs were barking so loud, she couldn't [sleep]. She finally had had enough. She got up and told her husband she was going to do something about it. She came back a few minutes later and the dogs were barking louder than ever. He said, "What did you do?" She said, "I put the dogs in our backyard. Let's just see how they like it."

Good neighbors, can't live with them, can't live without them. A neighbor also is the person who works in your office, the students at your school, the waitress who serves your meal, other drivers in morning traffic, etc. Even Mae West, an American blonde bombshell actress, oozed, "Love thy neighbor—and if he happens to be tall, debonair and devastating, it will be that much easier." Think of your neighbor as folk outside of your ethnicity, country, political party, or religion; they can suddenly include foreigners, strangers or enemies.

Many people may not have heard of President Franklin D. Roosevelt's Good Neighbor Policy; it was a United States foreign policy doctrine, adopted by in 1933, designed to improve relations with Latin America. You may also not be aware of National Good Neighbor Day, observed annually on September 28. This day was created to acknowledge and celebrate the importance of a good neighbor. It is a blessing to have a good neighbor, but it is even a greater thing to BE a good neighbor. You're great! Some are born great, some achieve greatness, and some have greatness thrust upon them.

Additionally, Philadelphia has long been nicknamed "The City of Brotherly Love" or "The City of Brotherly Love and Sisterly Affection" from the literal meaning of the city's name in Greek. "Brotherly love" also derived from the Ancient Greek terms *Phílos* (love or friendship) and *adelphós* (brother, brotherly). Love thy neighbor as thyself.

It's the people all around you – in every area and aspect of your life. People say to "love thy neighbor: thy homeless neighbor; thy Muslim neighbor; thy black neighbor; thy gay neighbor; thy white neighbor; thy Jewish neighbor; thy Christian neighbor; thy Atheist neighbor; thy racist neighbor; thy addicted neighbor." I'm reminded of a story of showing compassion and care by participating with my church's homeless ministry.

As one of fifteen teams, my spouse and I served on the Hospitality and Greeters Team. After the meal, I made a blooper when talking with a guest. He had a medical condition and asked for assistance from potential resources nearby. I was amiss in asking a homeless person, "Where do you live?" He said, "I live under a bridge." My wife wouldn't let me live down my embarrassing slip-up. We led the guest to our prayer team. In short, we helped out with the clothing team the next year.

Jesus meant 'love thy neighbor' to include all mankind! He willingly related with all kinds—society's outcast and ostracized, sinners, tax collectors, Pharisees, Sadducees, Romans, Samaritans, fisherman, women, children—with no regard for society's view of the respectable or deplorable. Imitation is the sincerest form of flattery. Love all persons, everywhere - not only our friends, allies, countrymen, etc. Every soul matters! The Bible tells us God's will is for us to love other people with a godly love – Love God, Love People.

You are called to "love your neighbor as yourself" (Luke 10:27) and even to "love your enemies, do good to those who hate you, bless those who curse you, pray for those who mistreat you" (Luke 6:27-28). Similar to the prodigal son's return home, respond with forgiveness, love, and inclusion. Love thy neighbor as thyself is a version of the Golden Rule and first found in the Old Testament. Jesus tells the parable of the Good Samaritan to illustrate this commandment:

> *One day an expert on Moses' laws came to test Jesus' belief; he cast the first stone by asking him this question: "Teacher, what does a man need to do to live forever in heaven?" Jesus replied, "What does Moses' law say about it?" "It says," He replied, "you must love the Lord your God with all your heart, and with all your soul, and with all your strength, and with all your mind. And you must love your neighbor as much as you love yourself." "Right!" Jesus told him. "Do this and you shall live!" The man wanted to justify (his lack of love for some kinds of people), so he asked, "Which neighbors?"*

A picture is worth a thousand words and Jesus replied with an illustration:

> *"A Jew going on a trip from Jerusalem to Jericho was attacked by bandits. They stripped him of his clothes and money, and beat him up and left him lying half dead beside the road. "By chance a Jewish priest came along; and when he saw the man lying there, he crossed to the other side of the road and passed him by. A Temple assistant walked over and looked at him lying there, but went on. "But a despised Samaritan came along, and when he saw him, he felt deep pity. Kneeling beside him the Samaritan soothed his wounds with medicine and bandaged them.*

He put the man on his donkey and walked along beside him till they came to an inn, where he nursed him through the night. The next day he handed the innkeeper two twenty-dollar bills and told him to take care of the man. 'If his bill runs higher than that,' 'I'll pay the difference the next time I am here.' "Now which of these three would you say was a neighbor to the bandits' victim?" The man replied, "The one who showed him some pity." Jesus said, "Yes, now go and do the same." -- Luke 10:25-37 (TLB)

Given the tense, hostile relationship between Jews and Samaritans at the time of Jesus, the parable of the Good Samaritan may have shocked its first listeners. Amazingly, no one would have expected him to answer the Jewish scholar's question, "Who is my neighbor?" with the example of a Samaritan. The scribe was an educated man and he could not possibly keep the law of love; he couldn't practice what he preached.

There would always be people in his life he could not love. Thus, he tried to restrict the law's command and asked the question "Who is my neighbor?" To further broaden your subject matter knowledge, view the proven case studies: *"Love Your Neighbor as Yourself, Part_1 and 2" and "You Must Love Your Neighbor as Yourself."*

The word "neighbor" in the Greek means "someone who is near," and in the Hebrew it means "someone you have an association with." This reading of the word, referring to a fellow Jew, appears to have excluded Samaritans, Romans, and other foreigners. Jesus gives the parable of the Good Samaritan to correct the false understanding the scribe had of who his neighbor is, and what his duty is to his neighbor. The Samaritan's love in this story showed an important and lasting change to his Jewish neighbor. The "neighbor," it would appear, is the man going from Jerusalem to Jericho. He may have put up his dukes, but was robbed of everything he had, including his clothing. They beat the living daylights out of him; he was beaten to within an inch of his life.

That winding road was dangerous and thick with thieves; the usual suspects in cloak and dagger wreaked havoc. The neighbor was the object, the one of whom the three other chaps came across. The priest showed no love or empathy for the man by failing to help him; he passed over to the other side of the road so as not to get involved; the man seemed out of sight, out of mind. I'll say it: The priest knew God's law of love -- you think? Was he not playing with a full deck? By nature of his position, a person of compassion desires to help others.

A Levite passed by the man who was beaten and left for dead. And it's no laughing matter that joker was caught red-handed; he did exactly what the priest carried out: passed by and showed compassion fatigue. That's a case of man's inhumanity to man. Common sense tells us he would have known the law, but he also failed to show the injured man sympathy.

Afterwards, the Samaritan, least likely to have shown kindness for the man, stopped. I'm sure he was a sight for sore eyes. Because Jews considered Samaritans low class, it would seem they would not let bygones be bygones; they would have nothing to do with them. The "Good Samaritan" saw only a fellow human and neighbor in serious need of assistance now – a no brainer. One good turn deserves another; he instantly aided him above and beyond what was required. A friend in need is a friend indeed.

Because the good man was a Samaritan, Jesus comparably drew a strong contrast between those who knew the law and those who truly abided by the law in their way of life and behavior. He now asks the lawyer if he can apply the lesson to his own life with the question "Now which of these three would you say was a neighbor to the man who was attacked by bandits?" (Luke 10:36).

Once again, the lawyer's stony heart hardened more. He cannot bring himself to say the "Samaritan;" he startlingly refers to the "good man" as "he who showed mercy." His dislike for the Samaritans (i.e., his neighbors) was so strong, it was a challenge to refer to them in a proper way. Jesus tells the lawyer to "go and do likewise." Thus, he should live what the law tells him to do. But in the end, thumbs up to the Samaritan who helped his man; he "proved to be the neighbor." So, what are you like?" "Who are you?" — that's the question. Which is which? Are you like this Samaritan who gives help when help is needed? Or are you going to still question who you're supposed to help? And when and where and how and what if?

Jesus made it rain in telling this parable that broadened the outdated definition of who is your "neighbor?" A neighbor is more than the person who lives next door; the neighbor is over and above someone in your extended family or community. Whatever social categories you may have that define "neighbor" are thwarted by all people's needs you encounter. In this way, anyone in need is your neighbor. His startling parable is telling us, "You do not have a neighbor. You make yourself someone's neighbor."

Now you have a historical context of this parable, you can bring to bear your present day situation for this reason. Accordingly, in loving your neighbor as yourself, do you uphold the dignity and gift of all people?

Are there communities whom people appropriately "write off?" How does your community treat those on the margins of society: immigrants, refugees, those living in poverty, those with disabilities, etc.? Do they ask, "Won't you be my neighbor?" We are to love as he loved us -- "But God showed his great love for us by sending Christ to die for us while we were still sinners." (Romans 5:8). And Jesus told his disciples the night before his crucifixion, "A new command I give you: Love one another. As I have loved you, so you must love one another" (John 13:34 NIV) – Love God, Love People.

Gee whiz, we will not like everyone, nor are we called to. You can love people who don't love you, love people who irritate you, or love people who stab you in the back, ostracize you, or gossip about you. You can love the unlovely, love the difficult, love the irritable, love people who are different or demanding, or fancy the love that dare not speak its name. God's grace also empowers us to love others. Even so, when you love someone with God's love, know your attitude toward that person suddenly changes.

For example, I heard about this country grandmother. She'll go out on her front porch every morning and thank the Lord for another day. Her neighbor didn't believe in God. He'll shout back: "There's no such thing as the Lord." One day he overheard asking the God to give her groceries for the week. He snuck over the next morning and put some groceries on her front porch. She got up and said, "Thank you Lord, you did it again!" He laughed and laughed and said, "God didn't give you those groceries, I put them there." She said, "Thank you Lord! You not only gave me the groceries, but you made the Devil pay for it."

Love is a choice and when you show love by your actions, discover your attitude will follow. Similarly in a racially-divided nation like ours today, many people have culturally-constructed definitions of "neighbor." We have expectations about what our neighbor looks like. If a person moves into our community and doesn't 'fit' our category of neighbor, we may say the community is "changing." Folk don't won't to go there. Applying this parable isn't about: standing beside the road and waiting for people who are in need so you may help them; picking up drifters or giving money to beggars down in the dumps; or indicting religious leadership or the upper class.

Jesus tells a powerful story that changes the question from "What kind of person is my neighbor?" to "What kind of person am I?" Don't have a clue? You move from "What sort of people are worthy of my love?" to "How can I become the kind of person whose compassion pays no heed to status?" The focus of the story changes from what kind of man is dying to the kind of people who are passing by. What kind of person are you? Do you put aside all forms of discrimination and feelings of superiority?

Martin Luther King, Jr. encouraged love your neighbor -- "Hate cannot drive out hate; only love can do that." The Samaritan didn't pause and beg the question: "Does this dude believes the same things I do?" He didn't delay and say to himself, "I'm not about to help him, after all, he's a Jew, and I'm a Samaritan." Are you the kind who first wants to try before you buy and decide whether a person is worthy of your love and care? Or are you the sort who wears your heart on your sleeve upon others regardless of their position in life and society?

Bite the bullet, you may find it better to have loved and lost than never to have loved at all. In other words, Christ-like love does not permit us to choose whom we will or will not love. Avoid categorizing people so you only feel responsible to love "our kind" or "our sort" – "us" versus "them." When a hot opportunity to show kindness and love comes along, can you get off your high horse because of one's clothes or culture? Are you put off their skin color is not the same? Do you find an excuse not to help those folk from the inner city or third world country? We aren't obligated to help and to love only those who share our faith. Share and share alike. Hear, hear!

To whom can you, to whom should you, be a neighbor today? Maybe an irritating dirt bag who lives next door to you? Perhaps a co-worker who is a Democrat, Republican, or Independent? Maybe a family receiving government or public assistance? Possibly the goody two-shoes yuppie in the suburbs born with a silver spoon in his mouth? Per chance an at-risk youth or person ending up on skid row? Conceivably a woman or man struggling with sexual orientation?

It could be a high on the hog executive or those suits (e.g., manager, boss, etc.) riding you all day at work? Feasibly the divorced single moms' kids who eats you out of house and home? Whatever the case, the issue isn't about who they are or what they are like. Enough is enough; know the result is about who you are and what you are like. The issue isn't whether they qualify to be your neighbor. Like a good neighbor, the result is whether you will choose to be a neighbor to them. Won't you be a neighbor?

In times where we come home and park in the garage without greeting neighbors, how well do you know your neighbors? Do you see them as strangers, acquaintances, or in relationship with them? When you're in relationship, you can live well among irreligious folk that they see your good deeds. Make it an opportunity to be rich in relationship and diversity. Be a good neighbor to the overlooked, ignored and forgotten – the least of these. Love as brothers: the poor, hungry, thirsty, strangers, sick and shut-in, jobless, disabled, addicts, orphans, abused, abandoned, homeless and immigrants.

All in all, Jesus is also telling us to follow the Samaritan's example. Show compassion and love for those you meet up with in everyday activities. Love others regardless of race or religion; the standard is need. If they need and you have what they need, give generously and freely without expectation of return. This was a challenging task for the lawyer, and for us. We cannot always keep the law because of our human condition; our heart's content and desires are mostly of self. When left to our own, we most likely do the wrong thing and fail to meet the law. A personal savior can save oneself from selfishness. So, the parable is a basic lesson on what love means for real --Love God, Love People.

Go and Do Likewise

All of a sudden, you can walk the walk now. You can stand and deliver; you can help talk the talk and walk the walk of suggested changes and succeeding action steps denoted in this book hands down:

1. **Love your neighbor as you love yourself.** Leviticus 19 tells us loving your neighbor includes sharing with the poor and the alien; demonstrating compassion, absolute honesty, and justice in your relationships with others; showing impartiality; declining to take part in gossip or slander; exhibiting an absence of malice toward anyone and refusing to bear a grudge; taking care never to put another's life at risk and never personally taking revenge upon another. It is also interesting to note when you have an issue with anyone, you should strive to make it right by going to him or her directly. Show your mettle. Talk with and greet each other, with get together or deliver goodies at holidays, go to events together, or share a meal or your table others. Show up regularly and frequently, intentionally engage in and build relationships, and invest in people's lives. Do as you would have them do to you (Matthew 7:12).

2. **Choose to love** your opponent's no matter their actions. Take the upper hand and open your hearts to them and act toward them with kindness. Jesus realized every sincere example of love grows out of a constant and total surrender to God. The writing is on the wall; love grows into an action rather than a feeling. And pray for them too; the sky's the limit! Pray for him to transform their hearts by the Holy Spirit. Walk out love for enemies by living out forgiveness. The jury is still out; see the goodness in people and search for their understanding. With God, all things are possible.

CHAPTER 4

Am I My Brother's Keeper?

In loving your neighbor, you see the dignity and ability of "the other"—Love God, Love People. As you go and do likewise, following the Samaritan's example in your own conduct, you can be in like Flynn and practice loving your neighbor. You can grow into your brother's keeper. Unlike Cain (Genesis 4:9), you can show a willingness to accept responsibility for the welfare of your fellow humans — your "brothers" in the extended sense of the term. We are our "brother's keepers." You are to "think of others as better than yourselves" and "take an interest in others, too" (Philippians. 2:3-4).

Throughout the Bible, a central faith principle is to welcome the stranger by loving and caring for them like you would love and care for yourself. In a nutshell, this is the law and the prophets and Jesus came to fulfill the Law. He's a man who loves God, his neighbor as himself, and welcomes the strangers no matter who they may be or where they come from. For him, loving your neighbor looked like Leviticus 19:9–18 (ESV):

> *"Lord When you reap the harvest of your land, you shall not reap your field right up to its edge, neither shall you gather the gleanings after your harvest. And you shall not strip your vineyard bare, neither shall you gather the fallen grapes of your vineyard. You shall leave them for the poor and for the sojourner: I am the LORD your God.*
>
> *"You shall not steal; you shall not deal falsely; you shall not lie to one another. You shall not swear by my name falsely, and so profane the name of your God: I am the LORD.*

"You shall not oppress your neighbor or rob him. The wages of a hired worker shall not remain with you all night until the morning. You shall not curse the deaf or put a stumbling block before the blind, but you shall fear your God: I am the.

"You shall do no injustice in court. You shall not be partial to the poor or defer to the great, but in righteousness shall you judge your neighbor. 16_You shall not go around as a slanderer among your people, and you shall not stand up against the life of your neighbor: I am the Lord.

"You shall not hate your brother in your heart, but you shall reason frankly with your neighbor, lest you incur sin because of him. You shall not take vengeance or bear a grudge against the sons of your own people, but you shall love your neighbor as yourself: I am the Lord."

Scripture also tells us of Jesus' expectations of service to the needy in the form of six works of mercy: Food, drink, hospitality, clothing, nursing care, and visitation. "For I was hungry, and you fed me. I was thirsty, and you gave me a drink. I was a stranger, and you invited me into your home. I was naked, and you gave me clothing. I was sick, and you cared for me. I was in prison, and you visited me" (Matthew 25: 35-36). Not your cup of tea?

The possibilities for mercy are boundless, as human needs are boundless. Are you in a quandary? You have the potential to provide these kinds of mercies. They do not require great sacrifice on your part, but they suddenly lessen the recipient's need.

Through Marah's perspective, she continued to witness a divided nation, "us" versus "them. Real talk, she also saw how this story of the Samaritan is relevant for today. She viewed people like the Samaritan viewed this man, who got the short end of the stick because outlaws had robbed and beaten him. They left him for dead like in the Old West. For example, an unwritten guide of the Code of the West was 'A cowboy always helps someone in need, even a stranger or an enemy.' In addition, like back in the day when residing overseas in Turkey, Marah looked at people fleeing economic violence and economic depression.

The migrants are trying to find a new life; yet, folk seem unmoved and unresponsive to declare the law of love in their hearts.

The refugees are pulling up stakes and leaving grim situations; they're pulling out all the stops to find better security and peace. In many cases, they have nothing to offer but blood, toil, tears and sweat. They're down to the wire seeking an improved place from themselves and their families. Yet, we've separated children from families, drawing a blank on how to take care of each other – to love your neighbor as yourself.

Marah was also a part of this Syrian refugee crisis first-hand. Most of us have had experiences that have forever changed our lives, either for better or for worse. We didn't know when we got up for the day, something or someone would alter our life. But that's what happened; this mission trip was such a day for her. Imagine you were traveling at dusk in a mountainous border area. You are attacked, beaten up and seriously injured. People ignore you because they are frightened, cold as any stone, or offer you a cold shoulder. A gung ho, boss-eyed, young man grinds to a halt to help you. He takes off his coat, puts it under your head, and calls for medical assistance. When you're recovering in the hospital, you discover he is a redneck and narrow-minded. Yet, he was Marah's helping hand and 'Good Samaritan'-- a thing of beauty is a joy forever.

Over the horizon, the sun shined bright as Marah made it to her destination. To travel hopefully is a better thing than to arrive. Her true contentment derived from the journey, not its end point. And that's not the end of the story; every cloud has a silver lining and love conquered all – life begins at forty! By faith and forgiveness, family members overcame divisiveness and adversity and restored their relationships. We shine the brightest when we get along with each other. The writing was on the wall; Marah transformed her life because she rose above others' selfishness. She loves God and loves people! And he and people continued to love her. She is worthy of love, especially when loving her is right!

You can apply the law of love to the circumstances of your day— race, color, creed, climate, gender, status, income, life style, etc. Let it penetrate into your heart; read it like it's something brand spanking new, something for you today. Like the unselfish Samaritan man of Jesus' parable, you are called to extend your love and concern to all people everywhere. Love your neighbors across the board as much as you love yourself.

Are you stumped about including anyone or any group as your neighbor regardless of social status, an alleged character flaw, religious difference, racial disparity, ethnic diversity, citizenship variation, etc.? Straight from the horse's mouth, C.S. Lewis heartened, "Don't waste time bothering whether you 'love' your neighbor; act as if you did. As soon as we do this, we find one of the great secrets. When you are behaving as if you loved someone, you will presently come to love him."

God has given each of you unique talents and gifts to use in his service. His work for you on earth is to use your gifts and talents in the service of others! You have something to offer to someone in need. You can give your money and your time to charity, help the sick and shut-in, do volunteer work, etc. If you think it's about how much you give, you have another thing coming. In my mind's eye, it's about the spirit in which you give that counts with him.

You're called to give generously of what wealth and talents you own-- whether it is a little or a lot. Jesus, The Bread of Life, compared a poor widow, who gave only a little, to the wealthy men who gave much more. The filthy rich men gave a token amount from them living high on the hog. In his eyes, the widow gave much more because she gave from the heart (Mark 12:41-44). Hold your horses. Scripture also tells us: "Owe nothing to anyone—except for your obligation to love one another. No man is an island and if you love your neighbor, you will fulfill the requirements of God's law.

For the commandments say, "You must not commit adultery. You must not murder. You must not steal. You must not covet." These—and other such commandments—are summed up in this one commandment: "Love your neighbor as yourself." Love does no wrong to others, so love fulfills the requirements of God's law (Romans 13:8–10).

To get a word in edgeways, we fulfill the law—loving our neighbor as we love ourselves—by the Holy Spirit instead of pride. You may assume pride aids you to eat, drink and be merry without depending on God; he is the source of your happiness. You find your happiness in him. Pride is the pursuit of happiness anywhere but in his glory and the good of other people. This is the root of all sin.

To hit the nail on the head, as you love yourself, so love your neighbor. In other words, in place of you longing for food when you're hungry, so want to feed your neighbor when she is hungry. As you bang on about nice clothes for yourself, hence wish for nice clothes for your neighbor.

As you work for a comfortable place to reside, therefore pray for a comfortable place to live for your neighbor. As you seek to be safe and secure, seek accordingly your neighbor's comfort and security. When you're active in chasing your own happiness, engage in your neighbor's happiness. Take up your neighbor's well-being the way you go in for your own well-being. Instantly love them the way you love yourself. Immediately show them, give them—through every practical means available—what you have found for yourself in God. Love God. Love people!

Go and Do Likewise

As fast as greased lightning, you can get underway now and not turn a blind eye. Cut to the chase and suddenly help put into practice the promised changes and following action steps hard and fast:

1. **Show brotherly love.** While you're not responsible for everyone's safety when you're not present, every man is his brother's keeper. You ensure they don't get the short end of the stick or allow others as a thorn in their flesh if you can prevent it. This sort of "keeping" is something God rightfully demands of everyone, on the grounds of both justice and love. As a believer, you're a keeper of fellow believers in two ways:

   - Avoid committing acts of violence against one another. This includes violence of the tongue in the form of "quarreling, jealousy, outbursts of anger, factions, slander, gossip, arrogance and disorder" (1 Corinthians 12:20).
   - Exhibit brotherly love toward our brothers and sisters in Christ with a tender heart and a humble mind (1 Peter 3:8). In this way, we "keep" those for whom Christ gave his life.

   Love is even greater than faith and hope. In loving one another, sometimes love must correct, admonish or reprove

(2 Thessalonians 3:13-15; Matthew 18:15). However, when you use correction, do it in the spirit of love with the goal of reconciliation. Tomorrow is another day and pursue what is good both for yourselves and for all. Chase the things which make for peace and the things by which you may edify or build up another (Romans 14:19).

2. **Generously give to the poor** (Deuteronomy 15:10). Most of us don't find giving to the poor or caring for the ill difficult. Jesus was also moved by passion to help a person, even if it was inconvenient (John 11:33). You don't have to agree with people to be kind to them. Most folk will feed or pray for the homeless; you can show passion and take the next step and establish a friendship and aid a life change (Luke 14:13). It's my hope and prayer you continue to connect with God's heart for the poor. Many more areas of society can also benefit from fostering a compassionate view: civil rights, treatment of animals, or the environment, to name a few.

CONCLUSION

Like A Good Neighbor?

Some last words I'd like for you to take to heart is to reflect on Marah's story of two halves and the world around you and take the final step and carry out the call of Love God, Love People. Go and do likewise and show what love means in your own life and community. The truth is, he wants us to learn to be unselfish. He wants us to learn to love like him. Love covers a multitude of sins, including selfishness. In reading this story, it's my hope you can weave in the former world expressed in the parable of the Good Samaritan with your present day world to live the law of love – Love God, Love People.

In order to better recognize the parable of the Good Samaritan's call to action, consider it is less a story about boding well than it is about breaking boundaries. The powerful story insists there are no boundaries to neighborliness. Live a new standard of love.

Love your neighbor as yourself is about freedom (to love "Everyone!") instead of about limits ("Who is my neighbor?"). Let's not only reflect on why you should care about what love means, but let's go further in what do you do now – go and do likewise. We can fix attitudes of angry hearts and express words of life and love. We can promote life by stamping out prejudices and hate, and loving our neighbors. Rise and shine to a new outlook on the subject. Like Marah's change, you can also move the goalposts and set aside differences and show love and forgiveness, if applicable. Show love and kindness to others in speech and in deed. "My little children, let us not love in word, neither in tongue; but in deed and in truth" (1 John 3:18 KJV).

The most important reason to show brotherly love – love your neighbor as yourself -- is Jehovah tells us to do so. You cannot love him if you refuse to love your brothers. Show the same kind of love to others as he showed to us when he paid it all (John 3:16). God commands, "Don't look out only for your own interests, but take an interest in others, too" (Philippians 2:4). You can set aside your prejudices and show love; you can love all mankind, considering your neighbor is anyone you encounter.

You can learn to love the unlovable; they're human too. Don't you desire others to love you? You can learn to love your neighbor, when things go right and when things are foul play. State Farm's iconic slogan, "Like a Good Neighbor," is as old as Methuselah; it has been around since 1971 – you heard? People know State Farm as a car and home insurer – "a good neighbor company is always there when things go wrong; they help you fight the good fight and recover after a car crash, house fire or a natural disaster. Like State Farm, make being a good neighbor a part of your DNA [deoxyribonucleic acid] too.

This may seem like an impossible task and it is - that's why you need God's love in you, so you can love others: "And so we know and rely on the love God has for us. He is love. Whoever lives in love lives in God, and God in them" (1 John 4:16 NIV). It's no smoke and mirrors; he'll love on you and live in you! You cannot love people like a good neighbor the way he loves you without his power in your life because human love runs out. Lord, you're holy! We lift you up and magnify your name. If you don't receive his love, you'll have a hard time loving other people – Love God, Love People.

You can when you have God's love coming through you. Tune in to him and he will lead you on the right path. And "the fruit of the Spirit is love, joy, peace, longsuffering, gentleness, goodness, faith, meekness, temperance: against such there is no law" (Galatians 5:22-23 KJV). You need to know his love so it can overflow out of your life into others. That's good!

However, if you don't feel lovable, the writing is on the wall you can't love anybody else. God says you're lovable. You can't fulfill his commandment to "love your neighbor as yourself" until you believe this. I receive that! He loves you consistently and unconditionally no matter who you are or what you do. He loves you! Daniel 10-19 says, "Don't be afraid," for you are very precious to God." When you don't have to worry or be afraid of anything, you're free to give love to everyone around you. Love God, Love People.

And your convictions determine your conduct. They motivate you to act in certain ways. Dictionaries usually define conviction as a fixed or strong belief. Your convictions include your values, commitments, and motivations. The people who have made the greatest impact on this world, for good or evil, were the people with the strongest, deepest convictions. Their convictions moved them to move the world. The great Bible teacher Howard Hendricks avowed: "A belief is something you will argue about. A conviction is something you will die for!" Your convictions will help you determine and live: "Love God, Love People.

Love is also a choice and it represents a commitment. You must choose to love God; he won't put you between a rock and a hard place and force you to love him. You can also choose to love others, but he won't force you to love anyone. If you only love on and off like a light switch, you do not love others like he wants you to love. Jesus said, "If you only love those who love you what credit is that to you?" (Luke 6:32 NIV). If you love someone, let's see how you act toward that person – Love God, Love People.

Additionally, love is an action; love is a behavior. Love is something you do. It can produce emotion, but love is an action. The Bible says, "Let's not merely say we love each other; let us show the truth by our actions" (1 John 3:18). You can talk a good act and exclaim: "I love people. I'm kind and tenderhearted." But do you love them for real? Your love is revealed in how you act toward them. As 1 Timothy 4:15 declares, "Give your complete attention to these matters. Throw yourself into your tasks so everyone will see your progress." Love God, Love People.

Furthermore, love is a skill you can learn. In other words, it's something you can get good at; you get better at love by practicing love. Want to be a master lover or known as a person of extraordinary love? When people speak of you they might say: "He doesn't care who you are or what you look like." "She doesn't care where you've been or what you've done or where you're from." The only way you get skilled at something is to practice. It's an open season for you do it over and over. It ain't over till the fat lady sings. The first time you do it, it feels awkward, but the more you do it, the better you become.

If you want to connect with people, you've got to start with their needs, not your own. That's how you make the initial connection. There's an old Chinese proverb that says, "Seek to understand before seeking to be understood." The Bible talks about this in Philippians 2:4: "Look out for one another's interests not just your own." It's such a counter-cultural verse. Everything in our culture -- from the moment we're born – tends to train us to think "me first.' As a result, we're all disconnected because we're all thinking about ourselves and not thinking about the needs of other people. People kiss and tell that love without proof is fake.

The jury is still out so dare to be different and:

Let your brotherly love continue! Love your neighbor as yourself by giving. Giving is a proof of love. Scripture tells us: "For God so loved the world he gave his one and only Son, that whoever believes in him shall not perish but have eternal life" (John 3:16 NIV).

Let your brotherly love continue! Show what love means by serving others. It's a great privilege when you serve the less privileged as well as those that are privileged. The Bible says, "Greater love has no one than this: to lay down one's life for one's friends" (John 15:13 NIV).

Let your brotherly love continue! Love your neighbor as yourself by forgiving. Forgive one another as a true proof of love: "Jesus said, "Father, forgive them, for they do not know what they are doing." And they divided up his clothes by casting lots" (Luke 23:34 NIV).

Let your brotherly love continue! Show what love means by encouraging one another. Share out the Word of God and spark a positive change in one's life. Scripture tells us: "As iron sharpens iron, so one person sharpens another." (Proverbs 27:17 NIV).

Let your brotherly love continue! Love your neighbor as yourself by praying for one another. Focus on interceding for others than your personal issue(s). The Bible says, "After Job had prayed for his friends, the Lord restored his fortunes and gave him twice as much as he had before" (Job 42:10 NIV).

Let your brotherly love continue! Show what love means by being meek to others. Help restore versus cast out those who have fallen, especially when such individual is repentant. Scripture tells us: "Brothers and sisters, if someone is caught in a sin, you who live by the Spirit should restore that person gently. But watch yourselves, or you also may be tempted" (Galatians 6: 1 NIV).

Let your brotherly love continue! Love your neighbor as yourself by being a referral for others. Any position you find ourselves, and if/when possible, should be an avenue to recommend others. In Daniel 2:48 – 49 NIV, "the king placed Daniel in a high position and lavished many gifts on him. He made him ruler over the entire province of Babylon and placed him in charge of all its wise men. Moreover, at Daniel's request the king appointed Shadrach, Meshach and Abednego administrators over the province of Babylon, while Daniel himself remained at the royal court."

Let your brotherly love continue! Show what love means because it will help you to endure whatever trials you may have in the future. Whether natural disasters, persecution, or economic difficulties, the more problems our brothers have, the more opportunities we have to show how much we love them. Even though this world's love will grow cold, continue showing brotherly love. (Matthew 24:12 NIV).

Let your brotherly love continue! Love your neighbor as yourself because we need one another, especially during difficult times. When Hurricane Harvey hit, the entire Houston community came together as a whole -- unity in community and neighbors helping neighbors. Stranger's rushed to help strangers. It was such an overwhelming response to help others. No one thought they were going to do this before this happened; everyone did it. You should look at human nature this way.

Let your brotherly love continue! Show what love means to show hospitality or kindness to strangers (Hebrews 13:2). You can invite a brother and sister to your home for a meal or for some encouragement. You do not need to make a big meal or spend a lot of money. Your goal is to encourage your brothers, not to impress them with what you have. And you should not only invite those who can repay you in some way. (Luke 14:12-14).

Let your brotherly love continue! Love your neighbor as yourself and keep in mind those in prison [for their faith]." (Hebrews 13:3.) Brothers and sisters who live close by can help them with practical things. Brothers and sisters who live far from those in prison can pray intensely for them. Let your brotherly love continue! Show what love means and keep on doing it more fully. There is always room for improvement! Paul encouraged us to love our brothers and sisters even more. (1 Thessalonians 4:9,10)

Like a good neighbor and Marah's transition back to her daily life, you can also experience new life of loving your neighbor out of love for God. A change or shift happens – from self-absorption to God dependence. Wet behind the ears? Let there be light! Like Marah, you can move to a new normal. Unfold a brand-new story in your life. Will that work for you? Forever change the old way of life and into a new and different life – Love God, Love People. Can you imagine a world where people loved each other this way?

Even if we refuse to address the elephants in the room dividing us (e.g., race, immigration, etc.), we can have an open mind without having a hole in our head. Our minds are like parachutes: they function only when open. Put on your thinking cap and let's not close our mind to possibilities, new ideas, effective courses of action, and to change; we then may doom ourselves to fail. It's also not rocket science snowflakes are frail. And if enough of them stick together they can stop traffic.

You can't do a whole lot and I can't do a whole lot, but together in a group we can do something. Change starts with you; change starts with me. It begins not only with your words or action, but in your heart. God's blessings are not only to you, but also through you to others. Life's too short and we can have an influence and impact on this world now; love won't let you wait.

Thirsty? Wear your heart on your sleeve and dream big – not only where you are, but also where you can be. While the country may seem divided, every day people from all walks of life are coming together; they're rallying behind each other and standing up for complete strangers. Though silence is golden, let's not rest on our laurels. Get up and get going—get involved; you have the potential to change things.

Thumbs up! Uplift and transform the world by loving God and loving people now! Stand up and shape the next generation's worldview today. Loving your neighbor as yourself is not about loving black or brown people; it's about loving all people. Prejudice and hate devalue life. Instead, couple anger at an action with love for the person. Martin Luther King Jr. envisioned love as key to building healthy communities; display love at the center of your social interactions. There's a 'king in you.'

To be or not to be, that is the question. You can make haste and decide right now to 'king size' your faith even when you're going through the fire of facing skepticism about this new standard of love. Many are called but few are chosen! In a nutshell, people will know you're a Christian by your love -- the position and attitude of your heart. What's your reaction to this course of action? Faith is confidence in God's ability.

For good measure, trust is confidence in his agenda. Like being in love, take that leap of faith and go out on a limb. Faith will move mountains. O ye of little faith, it is impossible to please him. Like when Nebuchadnezzar summoned soldiers to throw Shadrach, Meshach, and Abednego into the fire (Daniel 3), you're not alone in the fire! They were alive and kicking! Know he is in control and he is bigger than the fire. Not by your faith only, but Love God, Love People by works.

PART IV
WORK

WORK EXCELLENCE

CHAPTER AND VERSE

Daily Devotions for Your Work Week

CONTENTS

Preface 243

Work Week # 1—Demonstrating Godly Character 247
One - Integrity 248
Two - Service 250
Three - Excellence 252
Four - Courage 254
Five - Loyalty 256

Work Week #2—Working Heartily 258
One - Ability 259
Two - Success 261
Three - Promotion 263
Four - Diligence 265
Five - Balance 267

Work Week #3—Modeling Attributes of Godly Employees 269
One - Prayerfulness 270
Two - Obedience 272
Three - Attitude 273
Four - Encouragement 275
Five - Faithfulness 277

Work Week #4—Leading and Beyond 279
One - Direction 280
Two - Communication 282
Three - Ambition 284
Four - Team 286
Five - Transitioning 288

PREFACE

Why You Should Read This Devotion:

Work is so important God gives this command:

Six days you shall work. Exodus 34:21 (NKJV)

The words "work" and "toil" are mentioned over 480 times in the Bible, supporting the importance of work to God. The Apostle Paul also underlines the significance of work:

If anyone is not willing [versus if anyone cannot—who are not physically or mentally unable to work] to work, then he is not to eat, either. 2 Thessalonians 3:10 (NASB)

You may spend 100,000 hours working over a lifetime and your job, regardless of profession, often comes with some degree of dissatisfaction. Your typical work week behavior may spiral from the "Monday Morning Blues" to "Hump Day Wednesday" to "Living For Friday." Become an insider and you can suddenly find greater and proven satisfaction in your job as an ambassador for Christ. *"We are therefore Christ's ambassadors, as though God were making his appeal through us."* 2 Corinthians 5:20

Unfortunately, the only and worst picture of Christ some people will see is you. Therefore, you want to immediately develop and improve your powerful platform as a remarkable witness in shining armor at your work for the glory of his kingdom, God's nation.

Whatever you do in word or deed, do all in the name of the LORD Jesus, giving thanks through him to God the Father. (Colossians 3:17 NASB)

Pursuing excellence is nothing more than mirroring his character and behavior. It's easier when you are excited about your job to instantly turn the focus of your work from "I'm doing this for my boss" or "I'm doing this to get paid" to "I'm doing this for the LORD."

Accordingly, start your day with God first, giving thanks, reading, or listening to praise music; I encourage you to focus on him from the time you get up until the time you leave from work. No, it doesn't end there, continuous worship is another book. This devotional fully equips you now to increase your role as an ambassador while at work, especially since most of your life is spent in the work place. It promotes spiritual truth in doctrine; reproof in showing shortcomings; correction by revealing lessons learned; and instruction in giving our best while at work (2 Timothy 3:16-17 NKJV).

Why You Can Trust What This Devotion is About:

Like opening an e-mail from a protected, secure source, you can trust the true blue sender with no risk. This hot message isn't from an anonymous informant; it's from God. And he has given you a big job to do. As one of the few, your job as his ambassador to the people around you is a distinguished one. And you need to first understand the job description before you can do a job well. According to Wikipedia, "An ambassador is the highest ranking diplomat who represents a nation." He or she has authority to represent their head of state and their own country.

You may ask how to promote his exclusive kingdom in an excellent manner? Completely walk in the fruit of the Spirit:

> But the fruit of the Spirit is love, joy, peace, longsuffering, kindness, goodness, faithfulness, gentleness and self-control. (Galatians 5:22-3 NKJV)

God wants you to accurately represent him to the world around you, those outside his kingdom. He clearly supplies you with the amazing message he wants you to take to the world. He brought us back to himself through Christ's death on the cross. And he has given us the task of bringing others back to him through Christ. (God) has committed to us to embrace and receive the message of reconciliation. (2 Corinthians 5:18 and 19)

Through you, God is urging all people to suddenly become reunited with him through the work of his son, Jesus. For this reason, you can instantly rise and shine as an ambassador and accept an extraordinary privilege on behalf of him to those around you. Work is one area where you can carry forth his message by buckling down and being your best.

> Slaves [workers], obey your earthly supervisors in everything you do. Try to please them all the time, not when they are watching you. Serve them sincerely because of your reverent fear of the LORD. Work willingly at whatever you do, as though you were working for the LORD rather than for people. Remember the LORD will give you an inheritance as your reward, and the LORD you are serving is Christ. (Colossians 3:22-24 NLT)

By opening this book, you've shown interest in where you are now and desire to be. In this inspiring devotional, you'll find its content structured into four, 5-day work week-based sections. Discover how each unit instantly inspires you to get what you want out of your job and be an excellent ambassador:

- Work Week # 1 encompasses **Demonstrating Godly Character**
- Work Week #2 reveals our part in **Working Heartily**
- Work Week #3 encourages **Modeling Attributes of Godly Employees**
- Work Week #4 examines **Leading and Beyond**

Why This Devotional is Relevant to You Now:

In your capacity as an ambassador, *Work Excellence Chapter and Verse* can immediately help you can make a kingdom impact now by meeting your pressing need to be the best you can be at your job. This encouraging devotional also faithfully represents and advances his reconciliation message.

- Do you want to be thoroughly equipped for every good work?
- Do you desire to be rewarded for your hard work?
- God gives you your abilities and controls success and promotion. How should this perspective affect your work?
- For whom do you work in truth? How will this understanding change your work performance?
- What steps will you take to earn more: job satisfaction, leadership skills, responsibilities and respect, significance and say about how things are done, and privileges, pay and prestige?
- In leadership, you gain more: position (you can become more); power and influence (you can do more); and privilege (you can have more). Are you aware *Work Excellence Chapter & Verse* can apply this to your situation now?

Work Excellence Chapter & Verse delivers solutions for your work goals now and instantly helps fulfill your job satisfaction needs, both materially and spiritually. You can make an impact now by becoming a GIANT ambassador for the 'home kingdom' of God versus a MIDGET for other 'foreign' lands and a CHAMP for him in your work rather than a CHOMP for men. The honor and reputation of the kingdom are in your hands and today is your new life of suddenly achieving victory and job satisfaction—with him all things are possible. Work hard so he can say to you, "Well done. Be a good workman, one who does not need to be ashamed when God examines your work" (2 Timothy 2:15).

WORK WEEK # 1.

Demonstrating Godly Character

DAY 1

Integrity

When a man makes a vow to the LORD or takes an oath to obligate himself by a pledge, he must not break his word but must do everything he said —Numbers 30:2

You may have watched the drama unfold from the "Honesty Pass It On" commercial. A teenager runs across town with a purse a woman forgot at a bus stop. You may wonder if the young man is taking or returning the purse—until the last triumphant moment. He instantly returns the purse and on-duty police officers reward him with a doughnut. We need more people doing the right thing and valuing integrity.

As a supervisor, I remember correcting workers who cooked the books or pencil whipped a safety or compliance inspection checklist or training record. You may find it reassuring too when your workers own their mistakes by immediately taking responsibility for having made it or admitting to something when no one knew they did it.

In Daniel 6:4 (NLT), we also see "*the other administrators and high officers began searching for some fault in the way Daniel was handling government affairs, but they couldn't find anything to criticize or condemn. He was faithful, always responsible, and trustworthy*". His 'haters' could find no dishonesty in him, and there was no "evidence of corruption" in his work. He was trusted by the king.

Integrity is the basis of trust. Trust makes leaders effective; integrity underpins trust, which involves character and competence. One of the primary purposes of work is to develop character. When you build your 'house' at work, the 'house' is also building you (e.g., your ability, knowledge, judgment and so forth). People who excel keep their word; they are reliable. You count on them to do what they say they'll do.

Father, thank you for your Word, which is a lamp to my feet and light for my path. To live is Christ and help me to do the right thing. May I be characterized by my integrity as it honors you, my Father in heaven. In Jesus name I pray, Amen.

Day 1 Prose Interpretation
By Shaun Nichols

Though we all fall short of the Glory of God, we must not allow our witness to become distasteful.
In the eyes of the public who's looking for reasons to condemn, criticize the Saints of the most High,
like Daniel under every circumstance,
we must remain Faithful.
Higher should be our desire
And when our heart is set on fire
to please the King
even the king grants us access
full authority to control and govern his entire empire

DAY 2

Service

Let each of you look not only to his own interests, but also to the interests of others. —Philippians 2:4 (ESV)

While I served in the United States Air Force, the oath of enlistment's language makes followership-leadership a necessity of service: *. . . and I will obey the orders of the President of the United States and the orders of the officers appointed over me according to regulations and the Uniform Code of Military Justice.* Service is a pathway to real significance. Significance isn't possible unless what we do suddenly contributes to the welfare of others. Dr. Martin Luther King Jr. once said, "Life's most persistent and urgent question is: 'What are you doing for others?'"

In John 13:12-15, Jesus also modeled an example of servant-leadership to his disciples. *When he had finished washing their feet, he put on his clothes and returned to his place. "Do you understand what I have done for you? You call me 'Teacher' and 'LORD,' and rightly so, for that is what I am. Now I, your LORD and Teacher, have washed your feet, you also should wash one another's feet. I have set you an example you should do as I have done for you."*

The night before Jesus was crucified; he washed his disciples' feet. The LORD performed what may be considered a lowly task. Likewise, when you shift your focus from serving your own needs and desires to serving from the heart the needs of others first, you truly experience your passion and giving your best for him. Real joy comes from serving Jesus, Others and Yourself last (JOY).

Heavenly Father, Allow me to humbly serve others with a joyful heart, always giving and never expecting to receive. Allow me to serve others as you serve, giving of my talents, time and energy. Thank you LORD, I give you all the glory, honor and praise. In Jesus' name, Amen.

DAY 3

Excellence

Daniel soon proved himself more capable than all the other administrators and high officers. Because of Daniel's great ability, the king made plans to place him over the entire empire. —Daniel 6:3 (NLT)

One role of a computer technician is to perform initial fault assessment and resolution in response to customer-reported incidents via trouble tickets. While working as a computer technician, assigned computer incidents frequently remained unresolved in the job tracking system. Technicians often kept a high number of incidents in their job queue without taking appropriate, timely action to resolve them. Managers may have perceived workers did the minimum instead of resolving current incidents to delay assignment of new incidents.

In illustrating excellence, the story of the 'camel test' is a familiar one. Abraham's servant would ask a young maiden for a sip of water, and if she offered to provide water for his camels as well, she would be the one—a suitable wife for Abraham's son, Isaac.

Genesis 24:17-20 tells us *"the servant hurried to meet her and said, "Please give me a little water from your jar." "Drink, my LORD," she said, and quickly lowered the jar to her hands and gave him a drink. After she had given him a drink, she said, "I'll draw water for your camels too, until they have had enough to drink." So she quickly emptied her jar into the trough, ran back to the well to draw more water, and drew enough for all his camels"*. Rebekah became Isaac's bride!

Booker T. Washington once said, "Excellence is to do a common thing in an uncommon way." Some say Rebekah may have drawn water for 10 thirsty camels; camels can drink up to 40 gallons in one session. Thus, Rebekah drew as much as 400 gallons of water! You can also raise 'your game' and give God your best. You can exceed what is expected of you. Do more than the minimum; don't just get by. You can receive more than you expect and rise to the top. *"If someone forces you to go one mile, go with them two miles"* (Matthew 5:41).

Father, you are the Most High. I make use of the gifts given me and let my light so shine before men so they may see my excellence and my praiseworthy deeds. To God be all glory, honor and praise. Amen.

DAY 4

Courage

Be on your guard; stand firm in the faith; be men of courage; be strong. —1 Corinthians 16:13

While I was deployed to Qatar, my commander and I performed a site visit to Iraq to get a firsthand look at forward operating bases' Airmen's welfare and mission contributions. Before departing, a friend dropped me a note to reflect God's protection. While confident him as my "rock," sun and shield from harm's way, the note was uplifting and thoughtful. It echoed divine faith and courage in him always.

In Hebrews 11:23-24, 27, we're also reminded courage always produces action. *"By faith Moses' parents hid him for three months after he was born, because they saw he was no ordinary child, and they were not afraid of the king's edict. By faith Moses, when he had grown up, refused to be known as the son of Pharaoh's daughter. By faith he left Egypt, not fearing the king's anger; he persevered because he saw him who is invisible.*

Upholding standards of conduct and personal ethics as a centerpiece in your life and work also demand a great deal of courage. Minimum standards are not enough. Strive to avoid even the perception of abusing your position, misusing time or funds, stealing, hazing or being deceitful or taking part in any other unprofessional or prohibited actions.

Step away from battles or giants holding you back from your goals: trying to be like others; trying to make everybody happy; too many hobbies or too much time spent on a hobby; nonstop browsing or viewing of social media, movies, or television, the wrong kinds of relationships; past mistakes, and so on. Build up your faith and keep your foot from their path.

Eternal Father, I am of good courage and pray you grant me with all boldness to speak forth your Word. I believe no weapon formed against me shall prosper. I trust in you with all my heart and lean not to my own understanding. In all my ways I acknowledge you and you direct my path and I walk in light of your Word. In Jesus Name, Amen.

DAY 5

Loyalty

Commit your work to the LORD, and your plans will be established.
—Proverbs 16:3 (ESV)

Most people recite wedding vows pledging commitment and loyalty to their new spouse till "death us do part." We all crave for such unwavering devotion in our marriages. In my marriage, my better half and I covenant and honor "*MO2-4L+*"—*Mark and Margarita Overton For Life Joyfully*. Commitment and loyalty are also reflected in faithful allegiances between lifelong friends, between college graduates and their "alma mater", between veterans and the armed services, and between citizens and their countries.

In 1 Samuel 20:13-16 (ESV), we see the remarkable friendship and loyalty between Jonathan to David.

> *"But should it please my father* [King Saul] *to do you harm, the LORD do so to Jonathan and more also if I do not disclose it to you and send you away, that you may go in safety. May the LORD be with you, as he has been with my father. If I am still alive, show me the steadfast love of the LORD, that I may not die; and do not cut off your steadfast love from my house forever, when the LORD cuts off every one of the enemies of David from the face of the earth." And Jonathan made a covenant with the house of David, saying, "May the LORD take vengeance on David's enemies."*

Similarly, as an employee, honor your employer with a sincere heart by rendering service with a good will as to the LORD. Likewise, make your chief commitment to God himself.

"For the eyes of the LORD range throughout the earth to strengthen those whose hearts are fully committed to him. You have done a foolish thing, and from now on you will be at war." (2 Chronicles 16:9).

Awesome Father, in the name of Jesus, I commit my way to you. You will cause my thoughts to become agreeable to your will and so shall my plans be established and succeed. I praise you and purpose to live according to your Word. Amen.

WORK WEEK # 2.

Working Heartily

DAY 1

Ability

And every skillful person in whom the LORD has put skill and understanding to know how to perform all the work in the construction of the sanctuary, shall perform in accordance with all that the LORD has commanded." —Exodus 36:1 (NASB)

When I led projects at work, I frequently heard "20% of the people are doing 80% of the work", which follows the Pareto Principle or the 80/20 Rule. In 1906, an economist observed 20% of the people in Italy owned 80% of the land. This same principle, 20 percent of something always is responsible for 80 percent of the results, can apply in various work situations.

1 Corinthians 12:27 (NLT) tells us, *"All of you together are Christ's body, and each of you is a part of it."* God has given each of us a specific calling or purpose. Ephesians 2:10 (ESV) underscores *"We are His workmanship, creating in Christ Jesus for good works, which God prepared beforehand so we would walk in them"*. Exodus 36:1 also illustrates this truth in the above Scripture.

God has given you unique aptitudes. He gives job skills. You are gifted uniquely— spiritual gifts, heart, abilities, personality and experiences. David was a shepherd and a king. Luke was a doctor. Lydia was a retailer of purple fabric. Daniel was a government worker. Paul was a tentmaker. Mary was a homemaker. Jesus was a carpenter.

Each of us has a role to play, and every role is important. Some are visible and some are behind the scenes, but all are valuable. You're given gifts for a purpose. You *are* responsible for the ones given to you. Develop your talents. Keep learning, growing and improving; sharpen your skills. Be a good steward of your gifts—not for selfish uses, but for the good of others. When you use your gifts to serve others, you help to ensure everybody is equipped to do something versus only the 20 percent. Rise up and give; rise up and build.

Father, I thank you for filling me with talents and skills and the knowledge of your will to be concerned for not only my own interests, but also the interest of others. I give you all the praise, honor and glory. In Jesus Name, Amen.

DAY 2

Success

May he give you the desire of your heart and make all your plans succeed. —Psalm 20:4

Even while rising in the early ranks as an Airman, one key to success received from supervisors was "to keep your nose clean". As long as you met expectations and stayed out of trouble, promotion eligibility was in your hands. This 18th century English phrase derived from 'keeping one's hands clean', which referred specifically to the avoidance of corruption.

God gives success. In 1 Kings 2:3, when King David was about to die, he gave his son, Solomon, the following advice: "observe what the LORD your God requires: Walk in obedience to him, and keep his decrees and commands, his laws and regulations, as written in the Law of Moses. Do this so you may prosper in all you do and wherever you go".

In 1 Kings 3:12-14, Solomon's success formula when he became King was to follow God and obey him. He asked the LORD for a discerning heart to govern his people. God answered: "*I will do what you have asked. I will give you a wise and discerning heart, so there will never have been anyone like you, nor will there ever be. Moreover, I will give you what you have not asked for—both wealth and honor—so in your lifetime you will have no equal among kings. And if you walk in obedience to me and keep my decrees and, I will give you a long life.*"

Likewise, you can define your greatest joy or legacy by giving to others and helping someone else grow, prosper and win. Strive to shift the focus away from self.

Father, you are my Rock, fortress and deliverer and I praise you for equipping me for success. I rejoice I am like a tree firmly planted by the streams of water, ready to bring forth my fruit in my season and everything I do shall prosper. In your name I pray, Amen.

DAY 3

Promotion

For I know the plans I have for you," declares the LORD, "plans to prosper you and not to harm you, plans to give you hope and a future.
—Jeremiah 29:11

As I was flying in on a C-17 military transport aircraft to Bagram Airfield, Afghanistan we began our combat landing approach—a steep dive, spiraling down to the airfield below and soon the pilot's voice came over the intercom "We have a situation there and must abort our landing and maintain a holding pattern over Bagram at a safe altitude until the runway can be cleared."

For the next two hours we circled high above our destination waiting until we were cleared to land. Life can be like that sometimes, we are eager to reach a destination, be it a personal destination like marriage or a professional destination like earning a college degree or a promotion, but we find we aren't ready to arrive at a destination and we find ourselves in what we think is a holding pattern, feeling like we are wasting our time. But the truth of matter is—we are still a work in progress and if we had pushed forward trying to accomplish he right goal at the wrong time we may have learned some hard lessons we would regret.

When we reflect upon the words of God to the nation of Israel spoken through the prophet Isaiah during a time of exile we realize even when things are not going well, he has a plan for us. Our frustration comes when the fulfillment of a plan seems needlessly slowed down by detours we take in life or other obstacles we run into, but these detours, obstacles and even hardships may be a piece to his plan for our life. There is no easy job in today's workplace; every specialty has its rigorous training requirements and you depend upon your fellow coworker to be a subject matter expert at their job. We may want to rush into a supervisory position we always wanted or get a promotion we think we deserve, but in the end, he may be slowing us down, placing us a holding pattern because he knows we may not be as ready as we think we are.

But understand this, even holding patterns can help prepare us for what lies ahead and sometimes we may not understand why we have to do all the things we do, but when our moment arrives and we finally get to be "the man/woman" or "the boss" we see how much we needed those lessons in life and how we may not have been as ready as we thought we were and had we pushed forward at the wrong time, things could have ended badly.

I am reminded of how Esther's cousin Mordecai reminded her in Esther 4:14b—*"you have come to royal position for such a time as this?"* Everything Esther had experienced in life up to that point, the good (being selected as the Queen of the Medes and Persians), the bad (the death of her parents) and the ugly (the threat of annihilation of the Jews) prepared for this moment. Esther rose to the challenge by drawing upon her faith and the strength she gained from the experiences she had. In fact, the greatest military, political or world changing leaders in our history are those who had to prove themselves in the face of adversity.

I am convinced there are no wasted experiences in God's great plan. There may be some bad experiences we have brought upon ourselves he would not have wished for us to go through. But one of the of things making him the one true God is he can take even the worst experiences we have or the most mundane we think is another holding pattern and weave it into the tapestry of our life. He prepares us for what opportunities lie ahead, in his time. —Andrew G. McIntosh

Father, I bless Your Name, El-Shaddai, the God Almighty of Blessings. You are All Bountiful and All-Sufficient. I praise in all things you work for the good of those who love you, who have been called according to your purpose. Hallowed be your name! Amen.

DAY 4

Diligence

Whatever your hand finds to do, do it with all your might. — Ecclesiastes 9:10

When I lived on Fort Myer in Arlington, Virginia, I'd visit Arlington National Cemetery on the weekends and watch the diligence and hard work of the "Old Guard" at The Tomb of the Unknowns. Guards are changed every 30 minutes, 24 hours a day, 365 days a year, humbly revering fallen American service members whose remains have not been identified. Every sentinel spends 5 hours a day perfecting his uniform for guard duty and commits 2 years of life to guard the Tomb.

In 2 Thessalonians 3:7-10, Paul also set an excellent example among church members of working hard.

> *For you yourselves know how you ought to follow our example. We were not idle when we were with you, nor did we eat anyone's food without paying for it. On the contrary, we worked night and day, laboring and toiling so we would not be a burden to any of you. We did this, not because we do not have the right to such help, but in order to offer ourselves as a model for you to imitate. For even when we were with you, we gave you this rule: "The one who is unwilling to work shall not eat."*

The only place success comes before work is in the dictionary. Your work should never be at such a level where people will liken idleness with God. The Book of Galatians heartens us to "Let everyone be sure to do his best, for he will have the personal satisfaction of work done well and won't need to compare himself with someone else." When you strive to be the person you were made to be, you'll find real meaning, purpose, fulfillment, and satisfaction. Stay focused; hard work pays off.

LORD, you are an awesome God. Thank you for the grace to remain diligent in seeking knowledge and skill in my work areas. My light shall shine before men they see my good works glorifying you. In Jesus' name, Amen.

DAY 5

Balance

Six days you shall work, but on the seventh day you shall rest. In plowing time and in harvest you shall rest. —Exodus 34:21 (ESV)

According to a financial company survey, roughly three-quarters of Americans are living paycheck-to-paycheck, with little to no emergency savings. To manage to pay for bills and other necessities or wants, I previously worked part-time jobs as a cook, waiter, security guard and valet parking. When your work is out of balance, it can contribute to your spouse's contempt or disrespect because he or she may feel unloved, insignificant, unvalued or 'second best'.

Psalm 1:1-2 tells us *"Blessed is the one who does not walk in step with the wicked ..., but whose delight is in the law of the LORD, and who meditates on his law day and night."* If we overwork ourselves, we end up spending lesser time with God. Likewise, Matthew 22:37-38 calls us to first love the LORD our God with all your heart, soul and mind because it is the first and greatest commandment. When overworking causes us to be away from him, we will have lesser time to meditate on his Word! Matthew 6:24 reminds us we cannot serve both God and money. Similarly, if you are overworking because you need money and it is taking you away from him, you have to choose between serving him and serving money.

At the end of the day, balance hard work with the other priorities of life. The result of overwork is more stress and neglected or fractured relationships. Determine whether the job itself if too demanding or whether your work habits need changing. 1 Corinthians 14:40 (NLT) tells us: *"be sure that everything is done properly and in order"*.

In order to stay balanced, you first have to help yourself to enable you to help others to the best of your ability.

Father, I am so thankful you know my needs. I make my schedule around your Word. With all my heart, I seek you first and your way of doing and being right, and all my needs taken together will be supplied according to your riches in glory. Amen.

WORK WEEK # 3

Modeling Attributes of Godly Employees

DAY 1

Prayerfulness

"When Daniel knew that the document had been signed [restricting worship to the king alone] ... He got down on his knees three times a day and prayed and gave thanks before his God, as he had done previously." —Daniel 6:10 (ESV)

"If you have ever thought about poisoning, choking, punching or slapping someone you work with you need to pray at work". During my military service, I remember a reference to this "You Need to Pray at Work" e-mail series, which also may apply to your workplace. Many employees also post motivators and scriptures in their work space to uplift and encourage each other.

You can make work fulfilling, but it can also make you feel as a cause of great frustration. Prayer can help put those 'dissatisfying' times in perspective. Prayerfulness proved effective from Jesus Christ (Hebrews 5:7) to Paul (Colossians 1:9) to David (1 Samuel 30:6). In 1 Chronicles 4:10, Jabez cried out to God, *"Oh, you would bless me and enlarge my territory! Let your hand be with me, and keep me from harm so I will be free from pain."* And God granted his request.

God wants you to pray about your goals. He wants you to be specific. The more specific you are in your prayers, the more quickly he's going to answer. He also dares us to ask for big requests. James 4:3 tells us, *"you do not receive, because you ask with wrong motives."* Jeremiah 33:3 (ESV) tells us, *"Call to me and I will answer you, and will tell you great and hidden things that you have not known."* In Matthew 7:7, Jesus said, "ask, seek, knock" (ASK). Ephesians

3:20 tells us God *"is able to do immeasurably more than all we ask or imagine according to His power at work within us."*

Prayer is important and draws you nearer to God. ASK to make prayer a priority instead of faulting your busy schedule. If you are not praying consistently, your work suffers. He gives job skills, success and promotion.

Father, This is the confidence I have in you, if I ask anything according to your will, you hear me. I am so thankful whatever I ask for in prayer, having faith and believing it will be granted to me, and I will receive it. You, Father, are honored and glorified. Hallelujah! Amen.

DAY 2

Obedience

Therefore keep the words of this covenant and do them, that you may prosper in all that you do—Deuteronomy 29:9 (ESV)

From the military I learned, you're expected to mind your Ps and Qs and comply with standards of conduct relating not only to the performance of military duties but also to the discharge of your responsibilities and your relations with other members of the military community as well. When I became a federal employee, I underwent a "probationary period" before my supervisor determined he had hired the right person and declared me a "regular" employee. It's important you conform or abide by job standards and expectations at all times, not only during this "trial period".

In Jesus Christ we find the perfect model of obedience. He lived a sinless life. He paid for the sins of the world and purchased the pardon of men. He also restored man's fellowship with God, opening the way to eternal life. As his 'disciple', you follow his example as well as his commands. Your motivation for obedience is love. He tells us in John 14:15, *"If you love me, keep my commands."*

From the Old to the New Testament, the Bible places strong emphasis on obedience. It's good to be involved in worship at church; continue to give him the praise through your daily obedience as you move out into the real world. In your job, obedience brings blessings.

Father, in the name of Jesus, I commit myself to walk in the Word. In your name and in obedience to your will, I yield my desires not in your plan for me. Amen.

DAY 3

Attitude

Whatever is true, whatever is noble, whatever is right, whatever is pure, whatever is lovely, whatever is admirable--if anything is excellent or praiseworthy--think about such things.—Philippians 4:8

According to a recent Gallup survey, 90% of the employees surveyed said they were at least satisfied with their jobs. Building and maintaining healthy, effective relationships in all directions—with people you work with and people who work for you—is one of the keys to job satisfaction. People who excel maintain a positive attitude. I strive to start my day with God first, shaping the spirit of my mind and to give my best and stay in faith throughout the day.

In Philippians 1:27, Paul also writes from a prison cell in Rome about the attitude a Christian should have: *"Whatever happens, conduct yourselves in a manner worthy of the gospel of Christ"*. He's telling us no matter what unexpected disruptions, frustrations, or difficulties come our way, we are to respond with a Christ-like attitude. Paul later writes in Philippians 2:5 (NLT), *"You must have the same attitude that Christ Jesus had."* He also encourages us in Ephesians 5:1 and Matthew 5:16 respectively to *"Follow God's example"* and *"In the same way, let your light shine before others, they may see your good deeds and glorify your Father in heaven."*

At or outside of work, strive to own a Christ-like attitude-- selflessness, humility and service. Regardless of whether the job is big or small, give it your best. Great performers give their best effort, no matter what the size of the audience. Your attitude determines your joy. Proverbs 12:24 (NASB) tell us: *"The hand of the diligent will rule, But the slack hand will be put to forced labor."*

Father, whatever is true, whatever is worthy of reverence and is honorable, pure, lovely and lovable, kind, winsome and gracious, if there is any virtue and excellence or worthy of praise, I will think on and weigh and fix my mind on them. Amen.

DAY 4

Encouragement

Therefore encourage one another and build one each other up, just as in fact you are doing.—1 Thessalonians 5:11

One of my responsibilities as a Base Communications Security Manager was to perform a combination change on a security container when needed. One time during this procedure, I missed a validation step. As a result, I locked out everyone from the safe container, both unauthorized and authorized users. I kept a secure environment!

Combination troubleshooting to open the high security, electromechanical lock was unsuccessful. I felt miserable about the situation; it wasn't one of my better moments. When a female coworker reported to duty from unit physical training, she saw my distress. After explaining the setback, she confided, "the world isn't over; we'll get the container open." I kept my chin up and her positive words encouraged me; the lock was drilled and replaced with a spare.

In John 16:33, Jesus also encouraged his followers, "*In this world you will have trouble. But take heart! I have overcome the world*". He did not shy from telling his followers about the troubles they would face. In fact, he told them the world would hate them (John 15:18-21). But his grim forecast was tempered with cheer; he followed his prediction of trouble with a sparkling word of encouragement: He has overcome the world. Jesus is greater than any trouble we face.

Scripture tells us to encourage one another. Similarly when providing performance feedback, you help ensure your employee know where they stand and how to improve. You can set people up for success or failure by your expectations. To bring out the best in those around you, treat them the way they could be. Tell it like it could be.

Father, you are great and greatly to be praised. I am the righteousness of you. I purpose to edify my neighbor, to encourage, strengthen and build up others according to their needs. Amen.

DAY 5

Faithfulness

A faithful man will abound with blessings, but whoever hastens to be rich will not go unpunished —Proverbs 28:20 (ESV)

When I lived in Guam, our men's ministry headed a bimonthly homeless feeding, monthly breakfast, prison fellowship ministry, family fun day and retreat among other outreach activities. I'm so grateful I was a part of a group exemplifying "as iron sharpens iron" and striving to be "complete in Christ." Actions speak louder than words and being in the men's ministry was a powerful way to spread the good news by demonstrating it in daily life. A faith lived is a powerful, attractive faith.

Scripture speaks often of God's faithfulness. When he says he will do something, he does it. With him, all things are possible (Matthew 19:26). He is the same yesterday and today and forever. If this were not the case—if he were unfaithful even *once*—he would not be God, and we could not rely on any of his promises. But as it is, "Not one word has failed of all the good promises he gave" (1Kings 8:56). God is faithful. Faithfulness is an essential part of who he is (Psalm 89:8; Hebrews 13:8).

The heroic men and women of the "Hall of Faith" or the "Faith Hall of Fame" in Hebrews 11 encourage and challenge you to grow your faith. In Daniel 6:4, he influenced his employer, one of the most powerful people in the world, to believe in the only true God. By doing a job well in your sphere of work, you can also practically "show and tell" others with whom you work about Christ.

Father, in the name of Jesus, I cast my care on you. I expect a life of victory because my actions are done on behalf of a spirit humbly submitted to your truth and righteousness. May your will be done on earth in my life as it is in heaven. Amen.

WORK WEEK # 4

Leading and Beyond

DAY 1

Direction

Trust in the LORD with all your heart, and do not lean on your own understanding. In all your ways acknowledge him, and he will make straight your paths —Proverbs 3:5-6

"What will I do when I finish high school?" is a question many students ask. For some, the answer is "get a job." For others, the answer is "to travel and see the world or to continue education." I decided to "continue my education" at a local college before enlisting in the United States Air Force to "see the world." The immediate result of my decision was gratefully serving my country.

However, I obligingly experienced many second and third order consequences, which were different yet directly linked to my initial decision: permanent change of station or assignment, unaccompanied tours, temporary duty including short or no-notice deployments, alerts, recalls, extended hours or shift work and the real possibility of making the ultimate sacrifice in the line of duty.

In Jeremiah 42:8-22, the people of Judah also stood at a crossroad and on the cusp of a major decision. Their nation had been inflicted with disaster. They believed Egypt to the south offered more stability and protection from the dreaded Babylonian armed forces. The people asked Jeremiah, a prophet, for God's advice. After ten days of waiting, Jeremiah returned with an answer. He promised them two things. If you stay here in the land I have given you, I will restore your land. If you go to Egypt, you will all depart this life. Their desired outcome propelled them to "pitch their tent" in

Egypt; they made a choice based on their own wisdom and direction versus his and they eventually passed away.

The decision of faith in your life, if done in obedience to God, will always lead you down the right path. He is with you: *"For I know the plans I have for you, declares the LORD, plans for welfare and not for evil, to give you a future and a hope"* (Jeremiah 29:11 ESV).

Father, in Jesus' name, I praise you are ordering my steps and instructing me in the way which I should go. I thank you for your guidance and leading concerning your will, plan and purpose for my life. As I follow you, LORD, I believe my path is becoming clearer each day. Amen

DAY 2

Communication

If as one people speaking the same language they have begun to do this, nothing they plan to do will be impossible for them. —Genesis 11:6

You may be familiar with the "Test Man" or "The Verizon Guy" character in Verizon Wireless' "Can you hear me now?" commercials. You may also feel frustrated: when you feel like you're not being listened too; others change the subject, thus invalidating your feelings; and when others clearly behave in a way showing inattention.

When communicating with my spouse, we don't always get it right, but my spouse and I strive to give each other our fully undivided attention. It's important to listen to what each person is saying in order to show value and give the appropriate response.

The Genesis account of building the tower of Babel also supports the importance of good communication. Everyone spoke the same language and adopted a common goal. The LORD makes this remarkable observation, stated above in Genesis 11:6.

When people have good communication and pursue a common goal, "nothing they plan to do will be impossible for them"—as long as it is within the will of God. Since building the tower was not what he wanted, construction stopped. He disrupted their ability to communicate, which was the foundation for successfully completing the tower. *"Come, let us go down and confuse their language so they will not understand each other"* (Genesis 11:7).

It is especially important to listen to employee complaints. *"If I have denied justice to my [employees] when they had a grievance against me, what will I do when God confronts me"?* (Job 31:13-14). A sensitive, listening ear is a tangible expression of care. When a problem and solution is presented, employers should take appropriate steps to solve the problem.

Father, I desire to be in accord with James 1:19 and be quick to listen, slow to speak and slow to become angry. I purpose to express truth in all things and be filled with your praise and with your honor all the day. In Jesus' name. Amen.

DAY 3

Ambition

Do nothing from selfish ambition or conceit, but in humility count others more significant than yourselves. —Philippians 2:3 (ESV)

When I became a high-level manager, I had the opportunity to conduct "Airmen Calls" or meetings. The junior enlisted frequently perceived the senior noncommissioned officers as being all about "me." Instead of taking care of their people and fulfilling duty expectations, subordinates sensed the senior enlisted as advancing on personal interests by showing "I want to get promoted." 'Number one', 'the best' and 'bigger and 'better' is analogous to ambition. Your desire for promotion and ambition isn't out of line; it's misguided what one esteems or honors.

In Galatians 1:10 (ESV), Paul also addressed ambition by posing an insightful question: *"For am I now seeking the approval of man, or of God? Or am I trying to please man? If I were still trying to please man, I would not be a servant of Christ."* Is your ambition to please him or to please man? In seeking and honoring him, you are assured of his profound promise: *"But seek first his kingdom and his righteousness, and all these things will be given to you as well"* (Matthew 6:33).

Scripture supports ambition. To please Christ, work hard and pursue excellence in your job. Your motive is in the right when your success helps others rather than others mistaken it as a selfish act.

When your peers are promoted right over your head and you're "passed over," celebrate and commend their success. Be grateful, not regretful. Scripture says, "It is better to be satisfied with what you have than to always want something else." Rejoice in what you have. Your time is coming, not now. Continue to do your own work well.

Father, you are the great "I Am" and I thank you for your grace to shine upon me. I seek first your Kingdom and ask you to help me to see my situation as you see it and as you want it to be. I claim your blessings and thank you for favor, increase and overflow at my place of employment, at home, or wherever I may be. In Jesus' name, Amen.

DAY 4

Team

Commit your actions to the LORD, and your plans will succeed. — *Proverbs* 16:3 (NLT)

A friend of mine shared this testimony: "As a military spouse for over 29 years, I accompanied my husband around the world working for several employers. I am an educator and worked in seven different school districts and nine schools. The LORD blessed me with a job for each of our military relocations. God is good: employers not only hired me, but I also begin teaching the first year school year after our transfer to each new base.

Looking back at each school I've taught in, I see the reason the LORD placed me at each school. Whether it was helping a child who was abused, befriending a lonely colleague far from home, supporting a child with a learning disability, or mentoring a young teacher and mother, I am thankful for the opportunities I have had to serve the LORD through my chosen field".—Tonya Byrd

Proverbs 31 speaks of "a wife of noble character." She worked hard to keep her house and her family in order. In providing for her family, her employment was secondary to the stewardship of her husband, children and home. (Genesis 2:18; Proverbs 31:10-31). However, no Bible verse prohibits a woman from working outside the home. From Deborah, Anna, Tabitha and Phoebe to Rahab, women maintained jobs outside of their homes.

Many couples and families struggle in making a determination to embrace this biblical "Proverbs 31" model of a spouse working outside the home. When you commit yourselves to building a successful lifelong marriage, you act as wise captains and recognize, lean on, and use each other strengths for the benefit of the entire family. *"Two people are better off than one, for they can help each other succeed. If one person falls, the other can reach out and help."* (Ecclesiastes 4:9-10, NLT).

Father, we decree and declare ourselves to live in mutual harmony and accord, to be of one and the same mind. We thank you our marriage grows stronger day by day in the bond of unity because it is founded on your Word and rooted and grounded in your love. In the mighty name of Jesus, Amen.

DAY 5

Transitioning

But I do not account my life of any value nor as precious to myself, if only I may finish my course and the ministry I received from the LORD Jesus, to testify to the gospel of the grace of God. —Acts 20:24 (ESV)

The dictionary defines retirement as "withdrawal from an occupation, a retreat from active life." Your culture may promote the goal of retirement as ceasing all labor to live a life filled with leisure. In 2011, serving as the Guam Retiree Activities Office Director, I wrote an article titled, *The Bottom L.I.N.E. How Retirees, Active-duty Stay Connected.*

The retirement years are becoming a time of high activity and purpose instead of unproductiveness. According to the Association of American Retired Persons, 45 percent of all pre-retirees expect to continue working into their 70s or later. Nearly half of all Americans age 55 and over volunteer. You may be out of the service, but you are not served out—still serving in heart and spirit. You may have "retired," but you are in no way tired. Though you grow older, you still use your talents and skills to help others. Like academic graduation, retirement is a time when you move on to new, bigger and better things.

In Numbers 8:25-6, the only reference to retirement in Scripture, God informed Moses the Levite priests working in the tabernacle must retire. In the passage, God tells us "they must retire from their regular service and work no longer" and "they [the retired

Levites] may assist their brothers in performing their duties …, but they themselves must not do the work."

While you are physically and mentally capable, don't let age stop you from finishing the work God has called you to accomplish. He will provide you with the necessary strength. Moses was 80 years old when he began a 40-year journey leading the children of Israel.

Instead of being put "out to pasture," shift gears and use your experience and wisdom to open the door to new and different ways to serve God and others. Every exit is an entry. "Retirement" is not the end; it's the beginning of your next chapter in life. Help others during your retirement years.

Father, I bless your Name, Jehovah-Jireh, the One Who sees my needs and provides for them. I commit this transition to you, knowing you shall direct my path. I praise you I am strong and continue in doing right, letting not my hands be weak or slack or my heart weary of serving you. Amen.

PART V
PRAY

LORD TEACH ME HOW TO PRAY

10 Petitions That Strengthen Your Relationship with God

CONTENTS

Preface...295
Introduction - Elevate Your Prayer Level from
    Religion to Relationship 297

PART I: GLORIFYING GOD........................**301**
One - Our Father 302
Two - Who Art in Heaven..............................307
Three - Hallow Be Thy Name..........................309
Four - Thy Kingdom Come 314
Five - Thy Will Be Done On Earth As It Is In Heaven 316

PART II: SUSTAINING YOUR NEEDS................**318**
Six - Give Us Today Our Daily Bread 319
Seven - Forgive Us Our Debts,
    As We Also Have Forgiven Our Debtors 321
Eight - And Lead Us Not Into Temptation,
    But Deliver Us from Evil............................324
Nine - For Thine Is the Kingdom and the
    Power and the Glory Forever........................327
Ten - Amen..329

Conclusion - Pray and Convey His Blessing for Others........330

PREFACE

The Bible says God wants you to talk with him now and have a personal relationship with him. But how do you do that? Communication with God is called prayer. The word "pray" Jesus uses throughout the New Testament is the most simple and basic of all the words for prayer, and it means to "wish forward" or "desire onward." As Dr. Tony Evans, a Christian pastor, speaker, author, and a widely-syndicated U.S. radio and television broadcaster, stated, "Prayer is the vehicle that connects the natural with the supernatural".

God wants to hear the desires of your heart now. And like communicating and giving fully undivided attention with your spouse, you can instantly strengthen your relationship with Christ by conversing often with him through prayer.

Normally we pray only when we need God's help with a particular issue. Surveys show more than 90% of America pray daily. For example, you may call out to him to help you when a spouse has a surgery or a family member loses a job. While requests are surely heard, his deepest desire is to continuously increase communion with you through prayer.

In his book, *Let's Talk,* Bill Crowder, Associate Bible Teacher and Director of Ministry Content for RBC Ministries, assures us, "Prayer is not something we say to God; it is something we do together *with* our God! Bill Crowder, who is also a contributor to *Our Daily Bread,* says "The Godhead joins us in our prayers and responds to our prayers:

- Because the Father, in compassion, sees and hears,
- Because the Son is constantly interceding for us at the Father's side, and,
- Because the Holy Spirit is interpreting our prayers in order to bring our hearts in line with God's good purposes for us."

The LORD's Prayer, one of the best loved and most spoken prayers on the planet, is important to you, as a Christian, because it is what Jesus gave to his disciples as a startling form of prayer when they asked him to teach them HOW to pray – about God and your needs.

As you set aside a specific time to pray today, the LORD's Prayer will inspire you to quickly and easily discover and increase its pattern of prayer. Thus, you may first pray: "LORD, I ask for your help and your divine power to assist me in faithfully and consistently teaching me how to pray with more focus over the next 10 days and every day."

INTRODUCTION

Elevate Your Prayer Level from Religion to Relationship

Millions of people, ranging from devout believers to worldly folk pray each day. Christians pray The LORD's Prayer 95% of the time. Do you know what you're praying? Do you understand The LORD's Prayer? For many when it's recited or memorized, they rehearse only words, traditions or a routine. For this reason, prayer suddenly becomes religion versus relationship. Similarly, some people recite the pledge of allegiance, but to a person in the military, the pledge represents a way of life and promotes a sign of honor and respect. Likewise, parents may teach kids to recount The LORD's Prayer like echoing the alphabets. They're so happy when their children learn The LORD's Prayer. And shameful, too often, we keep our children at the "LORD teach us to pray" level. And we never teach them relationship improvement with God, because we were never taught.

This devotional's simple purpose is to instantly offer you the proper method and new posture how to pray and discover insight on the remarkable words Jesus tells us in Matthew 6:9-13 (KJV). In Matthew 6, when the disciples asked Jesus to teach them how to pray, they instantly repeated what he said. Jesus provided them a revolutionary template on how to pray to help keep their prayer in focus – a no-brainer. It gives you a great outline for making contact with God.

It's encouraging to know God hears you regardless of the language, length or logic of your prayers. Many of us can't pray for 5 minutes nor amazingly 1 hour because our prayer gets boring and repetitive.

Roman 8:26 tells us, "We do not know what to pray for as we ought." And the same passage adds "the Spirit himself intercedes for us with groanings too deep for words." We lack focus and start wondering and thinking about everything else. Like a laser beam cutting through steel, you can also focus your prayer – from recite to ripe; its impact can suddenly cut down every stronghold in your life, or cut-up the enemy's plan. A sight for sore eyes, many folk fall asleep, increase attention deficit disorder, and forget what it is they prayed.

Abide with me to focus your prayer now, you may also compare the ACTS method as a miracle prayer strategy:

- Adoration (adoring God for who he is),
- Confession (being or getting right with him)
- Thanksgiving (taking time to show your thankfulness for what he has done for you)
- Supplication (presenting your requests to the LORD).

Well, enough of your authentic prayer being a mess – it's not a show, act or pretense; it's time to instantly organize it and talk with your heavenly Father about what's on your mind now. What if you and I were having a conversation and you continued to change subjects, nod, forget your thoughts or fall asleep. Would we have a productive talk? If our chat is disrupted and you asked for something, the challenge is to stay focused to receive your request. Accordingly, you may not get what you asked for.

Also, when Jesus said the Spirit already knows what you need to pray, it does not give you a way out of not having to pray -- not the case at all. It means God already amazingly knows your thoughts, but it doesn't relieve you from praying. For example, a parent of a child will sometimes know what their son or daughter needs. And they will get the child to ask nicely for it first with no strings attached. So by asking him for things in prayer, it teaches us to respect him and to see him as our heavenly Father.

Prayer is for you and not for God. He is fine and he has everything you need; but you need to understand he wants to work through you and others to suddenly give you your exclusive desires and needs. Therefore, prayer helps you keeps the things and acts of God a priority. He will immediately make your things a priority once you make the things of his a priority. Matthew 6:33, NKJV says, "*But seek first the kingdom of God and his righteousness, and all these things shall be added to you.*" Prayer is one of the ways you can communicate with him. Anytime spent with God our Father is important. Trust!

Unfortunately many people are uncomfortable or intimidated with prayer. Thus, use the LORD's Prayer, a powerful "model prayer," as a guaranteed example to all of a sudden improve your prayer. This is the proven template Jesus used when the disciples asked him how to pray -- not what to pray -- in Matthew 6: 9-13. Therefore, it's not a recital. So, if the disciples needed to ask Jesus how to pray, you shouldn't be embarrassed or afraid to admit you do not know how either. The problem is we never learned how to pray.

The bonus goal here is not to become an excellent prayer warrior by the world's or church's standard. More than anything God desires a sincere heart. So whenever you come to the Father, he will look at your heart and judge the sincerity in which you come. Never ever be afraid to come to him in prayer; he knows all and there aren't any secrets.

Satan wants you to be afraid, be very afraid and fear coming to God in prayer. His basic methods are guilt and inferiority, shame and doubt -- to make you feel he is not interested in anything you have to say. Ultimately, he also wants you to believe God does not exist and therefore ironclad prayer is not needed -- a lie from the pits of hell. Satan will do anything to keep you from having a strong relationship with God. Be enthralled always and remember God loves you and desires an intimate relationship with you. Master, teach us to pray:

Our Father
Who Art in Heaven
Hallow Be Thy Name
Thy Kingdom Come
Thy Will Be Done on Earth As it is in Heaven
Give Us This Day Our Daily Bread
Forgive us for our Debts, as we also have forgiven our Debtor
And Lead Us Not into Temptation but Deliver Us from Evil
For Thine is the Kingdom, the Power and the Glory For ever
Amen

No beating around the bush, *LORD Teach Me How to Pray* motivates you to see your prayer time as special, life-changing and memorable. It'll strengthen your faith and spiritually catapult you today. For God is a Spirit and we must worship him in spirit and truth now.

PART I

Glorifying God

CHAPTER 1

Our Father

This is how you should pray. Who are you praying to? Notice Jesus told the disciples to start with "Our Father." You're not praying to the porcelain altar. And you can make contact with him by saying, "Hi God. It's me" and then pray your heart and reveal yourself.

When you think of the word *father*, what word and feelings come to mind? Merriam-Webster's definition of 'father'; is: "a male parent, a man who is thought of as being like a father, a person who was in someone's family in past times." For all intents and purposes, your definition may be different. It may depend on whether you had a father or not or what kind of father he was.

If your father is/was loving, some of the words you may use: loving, warm, compassionate, safe, secure, trustworthy, acceptance, firm. If you've never had a father in your life, your feelings could be unworthiness, abandonment, emptiness, insecurity, poor self-esteem or a list of other negative emotions. If your father is/was a strict disciplinarian, there are other feelings such as harsh, pain, fear, rejection, unloving etc.

As a result, your earthly father could affect how you see your heavenly Father. No questions asked, your heavenly Father loves you. He wants you to reverence rather than fear him. Do you see reverence as respect? For instance, there are some things you will not do in your parent's home, out of respect. As an adult, folk usually don't fear their parents; they respect them. And it's remarkably the same with God. He wants you to respect who he is in your life. He's amazingly more than another person in your life. As good as gold, he is your all in all. Everything about your life starts and ends with him.

Accordingly, the key to having an effective prayer life and suddenly knowing how to pray is connected to how well you understand who you're praying to. You think this is simple, I'm praying to God our Father. Ah, but do you understand who God our Father is?

Let's go back to the drawing board like in elementary school -- you know a sentence like: "God is ___." The sentence becomes challenging because he is so much more; it's impossible to start a limited sentence and do justice to God. For this reason, is your mindset secure in understanding what and who you're calling upon at the beginning of your prayer when you say 'Our Father? Use of the word "our" instead of "my" shows unselfish prayer.

Thus, you're also reminded you're a part of his family. Others are your brothers and sisters in Christ as well as the world, because he is their Father too. You can bet your bottom dollar, he wants to be a part of everyone's life. Beyond belief, he is not a dead-beat dad or a father not wanting to have a special, meaningful relationship with his children. And you treat all others like family members. Additionally, the word 'Father' teaches you should pray to him [the Father].

First, let's cover God's omnipotence (his power, which means ALL power). In essence, all power belongs to him. He startlingly created the world. The first chapter of Genesis tells of its amazing happening. He suddenly spoke the world into being. The Book of Psalm tells us to look around and marvel at his new creations (Psalm 8). Become an insider and take a minute and look at the stars, he did it. Look around and see the sun and the moon. He did it.

Imagine how large and deep the oceans are -- God's miracle doing. Come along and think on how he remarkably separated the darkness to make day and night – sensational! Don't forget all the living things too – introducing the plants and animals. Most important don't forget the most important thing of all, man. He quickly and easily created man; he created you (Psalm 139:13-18).

Be one of the few and get into your head, soul and heart his ironclad power. I'm sure there are many, many more things can attest to his great power. Yes sir! This is who you're praying to. Extraordinarily, he created the world in 6 days; but truly it'll blow your mind he could have done it in 1 day. Why? Be the first to hear he did it to teach us about order. As you look at Genesis, each day and things created in each day builds on each other. Therefore, it's vital we make our prayer life orderly.

Second, let's move to God's omniscience or total knowledge. Psalm 139: 1-6 tells us how he is all knowing. Jeremiah 1:4-5 also gives us insight on how well he knows us. Sometimes things (e.g., sins) in our past make us hesitant to go to him because we feel unworthy, shame and guilt. Let me set your mind at ease; we are all unworthy. He knows this. Jesus died for us knowing we were unworthy.

So, let's go to God the way Hebrews 4:16 tells us -- boldly (even though we have sinned) to the throne of grace to receive mercy and find grace to help you in your time of need. He knows everything, there are no secrets or surprises. It's all good you have access to the Father. For instance, if you wanted something done in the city and had a difficult time getting it done, it may frustrate you. Yet, if you have a relationship with the city mayor, you have members only access to the mayor. A golden key can open any door.

As a result of you having quick access to the mayor, coupled with a special relationship, it is more than likely you can suddenly bode well. You'll get your request done before everybody else. Access is the key. Too often, we don't exercise our access to the Father as often as we should. To have access to the Father, means no limits, no boundaries. Access him daily. The Bible tells us pray morning, noon, and night. Hurry and use your access card today and visit the throne of grace.

Next, God is omnipresent. By and large, he is everywhere; the camera cannot lie. Psalm 139:7-12 asks where can we go to get away from his presence? You cannot go anywhere to get away from him. He tells the Israelites in Deuteronomy 4:31, he would not forsake them. He also will not forsake (i.e., desert or abandon) you.

You're an insider and first to get an idea about who God, our Father, is. He is love. Imagine love from your idea of a perfect earthly father. Now magnify your vision of love a million times – your heavenly Father's love. A love so perfect you could never achieve it from anyone else. The parable of the Lost Son (Luke 15:11-32) also instantly shows us the kind of loving father he is. Like a loving father, he listens to your prayers and always gives his best. Sometimes, this result may not always be exactly what you want -- sometimes a loving parent even has to use the word "No" or "Not Now!"

When you have a child, many parents' love is so strong, they will die for their child – a parent's love for their children. They'll do anything in the world for their child. As a parent, could you carbon-copy and do as God did? Give them up for someone else, someone so undeserving, someone so ungrateful, someone who can be so mean-spirited and hateful and most of all someone so unloving? He sacrificed for us.

Jesus is his only son. Think about it, his only child. He gave him up. There was a time when Jesus was on the cross, God had to turn away from him. The time on the cross when Jesus took on our lifetime sins, he had to turn away since he could not be a part of sin. He was seen and heard. When this separation occurred, Jesus cried out, "My God, My God, why have you forsaken me?" Imagine the pain he must have felt to be separated from his only child, even if it was only for a moment. Can you close your eyes and think of the pain of knowing your child is in so much pain, and calling out to you without answer? Could you do the same thing?

How amazing it is someone loves something so much they will pay full price (give their life) for damaged goods. He immediately paid cash on the nail for us. We are all damaged goods. Yet, Christ died for us. Would you pay full price for a damaged item at the store? Most likely, you wouldn't purchase the item or you'd ask for a discounted price. See, no matter how you see yourself, God sees you as his child. As a parent, no matter what terrible thing your children do, you still love them. You see a glimmer of hope in them. You can't hold a candle to he also sees us this way.

God did this because he loved us so much. He knew exactly the type of people we were and still are. He still loves you in spite of your ways. In Jeremiah 31:3, he tells us, "I have loved you with an everlasting love. I have drawn you with loving-kindness." His love is so perfect and unconditional; no one else comes close to giving us amazing love!

Don't have a clue and forgot who you were. But remember, you were adopted (i.e. (engrafted) by the Father. God chose us; he chose you. Before him, you were an orphan and fatherless. What a privilege our Father adopted us despite our shortcomings, issues, and handicaps.

Regardless of how bad the relationship or not having an earthly father, when praying "Father," you're blessed to have a father loving you more than you love yourself. God is such a good Father; you can call a spade a spade no father can come close. Also, now you've been adopted, you have the right to all of the inheritance, riches and glory Christ have. Like he obtained his glory by being obedient, you too must remember it's the obedient and trusting child instead of the rebellious and faithless child receiving the blessing. This is the Father you are to pray to. A reminder, he is also our provider and protector.

Let's bring it back to your earthy father. How do you feel when you disappoint him? Most folk don't feel good about it, right? Well, when you say "Our Father," think of all the things you've done today to please him. And now focus on the things you've done to not please him today. Daddy's girl or daddy's favorite son? Did daddy smile and say well done son or daughter—"My girl, you can do it." Or did daddy say, "Don't do it, you know better. I taught you better?" Is God always pleased with your relationships? Daddy-being omniscience knows everything.

So, when you pray, focus on God as your Father. Meditate on your charmed life relationship and set the atmosphere of being open and honest with your father. Ask yourself, what can you do to be a better child as well as obedient to the Father? Think on areas in your life in complete shambles and where you're not living to the standards of your Father. Pray about those things. Knowing him as your Father means you have access to him and he personally will take care of you. The first part of prayer is the establishing the right relationship with the Father. Remember, all he wants is you as a chip off the old block is to reverence him.

CHAPTER 2

Who Art in Heaven

You should not think of God being in a faraway place because God is everywhere. He is right there. Acts 17:27-28 reminds us "... he is not far from each one of us. For in him we live and move and have our being ..." This petition of the prayer reminds you to acknowledge his sovereignty over the prayer; it also distinguishes the one, true God in heaven from all the false ones worshiped by man on earth. Heaven, the Father's house, is the true homeland.

Heaven is a real place. The Bible speaks of heaven's existence—and access to heaven through faith in Jesus Christ—but there are no petitions giving us a MapQuest-style location. *Heaven is where God is.* He is always near you when you call on him (James 4:8), and you're encouraged to "draw near" to him (Hebrews 10:1, 22).

The Bible says God in heaven is always near to his children on earth. Our Father who is in heaven wants us to focus on heavenly things. During prayer and meditation time, focus on heaven. Avoid focusing your minds on earth and what you have to get done. Focus on heaven. Heaven is where you want to go; heaven is a place of peace, joy, happiness, love and all glory. During prayer, ask yourself did you let heaven down today? Did you glorify heaven today? Did you fly heaven's banner today by telling others about heaven?

See, the enemy does not want you to talk about heaven. Hell or high water, he wants to keep you down in the dumps. He desires you keep quiet so the world can think there is no heaven, nor hell. As a result, you may feel your heavenly Father isn't loving. During this prayer time, give the Devil his due and focus on things you can do to make heaven proud. As you think about heaven, are there loved ones, neighbors or co-workers you are not sure whether they are going to heaven if they died? Pray for them, but also pray God uses you in a way to help them in receiving Christ.

Let's commit ourselves to magnifying heaven today. Oftentimes, folk don't want to talk about heaven because it infers one has to die or have one foot in the grave. But the Bible tells us to *"set your mind on the things above, not on the things are on the earth."* (Colossians 3:2 NASV). So, during prayer, to keep your prayer orderly before the King, set your minds on heaven --permanent things and not temporary things.

Many people come in on a wing and a prayer and focus too much on things not lasting. As a follower, you're renting time here on earth; it's not your permanent place. Therefore, as renters, shun getting comfortable and realize you're only here a short-time. People lives are going down the tubes and folk are dropping like flies. 2 Corinthians 4:18, NKJV says *"while we do not look at the things which are seen, but at the things which are not seen. For the things which are seen are temporary, but the things which are not seen are eternal."*

CHAPTER 3

Hallow Be Thy Name

'Hallowed' means 'holy'. Keeping God's name holy means you should honor and respect and admire who he is and what he has done. "Hallowed be your name" is telling you to worship God and to praise him for who he is. Eat, drink and be merry; you should pray with worship to him because he is so worthy of it. So, as a review, when you pray: (1) focus on the father (2) focus on heaven and (3) focus on hallowing his name.

Israel reverenced God's name so much they would not even say his name. During prayer, now we've created a heavenly atmosphere, it's also time to worship him like the heavenly angels and saints. Face the music and see prayer is more than communication. Prayer is not an event, prayer is an experience. Anytime, you can experience him and his presence, it's time to bow down and worship him.

"Father, I praise you and I worship you. You are holy. I give you honor. I give you all the glory." Use your own words. God recognizes a sincere heart. He does not require pretty words, eloquent phrases, fancy language, or wordy, meaningless rituals. And you do not have to be so deep or sophisticated or use a wide vocabulary. Telling him what's in your heart with your own words counts a great deal to him. Keep it simple. You do not need to impress him.

Even though Israel had the glory of God overseeing them; they didn't act like they had his glory. Your praise everyday let's him know how much you love him and is satisfied with him as your Father. This petition 'Hallow be your name' serves as a reminder to praise and worship him daily. However, many saints are excellent in praise and worship, but their lives don't glorify or adore the Father. Therefore, whatever you do, fight the good fight and you do it in his name. Philippians tells us whatever you do, word of deed, do it in his name.

Publicly, by your walk (which is a Marahthon) and not a Sunday stroll, glorify the Father. If not, repent for the things not glorifying him or repent for the things you could've done better to glorify him —hallowed be his name. How wonderful and excellence is his name. Unfortunately for this world, the only Jesus unbelievers see is often in you.

God is no flash in the pan; our Father and his name is holy and hallowed. God has many names, each describing a different aspect of his multi-faceted character. His name isn't mud and here are some of the better-known names of God in the Bible:

EL, ELOAH: God "mighty, strong, prominent" (Genesis 7:1; Isaiah 9:6) – *El* appears to mean "power," as in "I have the power to harm you" (Genesis 31:29). *El* is associated with other qualities, such as integrity (Numbers 23:19), jealousy (Deuteronomy 5:9), and compassion (Nehemiah 9:31), but the root idea of might remains.

ELOHIM: God "Creator, Mighty and Strong" (Genesis 17:7; Jeremiah 31:33) – the plural form of *Eloah*, which accommodates the doctrine of the Trinity. From the Bible's first sentence, the matchless nature of his power is evident as God (Elohim) speaks the world into existence (Genesis 1:1).

EL SHADDAI: "God Almighty," "The Mighty One of Jacob" (Genesis 49:24; Psalm 132:2, 5) – speaks to his ultimate power over all.

ADONAI: "Lord" (Genesis 15:2; Judges 6:15) – used in place of YHWH, which was thought by the Jews to be too sacred to be uttered by sinful men. In the Old Testament, YHWH is more often used in his dealings with his people, while *Adonai* is used more when he deals with the Gentiles.

YHWH, YAHWEH or JEHOVAH: "LORD" (Deuteronomy 6:4; Daniel 9:14) – strictly speaking, the only proper name for God. Translated in English Bibles "LORD" (all capitals) to distinguish it from *Adonai*, "LORD." The revelation of the name is first given to Moses "I Am who I Am" (Exodus 3:14). This name specifies an immediacy, a presence. Yahweh is present, accessible, near to those who call on Him for deliverance (Psalm 107:13), forgiveness (Psalm 25:11) and guidance (Psalm 31:3).

YAHWEH-JIREH: "The LORD Will Provide" (Genesis 22:14) – the name memorialized by Abraham when God provided the ram to be sacrificed in place of Isaac.

YAHWEH-RAPHA: "The LORD Who Heals" (Exodus 15:26) – "I am Jehovah who heals you" both in body and soul. In body, by preserving from and curing diseases, and in soul, by pardoning iniquities.

YAHWEH-NISSI: "The LORD Our Banner" (Exodus 17:15), where *banner* is understood to be a rallying place. This name commemorates the desert victory over the Amalekites in Exodus 17.

YAHWEH-M'KADDESH: "The LORD Who Sanctifies, Makes Holy" (Leviticus 20:8; Ezekiel 37:28) – God makes it clear he alone, not the law, can cleanse his people and make them holy.

YAHWEH-SHALOM: "The LORD Our Peace" (Judges 6:24) – the name given by Gideon to the altar he built after the Angel of the LORD assured him he would not die as he thought he would after seeing him.

YAHWEH-ELOHIM: "LORD God" (Genesis 2:4; Psalm 59:5) – a combination of God's unique name YHWH and the generic "LORD," signifying he is the LORD of LORDs.

YAHWEH-TSIDKENU: "The LORD Our Righteousness" (Jeremiah 33:16) – It is God alone who provides righteousness to man, ultimately in the person of his Son, Jesus Christ, who became sin for us "we might become the Righteousness of God in him" (2 Corinthians 5:21).

YAHWEH-ROHI: "The LORD Our Shepherd" (Psalm 23:1) – After David pondered his relationship as a shepherd to his sheep, he realized God had the exact relationship with him, and so he declares, "Yahweh-Rohi is my Shepherd. I shall not want" (Psalm 23:1).

YAHWEH-SHAMMAH: "The LORD Is There" (Ezekiel 48:35) – The name ascribed to Jerusalem and the Temple there, indicating the once-departed glory of the LORD (Ezekiel 8—11) had returned (Ezekiel 44:1-4).

YAHWEH-SABAOTH: "The LORD of Hosts" (Isaiah 1:24; Psalm 46:7) – *Hosts* means "hordes," both of angels and of men. He is LORD of the host of heaven and of the inhabitants of the earth, of Jews and Gentiles, of rich and poor, master and slave. Expressive of the majesty, power, and authority of God, he is able to accomplish what he determines to do.

EL ELYON: "Most High" (Deuteronomy 26:19) – derived from the Hebrew root for "go up" or "ascend," the implication is which is the highest. *El Elyon* denotes exaltation and speaks of absolute right to LORDship.

EL ROI: "God of Seeing" (Genesis 16:13) – the name ascribed to God by Hagar, alone and desperate in the wilderness after being driven out by Sarah (Genesis 16:1-14). She also realized *El Roi* saw her in her distress and testified he is a God who lives and sees all.

EL-OLAM: "Everlasting God" (Psalm 90:1-3) – God's nature is without beginning or end, free from all constraints of time, and he contains within himself the cause of time itself. "From everlasting to everlasting, you are God."

EL-GIBHOR: "Mighty God" (Isaiah 9:6) – the name describing the Messiah, Christ Jesus, in this forewarned is forearmed portion of Isaiah. As a powerful and mighty warrior, the Messiah, the Mighty God, will accomplish the destruction of his enemies and rule with a rod of iron (Revelation 19:15).

As you can see, it's a foregone conclusion our Father has many names. For good measure, getting to know him personally tells you what name to use. An example, a guy was the head coach on his son's softball team. His son of flesh and blood normally calls him dad; he immediately remembers to call him "coach." Even though the son was right about his dad, in the capacity at the softball game, he is operating as a coach first, dad second. And the coach didn't fly off the handle. His son knew the difference because he knew his dad well. However, often times you may use a general term and say "God" instead of being more personal and referring to the name you want to revere The Father. If you're praying for the Father to provide something for you, flat out say "Jehovah Jireh." If praying for The Father to heal you, "Jehovah Rapha" fits to a tee. To many, this is a small thing, but you can call upon his name in capacity he's operating in.

CHAPTER 4

Thy Kingdom Come

God is King so he has a kingdom. His kingdom is the sign of what Jesus did on the cross and why he did it. Jesus died so we no longer bind ourselves by sin – happy as a lark. Then, justice and peace will reign in the world. Sin could be wiped out – hasta la vista, baby! We are to pray his kingdom will come -- Jesus will come back and make it so. The kingdom will come in glory when Christ hands it over to his Father. You can also pray for the growth of his kingdom in your life today.

God is a fair, loving king. By saying "thy kingdom come," you are saying "Be my king." So, you're asking hard and fast for help to act, talk, and think the way God wants you to. You're petitioning to guide you today in showing you how you can uplift his kingdom. You know he wants the earth to be as his kingdom. What can you do today to bring glory to his kingdom? Ask to be used as his witness.

Since you realize our Father is a King, you must be a prince or princess. Therefore, meditate on being an ambassador for Christ, representing your kingdom nation -- heaven. (2 Corinthians 5:20 NKJV). Let's talk about being a hoity-toity ambassador. He calls you to be an ambassador. Like a United States Ambassador, it's high time you must be a good citizen first.

The President of the U.S. will not pick a person having a history of illegal incidents to be an Ambassador. Most time, before one can be a high and mighty ambassador, they must go through the scrutiny of personal background checks or extreme vetting to ensure they're competent and credible to represent the U.S. Our King doesn't hold your past against you -- Thank God! However, because he doesn't hold your past against you, you don't have a license to sin or live below his standards. Because of his grace, you can show your appreciation of it by not abusing it.

Even though, God calls you as a heavenly ambassador, are you a good citizen of heaven? If good citizenship is needed to represent the U.S., it's horse sense you can envision your Christian goal as a good citizen representing heaven. During this time of meditation about the kingdom, meditate on your hot off the press responsibilities as an ambassador. If the world saw you, can they tell you are from another nation, or do you act like the world?

Often, like identity theft, you can tell someone is from another country by the way they talk, dress or behave. When you open your mouth, do you talk like you are from heaven? When you dress, do you dress like you are from heaven or have you blended into this world. Can anyone tell you are not from this world? If you have short-comings in this area, meditate on areas you need to improve.

Beware the Ides of March, many unsaved folk will not come to know Jesus because they have been poor examples and ambassadors of what Christianity is all about. Have you caused anyone to stumble because your lack of talk about heaven or your behavior was not Christ-like?

CHAPTER 5

Thy Will Be Done

For all intents and purposes, you are praying for the advancement of God's kingdom and remembering your role to carry out in this petition of the LORD's Prayer. Asking for his kingdom and for his will to be done is surrendering to him. His rule and his plans are the best things for your life – his will, his way, your faith. It's not rocket science, you are to pray for his plan in your life and the world, not your own plan. If the shoe fits, pray for his will to be done versus your own. In heaven everyone submits to him. There is no selfishness, no cruelty, no lies – but plenty of love, peace and happiness.

You are to pray for what God wants instead of what you want. Did you know he has a specific will for your life? Part of connecting with him is saying, "God, what is your will for me today? I want to your will." His will is forgetting about your wants, desires and needs – only concentrating on what will please our Father. And he wants earth to be like or as close to heaven as possible. All the good things in heaven can be here on the ends of the earth according to his will. We've all read or heard about what a wonderful place heaven is. No more dying, no sicknesses or diseases, no sin or conflict -- enjoying being with and praising our heavenly Father.

Pray his will: "Father I want what you want. Because you are God, what I want doesn't matter if it's not your will." Look at Psalm 143:10. David asks God to teach him to do God's will. Jesus prayed in the Garden of Gethsemane his will be done, not Jesus.

Do you know God's will for your life? This is an opportunity for you to get to ask him to show you his will for your life. However, many of us have asked him and haven't discovered our will. Time and again, we are looking for some great work to do to fully understand our will. Whatever you love doing is his will for your life. So, whatever it is, you must seek him to align your will in sync with his plan for your life. He created all of us and he made all of us different. Therefore, he has a specific calling designed for all of us. It matches our genetic makeup.

But too often, since you don't know what your will is, you may get involved in a lot of things the Father didn't tell you to get involved in. Therefore, pray and ask him his will for you. If you know his will for your life, pray he helps you to stay in his will. Also, when it seems he is taking you on a journey or another direction, pray he reveal his will if the cap fits. Pray you also remain patient and disciplined while he takes you to the next station of life on your journey.

It is vital you become unselfish and allow God to do his will in your life and assist him in doing it on earth. Strive not only as a fan of the kingdom, but also as a true participant. Stay thankful he is God, for he knows the plans of your life. *"For I know the thoughts I think toward you, says the LORD, thoughts of peace and not of evil, to give you a future and a hope."* Jeremiah 29:18 (NKJV)

PART II

Sustaining Your Needs

CHAPTER 6

Give Us Today Our Daily Bread

So prayer is not only for God's heavenly glory, but prayer is provided for our earthly good. He is not only interested in your spiritual life, he is interested in your physical and material life as well. Now, it may not seem all spiritual to ask him for "bread," but you must keep in mind his meaning here addresses not physical bread, but also "bread" of the spiritual sort.

When you pray, "Give us this day our daily bread," you are expressing your dependence on God and conveying your gratitude for his gracious provision in your life. "Daily bread" symbolizes the bread of life and everything you need for your life, for the day. It is not demanding he give you food but reminds you not to take for granted everything you have. You agree he is the one who gives life and sustains you each day. Your cup runneth over – you'll have more than enough for your needs.

Man does not live by bread alone; we depend on God for daily physical and spiritual food. Praying for daily bread reminds you to live one day at a time. Lamentations tells us his mercies are new every morning. Matthew 6:34 tells us we are not to worry about tomorrow; each day has enough trouble of its own. You ask him to give you today your daily bread. You are to pray for one day at a time.

Remember the song, "'One day at a time Sweet Jesus." Father give us today our daily bread. Father today I need your provision, I need your grace. I need your protection. This day, I need you. If you pray every day, you are telling God you need him always -- his love, guidance, and forgiveness.

Father, your word says you have never seen the righteous forsaken or its seed begging bread (Psalm 37:25 NKJV). Righteousness is not a state of being dressed a certain way, talking a certain way, or being so holy; you can't touch anything. Abraham was counted righteousness by God because of his faithfulness. Abraham believed him. Abraham wasn't perfect. As you recall in Genesis, he lied to King Pharaoh about the status of his wife, Sarah. Noah was also counted righteousness because he believed him.

Please don't take God's provision for granted. He has given us jobs; yet we complain. He has given us good health; yet we complain. He has given us a home; yet we complain. He has given us clothes; yet we complain. Truly, no matter how hard you work, how much you earn, and how cleverly you invest, save and buy in market forces, all you have is a gift from his hand. Every good thing and many happy returns come from him.

What is your greatest need today? Bring it to God in prayer. The Book of Psalm tells us the LORD is my shepherd I should not want — translated means I should not be in want of anything. He will provide. Psalm 100 tells us we are the sheep of his pasture. Therefore, as the Shepherd, he is obligated to see his "trusting and faithful" sheep are fed, sheltered and protected.

CHAPTER 7

Forgive Us Our Debts, As We Also Have Forgiven Our Debtors

We need to ask God to forgive us of our sins -- all the wrong things we have done, including our actions, our thoughts and what we have said. Let's not mince words. You have to be sincere in saying my bad or sorry to him and you must forgive others too. You should not keep something like being hurt by someone else a secret. Instead tell him and after you talk about it, he will help you forgive those who hurt you.

Jesus teaches if you don't forgive others, God will not forgive you. What are our debts? We know a debt is something owed another. What do we owe the Father? Simply, we owe him everything. What are our debts? In this case our debts are the multitude of sins we commit. We all commit sins and Jesus died such a horrific death on the cross because of our sins.

Matthew 6:14-15, NKJV states *If you forgive men their trespasses, your heavenly Father will also forgive you: But if ye forgive not men their trespasses, neither will your Father forgive your trespasses.* Ask Jesus to forgive you for your sins as he forgive others who sin against you. You don't have a right to hold forgiveness from others. In some cases it is difficult to forgive; some people have done horrible things to us.

This is where Jesus comes in to help us. Ask him to help you to forgive. Most of all unforgiveness keeps you from having a full relationship with Jesus. It causes bitterness in you. It can make you physically ill. It can cause you to have anger in your heart and interfere in your relationship with others. All of those things can keep you from fully enjoying your life.

When you forgive others, you are not telling them the sin committed against you is okay. Jesus is not telling us our sin is okay. What he is telling you is he will not hold your sin against you and you should nip in the bud and not hold sin against each other.

In Jeremiah 31:34 NIV, Jesus told the Israelites he would not remember their sins: "For *I will forgive their wickedness and will remember their sins no more.*" He will do the same for you with his forgiveness if you ask.

Also, Luke 23:32-34 NLT, shows: *Two others, both criminals, were led out to be executed with him. When they came to a place called The Skull, [e] they nailed him to the cross. And the criminals were also crucified—one on his right and one on his left. Jesus said, "Father, forgive them, for they don't know what they are doing."*

Additionally, Stephen asked Jesus to forgive the people who was stoning him to death (Acts 7:59-61, NLT): *And as they stoned him, Stephen prayed, "LORD Jesus, receive my spirit." And he fell to his knees, shouting, "LORD, don't charge them with this sin!"* And he died.

If Jesus and Stephen could forgive the people for killing them, the heart of the matter is you can forgive others for sinning against you. Surely if Jesus, while dying a horrific death, could find it in his heart to forgive the people killing him, you can forgive others for what they've done to you.

Reciting this scripture in The LORD's Prayer serves as a reminder for you to forgive those who have offended you. Do you forgive them? Think about those people you may not like. Do you forgive them? Are you praying for them?

It's critical you forgive them so the Father can forgive you. The fact of the matter is many of the people who you don't forgive don't even know you're holding a grudge. When you forgive, it feels like the thing holding you back has been released. Also, why meditating, don't forget to confess your sins before God (1 John 1:9). He is faithful and just to forgive you.

But as you ask God for forgiveness, focus on true repentance and not true repeat. Unless we truly repent, our motive for asking for forgiveness is because we are unhappy about sinning against the

Father, but keep asking for the "grace" card (get out of jail free-card) to remove our sins. Remember, your prayer time with him is about relationship and not religion. Religion says you recite and you don't have to mean it. Relationship says you are not reciting but speaking to him from a sincere heart.

CHAPTER 8

And Lead Us Not Into Temptation, But Deliver Us from Evil

This petition of the prayer asks God for protection so you will be able to stand against all the bad influences in the world and achieve victory over sin. Feelings of anger, fear or loneliness can make you want to break a rule or sense temptation. Pray and feed your faith so he can help you with your feelings. Breaking a rule hurts him and you. He still loves you. Pray he helps you know the difference between right and wrong.

You may be out of sorts or have a hard time with this petition. You may find it difficult why you would need to ask Jesus not to lead you into temptation. Jesus would never lead you into or tempt you to sin. It's against his nature.

Psalm 19:13, KJV declares, *"Keep back thy servant also from presumptuous sins; let them not have dominion over me: then shall I be upright, and I shall be innocent from the great transgression."* The NCV scripture puts it even simpler. It says *"Keep me from the sins of pride; don't let them rule me. Then I can be pure and innocent of the greatest of sins."* You're asking God to keep you away, guide you from, and protect you from sinning; deliver you from Satan's evil tricks and temptations.

To put this in context, you face a clear and present danger in your generation. Behind the scenes a battle is being fought for the hearts and lives of men, women and children across planet earth. Forces of evil and good are on the warpath waging an invisible war, between God himself and a created being known as Satan.

As a believer, you are in this battle and you're in it to the end. You are not a tourist on a vacation in this world if you're following Jesus. You are on the side of angels and a soldier on a mission for him. And the only way to win this war is to be on the ball, preparing and praying. Jesus taught us to pray in order to overcome the temptation of the enemy. When you pray, you are protecting your faith, your future and your family. In these times, you must remember you are fighting a spiritual battle; you can only win with the spiritual weapons he provides. He has promised deliverance for his praying children.

We are all tempted by so many things. The Bible tells us God will not let you be tempted beyond what you can bear. And when you are tempted, he will provide a way for you to escape or show you a way out. Some ways you're tempted include lying, cheating, fornication and adultery to name a few.

While praying, ask the Father to show you areas where your armor is weak. Was I tempted today? Father through your Spirit, show me where I was tempted. Did I find pleasure in a potential tempting situation? Remember, James 1:13, NKJV tells us, *"Let no one say when he is tempted, "I am tempted by God"; for God cannot be tempted by evil, nor does He Himself tempt anyone."*

Temptation is serious because if you succumb to it, in the end it will destroy you. Don't and put yourself in situations where you're tempted. Don't paddle your own canoe and trust your flesh, it will let you down, for the spirit is willing; but the flesh is weak. Ask God to show you -- spiritually search you – and reveal all your temptations, even the hidden ones you try to suppress or keep others from knowing. Satan cannot stop you from doing anything for his glory, but he can throw temptation into your life to trip you.

Temptation is a prelude to sin. If you subtly preview the trailer, eventually you will become the main attraction in your sin-filled action movie. If you don't want temptation to follow you, don't act as if you're interested. Satan couldn't stop Adam and Eve, but he used temptation to stop them from living a life of abundance. Is the same happening to you? Check yourself and find out where's your weak point. Is it the lust of the flesh? The lust of the eyes? Or the pride of life?

If you realize Satan is tempting you, you must strengthen yourself in these areas. Remember, temptation is a prelude to sin and evil. As a devil's advocate, don't do it—everything you've worked for you can lose it in a minute. All things comes to he who waits. In the end, to keep God's trust when you continually succumb to temptation:

- Think on the things you're tempted of?
- Did you come close to falling today?
- Did you willingly allow temptation to be around you today?
- Did you notice the escape/emergency exit door?

Sin promises to serve and please and in the end it comes to rule and destroy. Has one bite of temptation put you into a spiraling effect on the road to destruction? Is temptation now an addiction?

Finally "But delivers us from evil" means God gave you a way to escape or he'll snatch you out of a tempting and potential situation. His Spirit will not force you to take an escape or exit; it's up to you. Pray he will deliver you, for his spirit gives you victory over temptation. Sincerely ask yourself do you want him to deliver you or do you want him to forgive you? Do you see the things tempting you as evil or pleasure?

CHAPTER 9

For Thine is The Kingdom and The Power And The Glory Forever

God is the real King. If you want to be part of his kingdom, you must trust him to teach you to pray, to understand the Bible, and to help you love others. He is almighty and deserves glory. It's all about you Father -- your kingdom, your power and your glory forever, for all eternity. It's not about me. I exist because of you.

This petition of the prayer can remind you of your purpose in Life; it's not a pipe dream. You're prompted you exist for God's pleasure and not your own. It can ring a bell everything you go through, he has the power to overcome. When you truly believe you're walking in his will and purpose, you can have less concerns and more peace; you stress less and can experience happiness and joy in your life.

The words "thine is the kingdom" can continually remind you of God. You're encouraged to ask, "Father, show me areas in my life where I've put things ahead of you and your kingdom and don't give you glory." Did the words I say today give you glory? Did my actions give you glory? Did my thoughts give you glory? Does my new relationships give you glory? The roles you call me in as a saint give you glory? As your role as a wife, did I give you glory? As a husband, did I give you glory? As an employee on the job, did I give you glory? As a friend did I give you glory?'

Play it again Sam! This appeal also gives you the reassurance you'll see heaven and prompt you to think on heavenly things. Scripture says to "set your heart and mind on the things above." Hurricane Katrina gave us a daily reminder of what things are important. You can spend years storing up fine things on earth. However, you can lose it in a second, such as the hurricane victims did. Make your whole focus on where your position is in heaven.

Poetic justice is we're so rebellious if God has to give us a passing grade for heaven, it'll be a point-blank 'D.' Preposterous, it wouldn't be an 'F,' because everyone passes if you accept Jesus Christ. Preaching to the choir, it wouldn't be a 'C;' because Romans 12:1 reminds us it's our reasonable service we make our bodies a living sacrifice. Reasonable means it's average or ordinary; he is not asking you to do anything extraordinary or great ... be average—reasonable.

When Israel was in the wilderness, even though the glory of the LORD was with them (cloud by day and fire by night), they did not truly glorify God. They were pressed into service about pleasing their flesh and not about having an awesome relationship with almighty God. Even though you pray for his glory? Are you like Israel? Are you rebellious? Are you stubborn? Are you a complainer? Do you feel like sometimes you made a mistake by establishing this relationship with him? Are you fearful of where he wants to take you?

CHAPTER 10

Amen

The Hebrew word translated "amen" means "truly," "so be it" or "I don't know when or how, but I know Jesus will answer my prayer." In the Old Testament, "amen" is used by people answering to curses spoken by God on numerous evils (Deuteronomy 27:15-26).

In the New Testament, the apostles – John, Paul, and Peter -- utilized "amen" at the end of their letters. When Christians say "amen" at the end of prayers, we are following the model of the apostles, asking God to "please let it be as we have prayed." When you pray according to his will, you can be assured he will answer "so be it" and grant your petitions (John 14:13; 1 John 5:14).

"Amen" says you agree with what God wants to do. You assent with the Father's response to your prayers instead of a tall story. You're in agreement prayer will change you for the better. We should not live without prayer; we must pray ceaselessly. You say yes prayer draws you closer to the Father. Subscribe you are victorious. You are of the same mind; you are blessed and he will continue to be your provider, protector, guide, comforter, etc.

CONCLUSION

Pray and Convey His Blessings for Others

You can bet the farm peoples' number one poll response of what they want most from prayer now would be "answers." When you pray, you're seeking an immediate response from God. In agreement with my *LORD Teach Me How to Pray* co-authors, Rodney Perry and Diane Smith, we believe the most important lesson learned regarding prayer is it is far better to be an answer to prayer than to get an answer to prayer. Why? Because he wants to answer prayers through us, according to his miracle power at work within us.

When you pray for others you allow yourself to be a new channel of blessing. God has remarkably blessed you and through you, he can amazingly bless others. Luke 12:48, NLT reminds us, *"When someone has been given much, much will be required in return; and when someone has been entrusted with much, even more will be required."*

The Bible is filled with tested examples of God using willing servants to convey his powerful blessings to others now. Remember Moses? Out there in the desert, he was praying for the children of Israel as the Israelites were praying in Egypt. And God came to Moses in a burning bush and said, "I have heard their cry." He told Moses he was going to be used by him to answer the Israelites' prayers.

The Bible also names specific groups of people for whom you are to pray.

Public leadership. This includes the President and Congress, our national leaders, our state and local government leaders, police officers, teachers, and others in authority. Whether or not you agree with their policies and opinions, you are to pray they would suddenly come to saving faith in Jesus Christ.

Spiritual Leaders. The devil aims his biggest guns at God's leaders, and today, many are discouraged, hurting, and even falling into sin. His people need to pray for his leaders. Pray now for the pastors, missionaries, and Christian leaders in America and throughout the world.

Our Country. We need to cry out to God and pray for our country. And if you love this country you will pray for him to revive his Church. Pray he would renew families and communities. Pray for your fellow citizens and neighbors, and turn your prayers to action. Psalm 33:12, NKJV says, *"Blessed is the nation whose God is the LORD."* Join in prayer our nation will return to its roots of honoring God today.

The Lost. Are you praying for those in your life who do not know Jesus? Prayer is the ultimate means by which you help point others to faith in Christ. You and I know people who have yet to receive God's gift of grace, and the first step you can instantly take is to commit the matter to prayer. Only he, by his Spirit, can reach a neighbor, rescue a reckless child, and turn a strong-willed heart toward him.

While it is wonderful to pray, "LORD, help missionaries?" God's response may be, "Now I want you to go and share the Good News!" If you're praying, "LORD, save lost people," listen carefully because he may put your hot feet to your prayers and say, "You go and tell your friend about me." Are you willing to be a big answer to prayer?

As you pray 'The LORD's Prayer' today, open *LORD Teach Me How to Pray* and take time to soak in the proven meaning of each line. First, ask God to show you a specific way in which you can bless someone today. Keep the eyes of your heart open for opportunities he will place in your heart. Pray specifically for his complete will to be done on earth as it is in heaven.

Now, you've read this book, we pray you have increased your prayer life. Thus, you have put yourself on the road to spiritual prosperity which will manifest to material wealth and life success. Jesus continually prayed and we know the results. Every knee shall bow and every tongue shall confess he's LORD. All because he understands prayer and the effects of prayer. Matthew 6:9 was the essence of his ministry. As a final word, everything starts with prayer.

CONCLUSION

Welcome Home!

Last but not least, what do you think is one of the biggest fears for people who are away from God: When I do come home, what will he do? When I return to him, what will he say? We'll celebrate and throw our arms around you and say, "Welcome Home!" That's what he will do. That's what we believers will do --no lectures, no questions, just "Welcome Home!" It's time to quit running. Come home to a *New Day, New Life*! When away or home, *Live, Laugh, Love, Work, Pray.*

When you "come home," one becomes re-established in one's community after a stint in jail, prison, or any other correctional facility or halfway house situation (especially after a long period of detention). Similarly, "Welcome Home" is said to military men and women who have returned to the United States typically after serving abroad or being involved in a military conflict. This tradition started after disappointing returns so many troops received after the Vietnam War. Citizens tell returning troops "Welcome Home" and heartily shake their hand.

Like Bubba, you may also know someone who is severely directionally challenged -- totally, completely lost! I heard about this man named Bubba. He lived way out in the country. There was this stray dog that kept showing up at his house. His wife said, "Bubba, you have to put the dog in the truck and take him out to the woods and drop him off. That's where he lives."

Bubba drove him a mile down the road [and] dropped him off. When he came back home, the dog was walking up the driveway --practically beat him back. He did the same thing; it happened again. His wife said, "Bubba, you have to take him way out, drive him around in circles [and] get him all mixed up." Bubba drove him an hour away, crisscrossed country roads he never driven before [and] dropped the dog off. Two hours later, Bubba called his wife from the truck and said, "Did that dog make it back home?" She said, "Yeah, here he comes walking up." He said, "Do me a favor, [and] put him on the phone. I need directions."

Similarly when all hope of finding your destination is gone, you finally give up and call for directions -- like trying to find your way without a global positioning system. And when people ask for directions, folk normally tell them where they need to be and don't tell them how to get there (e.g., turn where the Shell Station used to be). We kind of do the same thing to people who have lost their way spiritually. Most of the time, they know where they need to be, they've just lost their way. What they need is someone to tell them "How – how to find their way back to God."

Lots of people tell you what you need to do, but not "how?" When you have completely messed up your life, how do you start over? What seemed like such a good idea obviously wasn't. You thought living without rules would be great. You thought you knew better. Doing things your way miserably failed. You have to make a decision – swallow your pride and go home. How can you ever be right and whole again? After everything you have done, how can you return to your heavenly Father? How do you find your way home?

Maybe you haven't yet hit rock bottom yet. Still, you are aware something is missing. You know where you need to be -- in right relationship with God. You know you need it, but how do you get there? Perhaps it starts with a breakthrough and you come to your senses. You realize where you are and where you want to be. You want to go home; you want to eat! Your condition is lousy and you don't like it. You don't desire this; you want to go home. Home is better. Home is better than running. You don't want to live like this anymore; you need help – you need God! You want to go home!

You realize you want to go home and decide, "I'm going to do it." You decide to go home. You make a decision based on your realization of the facts. Realizing you want to return to your heavenly Father is good, now decide to do it. Sadly, not everyone who wants to go home make this decision. Think of all the things we decide to do and never actually accomplish (e.g., lose weight, get out of debt, tithe, read the entire Bible, etc.). You get the picture. Lots of people make good decisions. The key is to act on those decisions. Get going. Do it -- take that step. Come home!

OK – you want to do it, you've decided to do it. Now, don't wait, don't hesitate, do it. Take the next step and go home. Every change starts with a desire ("I want to go home."). Your desire becomes a decision ("I'm going home."). Then, you turn your decision into action. You do it and act on your good decision. You go home – come back to God. For some of you this is walking in the door of church. For others, it is raising your hand or walking to an altar. For some, it's opening the Bible or praying a prayer. You've been gone too long. Make the decision and act on it – come home.

Real talk, you may be incredibly nervous. "What's going to happen? What will my family do? What if they're still angry with me? What if they won't even let me in the door? Then what? Where will I go? What will I do? How can family love me? How in the world will God accept me? How can he love me? How can I go back to church?" You might have some of the same fears – "How could he ever forgive me after what I have done?"

You knew you wanted go home. You decided to go home. You acted on your decision. Then, you took the next important step – you repented. Your broken heart became humble and submissive instead of arrogant and rebellious. Your heart changed. Repentance always produces a change of heart. The way home has to include repentance. This isn't always an easy step. There is a difference between being remorseful and being repentant.

Remorsefulness is sorry for the past, but doesn't want to change the future. You may be remorseful because you get caught. You don't want to be in trouble. Repentance is also sorry for the past, and you make a change in heart to ensure a different future. Repentance changes future behavior so one won't repeat past mistakes. Repentance is not only sorry, but also people don't intend to make the same mistake again. You're truly sorry and make a commitment to change. Repentance is in response to love.

Like the Prodigal Son in Luke 15, you are forgiven when you come home and repent. That's it. No conditions. No exceptions. When you come home, you are forgiven. The father's forgiveness of the prodigal cannot be anything other than God's forgiveness of sinners. He never gave up on you. He never will. Though the elder brother represents the Pharisees and scribes (e.g., judgmental and self-righteous) and another part of this story, come home. He is waiting for you. Similarly, the Israelites came home to Judah and Jerusalem after exile in Babylon. God watched out for them; He watches out for you. Look to Him and get back in the game. We're waiting for you to come home to feel welcomed and loved. And to *Live, Laugh, Love, Work, Pray*. Come home to a *New Day, New Life*.

ACKNOWLEDGMENTS

Many people assisted me in the preparation of this text, the fifth and final in *The Good Book Series – Live, Laugh, Work, Pray,* and *Love*. First and foremost, I thank almighty God! He enabled me with faithfulness, gifts, and favor. The pen is mightier than the sword and may all I put my hands to bring glory to the Kingdom.

I'm also grateful for the wise counsel and inspiring insights and expertise from ministers and pastors during their review of this devotional in manuscript form. Greater love hath no man than this, a man lay down his life [e.g., time] for his friends (John 15:13 KJV).

Additionally, I'm appreciative to those who prayed and supported me in writing this book. It's my hope these multiplied blessings touch your heart. LORD God Almighty, make your face shine upon me. Make it possible the greatest number of new and growing believers draw nearer to you!

ABOUT THE AUTHOR

MARK C. OVERTON is a retired Chief Master Sergeant from the US Air Force. He first wrote the *Airmen Series*.

By faith, Mark turned to the Christian Life Devotional category, penning *The Good Book Series: Chapter and Verse: Daily Devotions for Your Work Week*; *LORD Teach Me How to Pray*; *I Like to Start with Something Funny*; *You Only Live Once*; and *What Love Really Means*.

From leading laymen ministries – usher, television, media, information technology and a men's group – to continually reading the Bible helped him to build and spread his faith.

Mark actively practices his faith by attending the First Assembly of God in North Little Rock, Arkansas. He's currently enrolled in the Master of Biblical and Theological degree program with the Dallas Theological Seminary and also partnered with Joel Osteen Ministries as a *Champion of Hope*.

MORE THAN A ONE-HIT WONDER: OTHER BOOKS BY MARK C. OVERTON

The Good Book Series

What Love Really Means

You Only Live Once

I Like To Start With Something Funny

LORD Teach Me How to Pray

Chapter and Verse

Airmen Series

Career Progression Guide for Airmen: The Basics

Career Progression Guide for Airmen

LAST BUT NOT LEAST INSIGHT ...

If you enjoyed this book or found it useful, I'd be grateful if you'd post a short review on Amazon or Goodreads.com. Share God's Word! Your support does make a difference and I read all the reviews personally so I can get your feedback and pen books for you even better.

https://www.amazon.com/author/markoverton

https://www.goodreads.com/author/show/7647613.Mark_C_Overton

You can also request an Authorgraph at: https://www.authorgraph.com/authors/goodnewsbookset

Draw nearer to God and draw God nearer to you and 'Like' our page at: https://www.facebook.com/YourWordIsTruthAlways/ to help reach the masses.

Thanks again for your support!

Have you known someone once lost, but now found? Have you wondered why people run away from home, including God and their spiritual home?

Adventure must start with running away from home – you think? You may know rebels with a cause desiring to find meaning in life. In their quest, they consider the dead ends pursued and the alternative to that futility – a God-centered life of *Live, Laugh, Love, Work, Pray*.

In *New Day New Life*, framed by the story of the prodigal son in the book of Luke, you'll:

- Discover five inspirational books in one volume -- *Live, Laugh, Love, Work, Pray h*ome or away -- despite impulses toward the adventurous, rebellious, or indulgence of forbidden appetites
- Learn God-centered alternatives to bright lights and loose living away from home. You can reap his safety, security, blessings and love.
- Transform the very aspects of life (e.g., *Live, Laugh, Love, Work, Pray*) declared empty in the under-the-sun passages.
- Understand how you can draw you nearer to God and draw him nearer to you. Be happier in a *Live, Laugh, Love, Work, Pray* environment.

Real talk, stop running and come home. You're no longer far away from God. You're alive again; you were lost and now found. As you believe, "new life" will be born into you. If you want to celebrate the blessings of *Live, Laugh, Love, Work, Pray*, request your copy of *New Day New Life*.